Managing Without Power

"Why limit yourself to half the world, when you can find the space in your heart to open up to the entire world?"

MY MOTHER: HANNIE SAS 1946 – 2016

JORIS MERKS-BENJAMINSEN

MANAGING WITHOUT POWER

Creating high-performing teams and
organizations, in your own human way

Boom

© 2023 Joris Merks-Benjaminsen | Boom

Graphic design and cover: Justus Bottenheft
Editor: Rolandt Tweehuysen

ISBN 9789024457618
ISBN e-book 9789024451784
NUR 801

www.boom.nl

All rights reserved. No part of this book may be reproduced, stored in a database or retrieval system, or published, in any form or in any way, electronically, mechanically, by print, photo print, microfilm or any other means without prior written permission from the publisher.

The compiler(s) and the publisher are fully aware of their duty to provide as reliable a publication as possible. Nevertheless, they accept no liability for any inaccuracies that may appear in this publication.

Table of contents

Foreword *7*
Introduction *9*

Part I **Great managers, Brilliant Basics** *35*

Google's ten behaviors of great managers *37*
Improving yourself with manager-feedback from your team *52*
Five Brilliant Basics for great managers *61*
    Basic 1 Genuine conversations about career and personal growth *76*
    Basic 2 Collaborative OKR-writing, setting direction and expectations *92*
    Basic 3 Meaningful meetings and team norms *105*
    Basic 4 Tracking progress on OKRs and milestones *130*
    Basic 5 Fair and predictable performance evaluations *136*

Part II **Great team leaders, high-performing teams** *177*

Psychological safety *182*
Combining psychological safety with high performance standards *185*
DEI: Diversity, Equity, Inclusion *191*
Triple-A: Activism, Allyship, Action *205*

Part III **Great leaders, high-performing organizations** *209*

Universal limitations of data: a game of prison break *213*
Five enablers of organizational transformation *219*

Epilogue *239*
Appendix *250*
Acknowledgements *259*
Literature *261*

Foreword

The world of work is constantly changing and the skills required for success are changing with it. The days of relying on traditional power structures are fading and becoming increasingly outdated. It's time for managers to tap back into their humaneness to create the conditions for individuals and teams to thrive, and for organizational culture to enable sustainable high performance.

Have you ever noticed how working for a team or organization can feel like a completely different experience depending on who your manager is? I, for one, have had experience working with both the *best* and the *worst* of managers – and it's something that most of us can probably relate to. Interestingly, even when these managers exist within the same organization, the impact on my performance, engagement and overall wellbeing differed vastly.

Their ability to foster the conditions for my colleagues and I to flourish was enabled through their inclusivity, them setting the right levels of structure and clarity, setting a vision and objectives that inspire and motivate, rolemodelling the taking of ownership and accountability *and* holding others to the same standards for all of the above. *That* was how to build and maintain a culture that enabled each team member to perform at their best and the team to succeed.

However it is sometimes hard to know *how* to go about creating these conditions for your team – especially if you haven't been lucky enough to have had great managers throughout your own career who exemplify these behaviours.

Drawing on his extensive experience both within Google and working with organizations across the world, Joris provides actionable strategies and suggestions for creating a psychologically safe environment where individuals are empowered to take ownership of their work, collaborate with others, and drive innovation.

If you're a manager, whether you're new to the role or have plenty of experience, or you work for a large organization looking to upskill your managers or restore the good thing you may have lost while growing, or you're a scaleup, growing rapidly but eager to maintain the culture you've built, then look no further than Joris's Managing Without Power.

FOREWORD

The book is full of proven techniques, frameworks, guidelines, and practical advice that I highly recommend you engage with.

Enjoy!

Kim Wylie
Global Director of People Development & Change at Farfetch

Introduction

A high bar for performance *and* humaneness

In the early days at Google, the company was famously anti-management. They even decided to abolish all manager roles in an uncontrolled experiment in 2002. This quickly resulted in chaos, and manager positions were reinstated. The attempt to abolish managerial functions was just one of many signs that Google's founders Larry Page and Sergey Brin wanted to start a company unlike any other large corporation. In their manifesto *Ten things we know to be true* they already set the tone during the early years with statements such as "You can be serious without a suit" and "You can make money without doing evil". They wanted to build a company that achieved success by adding real value to the world. The overarching mission for that was (and still is): "to organize the world's information and make it universally accessible and useful." Besides the fact that they wanted to create real value, they also wanted to establish a unique organizational culture: a culture with a high bar for ambition and impact, but also a culture that had room for humanity, creativity and playfulness, and where there was as little hierarchy as possible.

I think Larry and Sergey realized fully well that it would be more difficult to maintain these ideals as the company grew. In 2004, Google went public for the first time. That is an iconic moment, when there is always the risk of shifting the balance from idealism to profit. Larry and Sergey therefore once again clearly underlined in a "founders letter" what kind of company they wanted Google to be. They opened this letter with: "Google is not a conventional company. And we do not intend to become one. Throughout Google's evolution as a privately held company, we have managed Google differently. We have also emphasized an atmosphere of creativity and challenge, which has helped us provide unbiased, accurate and free access to information for those who rely on us around the world." In the same letter, they again underlined their conviction that a sustainable business success can only exist if Google genuinely will make the world a better place, and continues to invest in the long term.

Even after Google went public, you could still see clear signs of the unique way Google's leaders wanted to run the company. In 2008, Google's People Analytics team made another attempt at proving that managers don't matter: yet this time they decided to dedicate a thorough study to it. This research became well known under the name *Project Oxygen*, but the outcome was different than expected. They discovered the opposite: they discovered that managers matter a lot! They published their research externally and identified the following ten behaviors of brilliant managers:

1   Being a good coach
2   Empowers the team and does not micro-manage
3   Creates an inclusive team environment, showing concern for success and wellbeing
4   Is productive and result-oriented
5   Is a good communicator, listens and shares information
6   Supports career development, and discusses performance
7   Has a clear vision/strategy for the team
8   Has key skills (also technical) to help advise the team
9   Collaborates across Google
10 Is a strong decision maker

These ten behaviors are still being used by Google at the time of writing this book, and they play an important role in this book. I will show how to put these behaviors into practice, and how to use them to build teams and organizations with a high bar for both performance and humaneness.

In 2010 I was hired at Google as *Head of Market Insights* in the Netherlands. It was a dream job, and the stories about Google's unique culture played an important part for me in deciding whether or not I wanted to work for this company. At that time, Google had long since ceased to be a startup. There were already about 25,000 people working for the company worldwide. I ended up working for Google for more than twelve years, much longer than I expected. When I left the company in 2022, it employed about 190,000 people, and Google had become part of a parent company called Alphabet. Across those twelve years, I held seven different positions in four different divisions of the company. I held both local and international jobs. I was a team manager about half of the time, and I worked with Google's largest clients in all roles. I worked with marketing teams and senior leaders of all the major brands in the world. The fact that the Google brand opened the door to work for so many great clients, was one of the best aspects of my job. I also got to work together with some of the smartest colleagues I ever met. In the early years, I focused mainly on research about changing consumer behavior, as a result of the rise of online shopping. However, I gradually became known externally by speaking at conferences and writing books on digital transformation I won the award for best marketing book twice during that time: in 2013 for my Dutch book *Schizofrene marketing* (Schizophrenic Marketing), and in 2015 for *Online Brand Identity*. That opened the door to a so-called "Evangelist role" for me: I became Head of Digital Transformation. In that role I ran workshops with Google's largest customers in order to solve digital-transformation challenges together.

In 2016, I made the move to my first manager position at Google. I had deliberately avoided this for the first six years, because I was afraid of becoming "too internal," and that this would make me less in touch with Google's customers. However, the team in which I was allowed to work was a special team with a special founder. Director Shuvo Saha had founded the so-called Google Digital Academy team about two years before I joined his team. That team did exactly the same thing I did, run workshops to help customers with digital transformation. Only they did it with more than twenty people on a larger scale. In addition, I had now unfortunately found that the unique Google culture I just wrote about was not so easy to find anymore. Much of the company had become as corporate and political as any other large organization. If you were lucky with who your manager or leader was, you could still experience the original Google culture in parts of the organization, but it had been a while since I experienced this. Shuvo was a leader, who was as fascinated by Google's unique culture as I was, and who made a conscious effort to create this culture in his team. I decided to embark on that journey, of creating the "real Google" with him. That choice gave me six more extraordinary years at Google.

Managing without power: a thought experiment

When I became a manager, I very consciously reflected on what kind of manager I wanted to be, and how as a manager I could create the "real Google". During those reflections, I came to an important insight. When you look at how Google is organized, it seems like they deliberately stripped managers from their powers. Hiring, performance ratings and promotions are all decided by committees. A hiring committee consists of at least three people. One of them is the hiring manager, and one needs to be from a team in a different part of the company. Each person in the hiring committee has a veto right, so a hiring manager can only hire a person if all people in the hiring committee rate the applicant positively. The underlying thought is that you don't hire for an individual job, but you hire people for a journey at Google. Performance ratings and promotions work in a similar way. Ratings and promotions are decided within a group setting: managers need to agree with peer managers what ratings to give and who to promote. You can't give a person a promotion or a particular rating, unless your peer managers agree. No manager can decide alone what rating to give or who to promote.

Managers don't only score their teams, but teams also score their managers, on the ten behaviors mentioned earlier. As a manager I got scored by my team every six months. The manager feedback from the teams influences the manager's performance rating. This means it affects the manager's bonus, pay increase, equity and opportunities for promotion. That's quite some power to give to a team, and it counter balances the power managers have over their teams.

Finally, salaries and bonuses are largely defined by fixed rules. Once performance ratings and promotions have been assigned (by committee as explained), for most people this defines almost entirely what their salary and bonus becomes. There are exceptions here and there, like any organization has, but most of the time the outcome is largely derived from the performance rating through fixed rules. Managers can't decide on their own to give a person a large raise because they think they performed well, or because they fear the person might leave. Google has a clear philosophy about compensation and reward that they communicate openly and even published externally in books and articles. They systematically apply this philosophy.

If you sum up all of the above, you see that Google has minimized the power of managers wherever it could. No manager can get away with hiring, promoting and overpaying their "favorites" or mistreating their teams. For the record: I've never read an article or heard anyone communicate that the goal was to reduce the managers' power, yet the fact is that this is still the net result. When I realized that, I found it a fascinating thought. Reality is that managers still have a strong influence on all of the decisions I just mentioned. Managers influence which people become part of the hiring committee, which influences the decisions of that group. And from among the candidates that have not been vetoed by the group, the manager makes the final call on who to hire. Managers are also the ones that represent their team members when they speak to peer managers about performance ratings and promotions. This means a manager can choose what information to share about a team member and what not to share. Thereby the manager shapes the perception of the group, and can influence decisions about ratings and promotions. Through their influence over ratings and promotions they also have influence upon compensation, because compensation directly follows from ratings and promotions.

It is impossible to entirely get rid of the power of managers. When you are in a manager position, you have power whether you want it or not. I personally find it a strange position to be in. Who am I to say whether another person is doing a good job or not? Whether they are talented or not? Whether they deserve a certain amount of reward or not? Whether their style of working is suitable or not? Whether or not they work hard enough? Whether they deserve certain opportunities or not? Who am I to decide about people's lives, their credentials, their income, their families, their careers and even sometimes their happiness?

For that reason, I decided to take on a thought experiment myself, and use the power I had as a manager as little as possible. So, I became one of Google's highest-scoring managers. During the six years I was manager, I was rated twelve times during performance reviews by my team as to the ten behaviors of brilliant managers. I scored 100 percent twelve times in a row. Getting a 100-percent score once is already quite special. Getting it two or three times is very rare. Getting it twelve times in a row is something probably only a handful of people in Google's history can say. That led to me getting a larger team relatively quickly, and in 2019 Director Shuvo Saha gave me the opportunity to lead the full Google Digital Academy team. He then went on to lead a broader team himself, which I was a part of with my team. Within the international Google organization, my unique track record was noticed. I trained many managers, and played a role in European and global working groups for career development, Diversity and Inclusion. An interesting additional fact is that I managed my team remotely during the entire six years: none of my team members worked in the same country as I did. This made me the living proof that remote managers can be effective. When COVID-19 hit the world, that experience of managing remotely came in handy, as I was unable to physically meet with my team members for three years during that period. Therefore, the principles in this book will certainly also be valuable if you, as a manager, need to manage a team remotely.

I think I can honestly say that together we created the "real Google". In addition, in a short period of time, we tremendously increased the impact of the team: in the end we ran about 1,000 digital-transformation workshops per year on forty different topics, ranging from data integration to marketing automation to organizational transformation, and we were successful in working with the highest-level leaders—the C-suite—of Google's largest customers. We proved that you can create Google's unique start-up culture as a manager and leader, even within the context of one of the largest publicly traded corporations in the world. It wasn't an easy ride though: to create the Google we envisioned for my team, I had to fight hard despite the unique reputation I had. That fighting was often necessary to create space within the commercial pressures that existed: space to continue to invest in the long term, and in what was right for customers. Fighting was often necessary to survive within a group of leaders, who competed for visibility and resources, and who competed because of their personal careers and ambitions. And unfortunately, I also had to fight for several years because fellow leaders exhibited harmful behavior, and somehow managed to get away with that behavior for many years. I had become a safe place for many people, who often came to me with stories of what had happened to them. I had to escalate those stories for several years, risking not being believed, and risking being attacked myself. Fortunately, eventually the right actions were taken, but it took a lot of energy, stress and patience.

Human cultures vs. performance cultures
I have seen the worst and the best of Google, and everything in between. I know that it is possible to maximize the most beautiful things, and minimize the worst, if you as a manager and leader pay conscious attention to it, and are willing to stick your neck out. I discovered that managers and leaders can heavily influence which version of Google people experienced by their ability to balance Google's high performance standards with the high standards for humaneness. That is however a skill which only few managers and leaders can reconcile. Yet the reality is that organizations can only perform at the highest level when emphasis on performance and humaneness go hand in hand. Only few organizations combine them, which means few organizations are genuinely high performing. Figure 1 shows what happens if the balance between the two dimensions isn't optimal.

I worked for highly human teams and organizations, yet they lacked accountability. The lack of accountability led to people pushing work around, or just not responding to requests and not delivering on tasks, without anyone remarking about it. When humaneness goes at the expense of accountability, one ends up in the top left cell of the matrix. That's a situation in which you can't rely on your colleagues. Not being able to rely on your colleagues is demotivating for your talented and motivated employees, who want to make a difference. They're likely to leave the organization, due to the lack of aspirational achievements. The people who survive in these organizations are nice people, yet they're not necessarily the ones that make an impact. That's why I called this cell "survival of the nicest."

I also worked for teams and organizations with a strong emphasis on performance, but the human side was often lacking. The tough culture led to competition between people, which undermined collaboration and fueled political behavior. When emphasis on performance goes at the expense of humaneness, you end up in the bottom right cell. The political behavior that often occurs in these organizations aren't easy to see for senior leaders: people who survive in

Figure 1 *An organization can only perform at its ultimate level if the emphasis on performance is balanced by high human standards.*

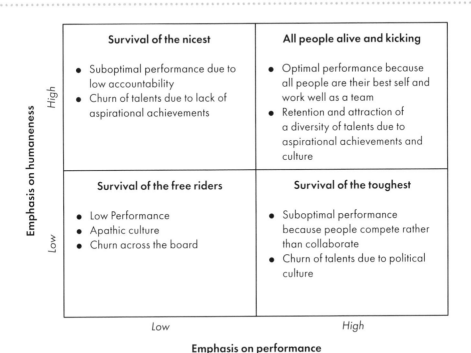

these organizations can skillfully manage the perception that they talk the talk that leadership speaks. Collaboration often won't be genuine, as their personal goals will always be a bit more important than the common goals. This situation again increases the odds that talented people leave. For those people, a political organization feels like walking through the mud, and they can afford to have higher expectations from the organizational culture. The people who survive in these organizations are the ones with a thick skin and a dominant style of working. They know how to take care of themselves, but not necessarily how to take care of *others*. These people shrug their shoulders at a bit of corporate politics. They can deliver impact, but they are not your top talents. Their main trait is that they are tough. That's why I called this cell "survival of the toughest."

The worst cell in the matrix is the one bottom left, with low humaneness and performance. Apathy is the best way to describe the culture in those organizations. Churn rates will be high, not just among talented people. The people who survive in an organization like this, are those who come to work because they get paid, not because of a sense of meaning. That also means they'll try to avoid accountability when they can, often by faking productivity and impact. Their impact doesn't match their salaries. That's why I called this cell "survival of the free riders."

The top right, of course, is where you want to be. And it's where you *can* be! An organization like this is a place in which all people are their best self and work well as a team. Your organization is no longer a place where some people survive and others don't. That's why I call this cell "all people alive and kicking." The only people who don't survive in these organizations, are the ones unwilling to deliver impact, or that willingly harm other people. Diverse and inclusive is the default state: because an organization can only perform at the highest level, if it attracts and retains the broadest talent pool available, and if a critical mass of these people are their best self.

Humaneness and performance are therefore *not* opposites. They can't live without one another. When I speak to people in non-profit organizations, they often associate the term "high performance" with hardcore commercial companies, where people do lots of overtime, and colleagues compete to be the best and earn the most money. To me the meaning of "high performance" is simple and human: all people are their best self, and they work well as a team.

> *To me the meaning of "high performance" is simple and human: all people are their best self, and they work well as a team*

Many organizations in the bottom right cell call themselves "high-performing organizations," but what they really have is a culture of swimming or drowning. The fact that people compete rather than collaborate and that political culture leads to a churn of talent, means they don't perform at the highest level. When some people can survive in an organization's culture and some cannot, this culture isn't high performing. When people are under continuous high pressure and do overtime structurally, they typically don't have the clearest minds that come up with the best solutions and creative ideas. When pressures at work aren't healthy and sustainable, an organization is not a high-performing one.

It's worth noting that, just like my experience at Google, no large organization is ever entirely in one of these four quarters. Different pockets in an organization can feel differently depending on which manager and leader people work under. It's also worth looking at this matrix through the lens of cultural differences. My observations are based on many years of work with people in European and African countries and America. I've worked a lot less with Asians, and it's very well possible that cultural differences would result in a different assessment there. When working across cultures, you will benefit a lot by the sharpened senses you acquire through the deliberate process of unlearning the unconscious use of power. It will help you tune into people with completely different backgrounds than yourself. The Brilliant Basics I will cover in part I of the book, will help you spend enough quality time with your team members to deeply understand where they "come from." Never assume, always be curious, always keep on learning.

Many companies have underlined in various ways the importance of a balance between "hard" and "soft" characteristics for building high-performing teams and organizations. Google's own research about high-performing teams that I will cover later in this book underlines the importance of psychological safety, but also of structure, dependability and impact. The ten behaviors of great managers from Google's Oxygen-research underline the importance of a focus on productivity and results, but they also cover inclusiveness, and concern for well-being. In consulting company McKinsey's view about high-performance cultures they advocate the authoritative and challenging leadership as well as the consultative and supportive leadership. They advocate accountability and structured performance reviews, but also openness and trust. Consulting company Gallup advocates getting the communication, values and rituals right, but also getting performance management right. So, many organizations have advocated a balance between emphasis on performance and humaneness, yet it is still hard to find. With this book I aim to make combining high performance and humaneness practical, because without making it practical, real change will never happen.

Critical points
- A team or organization can feel completely different depending on which manager or leader you work under.
- Only organizations that balance emphasis on performance with humaneness, can be truly high-performing organizations.
- If one of the two is missing, performance will be sub-optimal and talent is likely to leave.
- High performance means that all people are their best self and work well as a team.
- Diversity and inclusion is the "default setting."

Managers can make or break an organization

Because I experienced first hand at Google how different one and the same organization can feel, depending on what manager or leader you work under; and because I saw the large impact I personally had on the team I managed, I realized that managers make or break an organization. There's a reason why the phrase "people leave bosses, not companies" keeps popping up. Consulting firm Gallup published their *State of the American manager report* in 2015, that one in two employees left their job, in order to get away from a manager. Each year, Gallup publishes updates of their insights with additional nuances based upon employee research, with insights at the global level, as well as by region. In 2021, they found that a good manager can prevent people from leaving: it takes a twenty-percent salary increase to convince someone to leave a good manager. In 2022, they saw that the quality of managers is accountable for seventy percent of the variation in employee satisfaction scores.

I've had periods in my career where I was in a complete flow. I loved everything about my work. I did not feel structurally stressed, and was highly productive. My first years at Google were a perfect example of that. In my first role as Head of Market Insights, I worked on projects I wouldn't have been able to do anywhere else. I felt I was having a positive impact for Google's customers, for Google and even for the marketing and advertising industry. I even had a nice manager and team. Time flew by.

I also had periods when I felt structural stress and unhappiness. This could in most cases be traced back to my manager, or to a leader above my direct manager who had a negative impact on team culture. There was a point at Google where I left my Market Insights-role, because I didn't want to be in research my entire career. This meant I had to move to a different part of the Google organization. I went through a period of several years, where I felt stressed most of the time. I'd tried to solve the problem by moving into different jobs within the organization, but hadn't been happy at work for quite a while. I even started interviewing externally and seriously considered leaving, even though I still loved Google as a company and was being paid well. I then realized that the Google I experienced in my first few years, was different from the Google I was experiencing now. I analyzed the problem, and realized a leader a few layers up in the organization created a culture that was different from what I thought Google could be. I realized I had to move to a different management chain to find back the "real Google". I knew that it could take a while, so I needed to find a source of energy in the meantime. I found an adidas *sneaker configurator* online that allowed me to create my own custom sneakers. I created a set of sneakers with

Google colors. I wore these to remind myself that I was working for Google, not for this leader. I did the things I thought Google's founders would want me to do, and things I knew Google's customers expected from Google.

I designed full day workshops that helped teams from large customers solve digital-marketing transformation challenges. The Google Sales person would join these workshops to spend quality time with the customer, and step into a consultative role. An international sales leader heard about my workshops through his teams, and gave me the opportunity to run my workshops in his region and train other Googlers (Google colleagues) to run them as well. This made my workshops visible internationally. This was the moment when the Director of Google Digital Academy noticed my work, and offered me a role as manager in his team. I found back the culture I remembered from my first years at Google.

In all of those years I always worked for the same company, but I experienced that company in a completely different way depending on the manager I had, and the senior management chain I was under. The way I choose jobs has fundamentally changed as a consequence of this experience and knowledge. In the early years of my career the main determining factors for me picking a job were the job role, the company name and the industry the company was in. Nowadays when I consider a new job I make the assessment at a completely different level. First of all, I don't expect any job or organization to be perfect anymore. I also don't join a company for a single role, instead I join it hoping for a journey. I know the experience of that journey is heavily influenced by the managers I will have, the teams I will be part of, and the company's culture in general. Therefore, I try to speak not only to the future manager, but also to people who worked or have worked in the team and the organization. That way, I try to assess all factors mentioned, before making a decision.

Going back to the phrase "people don't leave companies, they leave managers." If you have too many managers who are abandoned by people, you will also have trouble attracting new talent, because people share bad experiences with one another. They do so in their networks, and on online platforms such as Glassdoor.com. The opposite is also true: great managers attract and retain great people. They create great teams and great teams make great organizations that people talk about positively.

In a time where finding great talent is becoming harder, great managers are critical for the success of any organization. As the world is recovering from the

COVID-19 pandemic we are facing a global labor shortage. HR services company Randstad published a meta- analysis in 2022, with the title *Why is there a global labor shortage*. It illustrates there are more open applications than there are registered unemployed workers in many places in the world. For example: in the United States, there are nearly eleven million job vacancies, but only 6.5 million workers are listed as unemployed in 2022. As of early 2022, employers in Europe were struggling to fill over 1.2 million open vacancies, while employers in Australia are working to fill nearly 400,000 vacant positions. Also, in 2021, Singapore saw 163 job vacancies for every 100 available candidates. Korn Ferry estimates that by 2030, more than 85 million jobs could go unfilled because there aren't enough skilled people to take them. At the same time expectations of employees have fundamentally shifted. Coming out of COVID they expect larger flexibility about when and where they work. Employers still struggle to find the right answer to these changed demands.

This makes great managers even more critical to organizations. An effective organization is one that attracts, retains and nurtures a critical mass of managers using the power that comes with the position in positive ways: at the benefit of the people, the organization and the organization's customers. That also means an organization needs to have the skill of neutralizing people who seek manager positions for the *wrong* reasons, who use their power in *negative* ways. It should be avoided at all times that this group becomes too large, because it takes a lot of time and effort to change an organization once too many of these people are in power.

If you picked up this book, I'm pretty sure you are in the group that aims to use the power of the manager's position positively. That intention already makes you a great manager. When a group of managers pulls together, an organization can turn around and feel differently soon. The positive impact this has on the organization and on people's lives is profound. Great teams leave great memories that last a lifetime—for you and for the team members that worked for you. People will remember that time as a period when they were at their best, being seen, feeling valued, and working with great colleagues having real impact together. You will have shifted the bar forever, because they now know what work can feel like. They will bring that to the future teams they are part of, or might manage. It's hard work, but the payoff is priceless!

My goal with this book is to help managers and leaders to magnify the best side of their organizations, and to minimize the worst. I know that most managers and leaders have sincere intentions of building a beautiful culture for their team and organization. Yet it doesn't happen as often as you might hope. In the years of training fellow managers at Google, I noticed that there are several problems going on simultaneously. For starters, managers rarely get the onboarding and guidance that equips them with a structured approach, to create a high-performance culture in their own human way. I experienced this myself when I became a manager. There was a lot of material, but it was very fragmented. Trainings usually focused on one aspect of management: for example coaching, performance management, or inclusive leadership, but no one had made an effort to bring it all together into one holistic applicable toolkit. I hope this book will show you that all topics lean on each other, and that lack of connection between topics almost inevitably leads to situations where words and actions don't match. There are also many topics where it is simply assumed that, as a manager, you will figure out for yourself how to do it right. You usually get no support on those topics. For example, as a manager, I didn't get any support on effective meetings and team norms.

The other problem was that the people who provided training for managers were fantastic facilitators, but most did not have extensive experience in leading teams themselves. This left a gap between theory and practical application. The reality of being a manager is that you juggle many things that require balancing, such as the balance between accountability and psychological safety. So, how do you hold someone accountable for making a mistake, but without creating psychological unsafety? You had one training on the importance of accountability, and another on the importance of psychological safety. In theory, both sound nice, but no one told you how to bring the two together. Very often I found sharing experiences with other managers during training more valuable than the training itself.

For that reason, I created my own holistic and practical toolkit: one that brings together all aspects of the manager's role in a model. I trained fellow managers to create a conscious connection between topics—such as career conversations, performance conversations, creating trusting relationships, writing OKRs (Objectives and Key Results), tracking progress, giving feedback, and so on. You will find all of these topics in this book. I have also incorporated my experiences from working groups, on diversity and inclusion and career development, into the model.

Figure 2 provides an overview of the entire model, and shows how a group of brilliant managers can build a high-performing organization together.

Figure 2 *Great managers start with five Brilliant Basics. By applying these consistently, they build high-trust relations and intrinsically motivated teams. That's the start of building high-performing teams and organizations.*

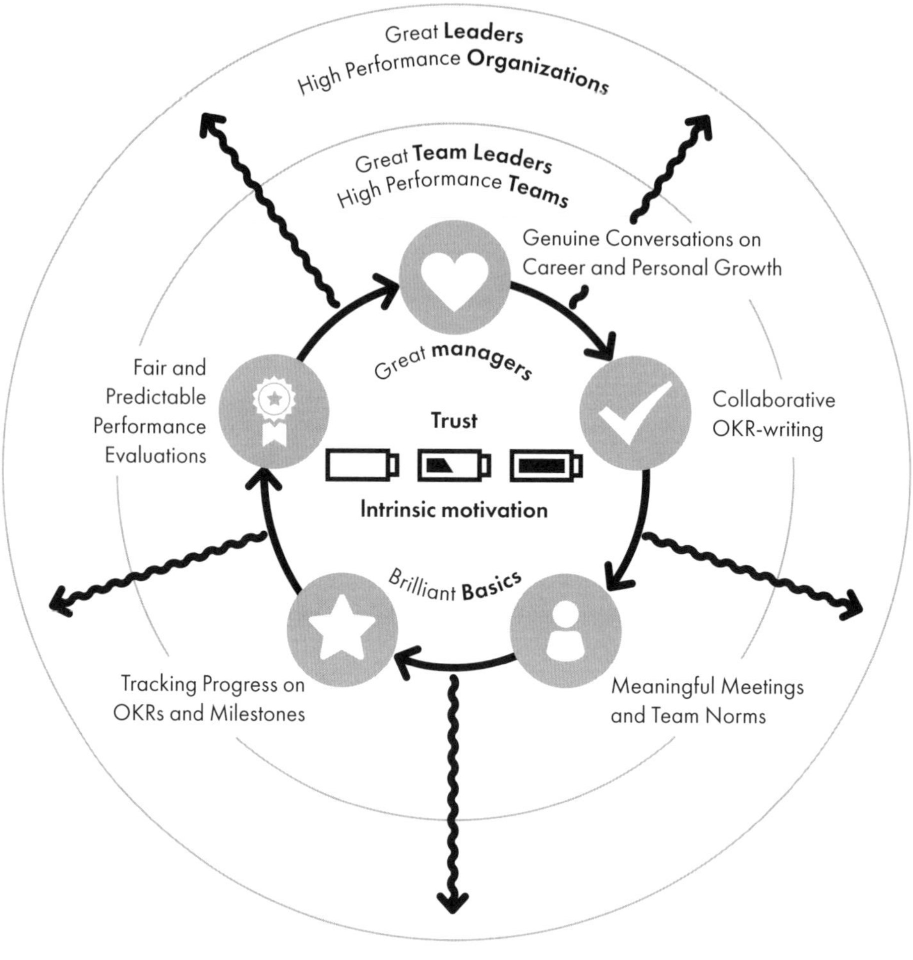

The model starts with five Brilliant Basics that you must have in place as a manager before focusing on other things:

- Genuine conversations about career and personal growth
- Collaborative OKR-writing (setting and prioritizing Objectives, and expectations for Key Results)
- Meaningful meetings and team norms

- Tracking of progress on OKRs and milestones
- Fair and predictable performance evaluations

When you systematically invest in these five Brilliant Basics, the battery in the middle charges: this battery contains the energy you get when you succeed in creating high-trust relationships between you and your team members and amongst team members, and when people work based on intrinsic motivation. You need that energy to build successful teams and organizations. Conversely, if the five Brilliant Basics are *not* in place, that will hurt trust relationships and intrinsic motivation: it depletes the battery.

Without a strong foundation of these five Brilliant Basics, there are few other things you can still do well. For instance, when you try to work on topics like culture of innovation, vision, mission, or diversity and inclusion, you very quickly end up in a situation where the words you speak aren't in line with the reality people work in. Inspirational concepts aren't real unless you consistently apply them in everything you do, because all aspects of being a manager are interconnected:

- A vision is meaningless if you don't show people how it guides consistent setting and prioritization of OKR's.
- Equal opportunity doesn't exist if the performance system doesn't result in fair ratings and promotions.
- Trust is damaged when performance ratings are unpredictable.
- Psychological safety doesn't exist if people get punished for mistakes in their performance reviews, yet consistent performance standards don't exist when people get away with making avoidable mistakes.
- Inclusion doesn't exist if it isn't for everyone.
- Equal opportunity doesn't exist if some people get more personal time with the manager than others, or get more high-profile projects.
- Work/life-balance won't exist in your organization if you say it's important, yet primarily promote and reward people who work five days and do regular overtime.

Without Brilliant Basics, the more you speak about innovation, vision, inclusion, culture, high performance, respect, transparency, etcetera, the more cynical people become. Vice versa, when a critical mass of managers demonstrates Brilliant Basics in their behavior, you'll see people drive organizational goals based on intrinsic motivation, while creating synergies with the people around them. People will invest in impactful behaviors, even when no one is watching. They come up with solutions you wouldn't have thought of, and they help one another to solve problems.

Because these Brilliant Basics are so crucial to all the success you can create as a manager or leader, part I of this book is devoted to these fundamentals. Part II helps you consciously nurture psychological safety, which Google discovered is the primary driver of team effectiveness. I will also cover principles of diversity, equity and inclusion in this part, because psychological safety is only real when it exists for all types of people. Part III is about driving change in your organization.

Challenging the boundaries of an organization comes at a price as well: it is hard work and you often take personal risk. There may even be times that you need to act against the wishes of senior leadership, hoping they will understand later on that you were doing the right thing. I will therefore conclude the book with reflections about yourself, about your values, your limits, and the ways that help you to find the energy in order to keep doing what is right, especially under pressure.

This book is for managers and leaders who genuinely want to create teams and organizations where all people can be "their best selves." If you are a manager starting out, the practical models and exercises will help you to get started quickly. If you are a manager who is strong on the human side, but finds it difficult to be strict at the right times, the book will help you balance both sides of the equation. Conversely, the book helps tougher managers and organizations make the balance more human. If you work in HR, or in a senior leadership position, the book helps create principles, processes and systems that balance performance and humaneness.

When you work in a non-profit organization, some of the language I use in this book may sound highly commercial, like the example of "high-performance culture." My background happens to be in commercial companies, but these are still groups of people trying to do great work together, like in any other organization. My hope is that through this book I can bust some myths: every organization wants their employees to be impactful and happy at work. The fact that you work in a non-profit organization doesn't mean principles of high effectivity don't apply to you, as if it would mean that you are too soft and ineffective. If you are a person who works within a highly commercial and competitive organization, you shouldn't assume that your organization would perform better than most non-profit organizations. What's more, when empathy remains lacking due to high levels of competition, your organization is likely to perform less well than many non-profit organizations. The notion that non-profit organizations are less competitive, is already an assumption that is probably not true. So regardless of where you work, please look beyond what you are used to, and allow me the opportunity to bust some potential myths.

Managing Without Power is about genuineness: none of the tools or ideas can be used in itself, or as a "trick" to make you look better as a manager or leader. There are no shortcuts. It only works if you apply the principles and tools with genuine intent, discipline and great situational awareness. That also means you need to make them to your own. My way of working is inspired by the work of Google's people analytics team about great managers and high-performing teams. I applied these principles with self-made tools in a way that is completely personal to me, and is tailored to the teams I worked with at the time. You have to find the way that is personal to you, and is adapted to the team(s) you are working with. My aim is to empower you to build high-performing teams in your own personal and human way, and leave a legacy you can feel proud of.

Critical points
- Managers make or break an organization.
- When a group of managers pulls together, they can make a positive difference in the organization really fast.
- Managers that can manage without power, and that consistently apply the five Brilliant Basics, create high-trust relations and intrinsically motivated teams: the foundations of high-performing teams.
- When there's a critical mass of those managers, their teams become a source of energy that fuels a high-performing organization that can reinvent itself over and over again.

Unlearning the unaware use of power
Before we move on, I want to underline one more aspect of the subject of power: the process of unlearning the use of power. I achieved my track record of 100-percent manager scores with a thought experiment in which I consciously used my power as little as possible. When I started training managers to apply my toolkit, I noticed that this is not an obvious step for everyone. Power is so inextricably linked to the role of manager or leader that it is very easy to forget you have it, and people therefore use power unconsciously. Using your power less therefore starts with unlearning the *unaware* use of power. That starts with

being conscious of the sources of power you possess, and about the effect they have on people. So what are these sources of power? Some of these I already covered in the previous sections, but let's just make a list. Below are examples of topics where managers have decision power, and that can have large influence on the careers and lives of the people working for them:
- Hiring
- Firing
- Compensation
- Promotion and progression
- Assignment of high-profile work
- Assigning opportunities for mentoring, talent programs and education
- Visibility & connections
- Endorsement (or lack thereof)
- Punishment
- Sharing (or not sharing) information top-down
- Sharing (or not sharing) information bottom-up
- Ownership of communication channels
- Levels of resource and support
- Prioritization of projects, or killing of projects

If you see it listed like this, it's easy to see that managers have a lot of power over people who work for them, and it's almost inevitable that this affects the relationships between managers and their teams. It's worth thinking about some of the subtle ways in which power manifests itself in the interactions between managers or leaders, and the people working under them in the hierarchy.

Senior shortcuts
There is a subtle way in which the unintended use of power manifests itself in interactions between senior and junior people: I call it "senior shortcuts". These are behaviors that you easily get away with as a senior person within an organization, yet that you wouldn't be able to display if you didn't have the power you have.

The problem is that power makes you less sensitive, often without you realizing it. It starts with the fact that, if you are senior person, many people will treat you differently: they will be a little more friendly and socially correct, and will listen to you a bit more attentively, accepting your opinion a bit easier, will be a bit less likely to give you difficult feedback, et cetera. As a result, you get a less unadulterated feedback about how you come across, and about the impact of your actions. This gets worse the more senior you become. On top of that, your work starts being more fragmented, you are often under more pressure, and have to make trade-offs more often when many interests come into play. That means you make decisions quicker, and get used to the fact that you can never make everyone happy. It is therefore very easy to develop "small habits of power" without noticing it: you refer to people more easily, make a bit less of an effort to involve them in decisions, listen just a little less attentively, and so on. Nothing seems wrong, because most people don't tell you that you're doing this. You're the boss after all. Yet gradually, you become the manager or leader you don't want to be. Your team will feel the difference: in the least favorable scenario, your team experiences a manager that is ticking boxes when talking about the team, the vision and the culture, whereas most managers aspire to be leaders with genuine intent and purpose.

There's one simple question that can sharpen your senses, and help you avoid senior shortcut behaviors. Would I demonstrate this behavior if I were interacting with a person two layers higher than me in the organization? Imagine having your weekly one-on-one meeting with one of your team members. You show up five minutes late. Would you have done that if this person was your boss's boss? Your team member has shared some information with you, ahead of the meeting. You didn't have time to read it, so you ask your team member to talk you through it. Would you have failed to read the information ahead of the meeting if this were the boss of your boss? Your team member wants to suggest an idea to you. You notice you have difficulty listening, because there's an important leadership meeting right after this one that is absorbing your mind. Would you struggle to listen if this were the boss of your boss speaking? You give your opinion about what the best way forward is. Your team member says "thank you for your feedback." You move on to the next topic. Would you have assumed so easily that your opinion is the right one, if this were your boss's boss? Or would you have provided more context, asked more questions, taking the opinion of your boss into account? During the meeting you promise to share some slides with your team member. After the meeting you are closely involved with meetings the rest of the day, and an important deadline is emerging for a senior leadership update. You forget to send the slides. Would you have forgotten to send the slides if this were the boss of your boss?

There are many more examples where this switch of perspective works well. For example, if your team members were two levels higher than you in the organization, would you...
... reply to their emails more often, or faster?
... interrupt them so easily when they speak?
... send them chat messages in the evening about something you need from them?
... arrive at a meeting without agreeing upon an agenda in advance?

If you reflect frankly upon moments like these, it's likely that you will have to admit that at least some of the time you demonstrate behaviors to your team members that you wouldn't demonstrate if you didn't have the position of power you in fact have. It's easy to slip into that behavior, because we've got a lot on our plate. Often it seems like the faster way. For instance, telling your team what your decision is, is often done faster than bringing them along on the basis on intrinsic motivation. But the more you push your decisions onto the team without winning them over, the more you erode their sense of meaning and ownership, and the less output you get back from them in the long run. The damage is often hard to see, because the people who work for us are polite to us. They depend on us for approval, reward, recognition, career, and for having a job in the first place. Even when people don't object, there is still damage that accumulates over time.

Applying micro-pressures
A second form of an unaware use of power is what I call "micro-pressures." Because managers have so many sources of power, it is easy to use them without realizing it. Micro-pressure is about the moments when you as a manager create more pressure than you realize, usually because you have underestimated your power. You can damage people that way, without wanting to or even noticing it. I think many managers underestimate how much power they have, and that they put more pressure on people than they realize.

A simple example to illustrate what micro-pressure is, is sending emails outside working hours. That doesn't sound very harmful, but it can have more negative impact than you think. When I started as a manager, I often sent emails in the evenings. As a parent of young children, it was convenient for me to start work later in the morning, so I could first take my children to school. I often stopped work earlier so I could have dinner with my family. I made up that time by sending a few emails early in the morning, and after dinner when the kids were in bed. That gave me a better work-life balance. I felt that by doing this, I was setting an example of flexible working for my team. I hoped that encouraged people could decide for themselves how they preferred to work. I had a "disclaimer" at the top of my emails that said it's OK to reply at your convenience. But one evening I sent an email to a junior team member. That person responded immediately, and that response led to an email exchange between several people. The subject of the emails turned into something stressful for the person to whom I had sent the email. I realized that I had caused a moment of stress on an evening when that person might have been relaxing at home. I realized that the rules work differently when there is a difference in hierarchy: If a senior person sends an email, people lower the hierarchy will always feel a pressure to read it and respond to it, even if you explicitly say they need not respond right away. I decided that from then on I would lead by example. I no longer sent emails outside normal working hours, so no one could feel pressure to read them.

> *If a senior person sends an email, people lower the hierarchy will always feel a pressure to read it and respond to it, even if you explicitly say they need not respond right away*

Then I went on vacation. During my holiday, I occasionally checked my emails, to see if the team was okay. Sometimes I replied, hoping to be helpful to the team. When I returned from vacation, one of my team members pointed out to me that the example I set, while well intentioned, created the expectation that people would check their work email during their holidays. So again, I was creating pressure without meaning to.

So you can easily put pressure on people as a manager or leader without intending or noticing it. When I look around me at how other managers and leaders work, I see many of them making overtime most of the time, sending late emails regularly. Sometimes, a leader may speak about work-life balance and mindfulness at work, but most of the time people can see that the real behavior doesn't match those words. As a consequence, despite those words people still feel pressure to work evenings, in order to respond fast to mails regardless of when they receive these. People then struggle to detach from work, which can lead to high levels of stress at intensive periods.

To make things worse, colleagues that achieve great accomplishments through systematic overtime are in many organizations more likely to be rewarded and get promotions. Making systematic overtime may not be a problem for these particular people, but it does create pressure on peers to work more hours as well. Particularly when working with ambitious young people, the risk of creating high-pressure situations without realizing it is considerable. These people are keen to make an impression, and don't always set clear boundaries when it comes to workload. Many won't object until it's too late. They don't want to look weak. It is your job as a manager and leader to protect ambitious people like that against themselves, and against each other.

My experience is that the team as a whole is much more productive if all individuals work within the boundaries of the workload they can handle, while having autonomy to prioritize their own work

I think some managers fear the team won't be as productive if they consciously reduce pressure, yet my experience is that the team as a whole is much more productive if all individuals work within the boundaries of the workload they can handle, while having autonomy to prioritize their own work.

Death by a thousand cuts

Senior shortcuts and micro-pressures can be a damaging combination, because they can lead to a situation of "death by a thousand cuts." Most "micro-pressures" aren't damaging if you isolate them from their context. No one gets a burnout from one person sending emails after working hours. The problem is that it sets a norm, and that these behaviors become an unwritten part of the culture of the team and the organization. If the manager then also displays too many "senior shortcut behaviors" the general level of care about team culture, and about each other, becomes lower amongst the team members. Bit by bit people start demonstrating small signs of crossing each other's boundaries, competing with each other for attention of leadership. Some people will notice the culture is sliding, but it's unlikely they will tell the manager, because senior shortcut behaviors send signals that the manager doesn't care enough. In the best-case scenario you'll end up with a team that just cares a little less about the impact of their work, and about one another. They might care a bit *more* about their visibility, their career progress and their compensation. You end up with a team that just isn't as engaged as they might be, and their combined impact is unlikely to be the best they can achieve. The worst case scenario is a toxic political culture that grinds people down, and that triggers your most talented staff to leave your team. This is why role-modeling of managers and leaders is so important: everything they do is under a magnifying glass, and this affects what people think, feel, and do.

What managers can learn from top sports
So power can lead to situations where you unintendedly create damage as a manager or leader. If you don't counter certain micro-behaviors intentionally, you gradually become the manager or leader you don't want to be. But the opposite is also true. Power can be used in positive ways: to reward the right behaviors that lead to a healthy team culture, to give opportunities to talented people who are making a positive difference, or for instance to discourage or even eliminate behavior that damages people and culture. When used well, power is a beautiful instrument that helps you create a magical experience, and highly effective teams.

When leaders talk about high-performance cultures, they often make references to sports; in both cases people aim to play at the highest level. In particular they then emphasize the need for discipline, hard work, and sometimes principles like "no pain, no gain." This is all true, but by overemphasizing the importance of strength and discipline, other important things get overlooked. I've been a competitive judo fighter for twenty years, and I was a judo teacher for children several years as well. When kids grow up doing judo, there are always a few that have the luck to be born with brute physical strength. They discover at an early age that they can easily overpower opponents, and win almost all matches this way. Yet as they grow into competitive fighters, there's always a moment when they start to discover this strategy no longer works for them. The closer you get to higher levels of competition, the more people are also physically strong. And at the highest level, there are no exceptions anymore: all single players have brutal physical strength available to them. The ones that keep winning are the ones that learned early enough in their journey to practice without using their strength. By doing so, they learn to develop the skill of feeling the movements and tensions of their opponent, surprising the opponent, acting spontaneously in the moment, and coming up with strategic game plans. If a young judo player discovers at the age of twenty that physical strength is no longer sufficient, they typically get stuck. Their learning curve on all other topics is several years behind other competitive fighters at that moment, and the other fighters aren't standing still in their growth either. So there's no catching up anymore. You can't compete at the highest levels if you don't learn to fight *without* using your strength as early as possible in your growth journey.

The same is true for leadership. Yes, to lead at the highest levels you need to be able to make tough decisions, you need to be strong, resilient, often thick-skinned, work hard, and be willing to push people every now and then. But you also need to develop the skills to listen, to build trusted relationships, to empathize, to extend trust and autonomy, and to create space for people who disagree with you. You need to learn to express gratitude and appreciation, to share your doubts and fears, to admire team members and learn from them. The less you use the power you have, the more you train all these other skills. The earlier you start practicing with this, the steeper your growth curve is. Your leadership skills will become more versatile, and both you and your teams can thereby perform at the highest level.

> *Learning not to use your power sharpens your senses, it helps you tune in on people more attentively and increases your situational awareness*

Learning to use power the right way, starts with becoming fully conscious about all ways that your power manifests itself in interactions with your team members. The process of unlearning behaviors where you apply micro-pressures, and unlearning senior shortcut behaviors is a powerful starting point: learning not to use your power sharpens your senses, it helps you tune in on people more attentively and increases your situational awareness.

The less you use the power you have, the *more* you role-model behaviors set the highest bar for integrity, respect and discipline. You'll connect to people on a deeper level, because you prioritize them, you listen to them more attentively, you bring them along at important decisions so their work is based on intrinsic motivation, they feel safe to challenge you, and they feel seen, heard and valued. At the moments when you do choose to use your power, the impact will be much stronger, because you've developed a strong sense of situational awareness by listening more attentively to your team. This is why Managing Without Power is so powerful.

Critical points
- Senior shortcuts and Micro-pressures are common examples of the unconscious use of power.
- These can cause "death by a thousand cuts", because the role model leaders lower the bar for the culture of the team and organization.
- When you unlearn the use of power, you sharpen your senses that help you tune into your team more attentively, and increase situational awareness.
- If you can manage without power, you create an environment where people feel safe to challenge you, and feel seen, heard and valued.
- After that, when you purposely do choose to use power, you'll have much more impact, because you do it with personal and situational awareness.
- This is the foundation for creating high-performing teams, and organizations that can reinvent themselves over and over again.

PART I

GREAT MANAGERS, BRILLIANT BASICS

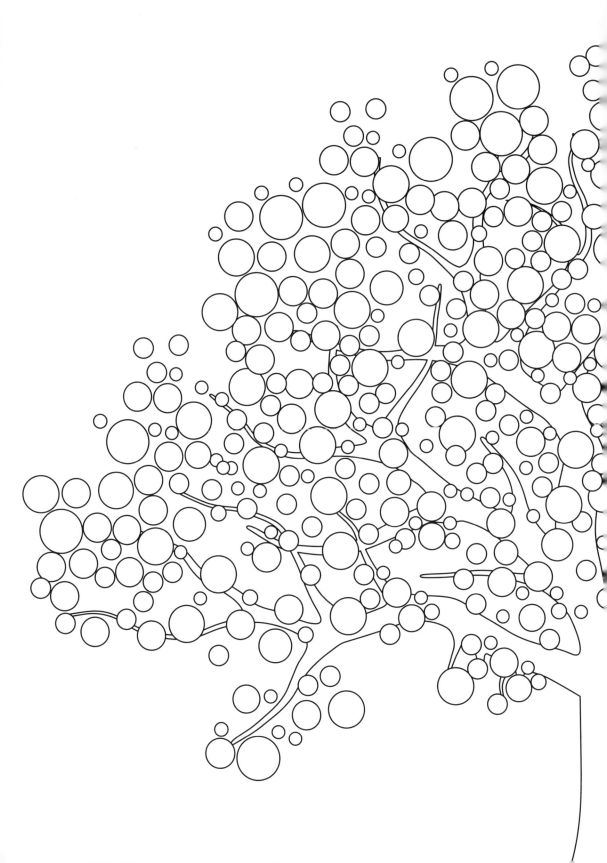

In this part of the book, we lay the foundations on which you can build successful teams and organizations. We do this by using Google's ten behaviors of great managers to measure manager feedback, then using five Brilliant Basics to build high-trust relationships and intrinsically motivated teams. The principles of Managing Without Power help you to apply the behaviors of brilliant managers, and the five Brilliant Basics with attention and care for all types of people on your team, so all people are at their best and are working well as a team.

Google's ten behaviors of great managers

My most valuable source for personal and professional growth as a manager at Google, was getting manager feedback on *Google's ten behaviors of great managers*. Team members filled in a survey that covered the behaviors every six months, and they also answer open questions about what they believe is going well and what could be done better. The open answers were the most valuable source of feedback for me. Sometimes this was because team members made me aware how much they valued the things I did. For example the fact that I always reserved one hour a week for the one-on-one meetings with every individual that reported to me, consistently came up in the comments people wrote. This gift of time, the fact that I rarely canceled these meetings, and that I always showed up with attention for their work as well as for them as persons, was seen as an indication that I genuinely cared. Other topics that consistently came up were the full day of career conversations I ran with people, and the clarity of goal setting and communication. When you run this manager feedback-survey with your team, you will see that people in their comments actually refer to the ten behaviors of great managers, because they are so relevant. The comments by people show you what these ten behaviors mean within the context of your team. And that helps you to apply them more consistently.

Sometimes people made me aware that something I did, came out differently than intended. For example, my responsiveness to email is much greater than average. Underlying reason is the fact that I work in a highly disciplined manner with a zero inbox-policy, and I wanted my team to know that I'm always there for them. I felt I was giving them fast and reliable communication—no matter who sent me a mail, they would always get an answer the same day, and very often within minutes. One of my team members joked that I have a secret twin brother who adds to my productivity. For some people however, that created feelings of pressure. Not everyone prefers email as a communication channel, and my fast emails also made some people feel that I expected the same intensity from them. I became more selective as to when, how often, and to whom I sent emails. I still made sure every person always got an answer fast, but I tuned my style based on the preferences of the individual. For instance, I'd write a short sentence saying "Thank you! I read your mail and have put the topic in the agenda document for our next one-on-one conversation. The idea sounds promising!" That way I could show people I digested the information they sent me, without triggering the need for lengthy email exchanges. The last short sentence prevents people from worrying that I'm going to tell them in a one-on-one conversation why I think the idea is a bad one. If I thought the idea was a bad one, I probably would have planned a quick meeting to check whether I understood the idea correctly.

> *Some of the manager feedback you get, might not feel fair. Nevertheless it still helps you to understand the sentiment of the people on your team. You don't have to agree with everything*

There was also a period when the leadership team I was part of went through difficult dynamics. A peer manager of mine had joined the team, and turned out to be a tricky personality. Because I had become a "safe haven" for people, they came to me with stories about things that happened. Political behavior from this peer manager complicated the collaborations between the sub-teams that had interdependencies with one another. I ended up escalating these stories across a period of more than two years, often at personal risk. This took a toll on me. At one point I chose to share with my team the pressure I was under, and what it did to me. I didn't share full details about all things that had happened, because situations like these come with a lot of confidentiality-issues. I shared enough for people to understand why the situation was hard. I made them aware of their own responsibility (and rightly so) to escalate into all relevant channels, while also making sure they knew I would have their back. In the manager evaluations afterwards, this moment consistently came up as something that people had highly valued. Partly from a perspective of transparency, it empowered them to take control of their challenges. Yet they mostly valued my vulnerability. Until that moment, many of them had formed an image of me that was a tad "superhuman." The downside of this is that people might feel they need to be perfect. Everybody has bad days, or bad periods. No one is productive and happy all the time. The fact I shared that I wasn't perfect, made it OK for people to have bad days or even bad periods, and share these with one another and with me.

Sometimes people wrote feedback that I fiercely disagreed with. It could make me feel misunderstood. As a manager you always juggle conflicting needs, and you can't give them everything they want. Not everyone understands that. So some of the manager feedback you get, might not feel fair. Nevertheless it still helps you to understand the sentiment of the people on your team. You don't have to agree with everything. It feels scary to be evaluated by your team as a manager, but the insights easily make up for that. Now, let's have a closer look at what these ten manager behaviors mean. A great manager...

...Is a good coach

Coaching and feedback are covered in the chapter about the fifth Brilliant Basic, fair and predictable performance evaluations, so I will keep it short here. This statement relates to your ability to give people actionable thoughts, ideas and feedback that help them to do their work better, being a better professional and person. A lot of that is achieved by asking questions that help people reflect, and that trigger ideas. It's a risky territory as well, because you can't coach someone who doesn't want to be coached (by you). This is where a foundation of trust is so important.

...Empowers the team and does not micromanage

This phrase means different things to different people. What is micromanagement to one person, might feel like valued supportive behavior to another. Where one person might feel a broad briefing, and lots of space to make their own decisions, is empowering—other people might feel lost and stressed because of a lack of guidance. Empowerment and micromanagement are also situational. One and the same person might need lots of support and guidance when working upon a project that has high ambiguity, or that the person has less affinity with, whereas the same person might want lots of autonomy when working on a project one feels confident about. So this statement is very much about your understanding of the individuals that work for you: their skills, working styles and experience levels with different topics. And it's about your ability to flex your management style as to different people and situations.

You have a lot of influence upon the outcome of this statement by being aware and explicit as to how decisions are made, and who makes them. Some decisions need to be made by you—top-down. That's OK, as long as it's clear why a top-down decision is needed. Many decisions can be made by your team members. The principle I work by is that decisions should be made by the smallest group of people who collectively has all the relevant knowledge, which oversees all implications, and cares about these implications. Depending upon the topic, a group of two or three people typically brings all the critical perspectives and knowledge to the table. They should therefore be trusted to make accurate decisions. In some cases you can agree that they do a final sign-off with you. This only works within a context where structure, direction, roles and responsibilities within the team are clear. OKRs, one of the five Brilliant Basics, play an important part there.

Your communication about who makes decisions, when and why, is what defines the experience people have. If you say you will make a decision and you don't; or you say people can decide for themselves—but then you overrule them without good reason and explanation, your score on this attribution will go down.

…Creates an inclusive team environment, showing concern for success and wellbeing

This statement combines several things. For instance, your actions are what matters here, more than what you say. Showing concern for success and wellbeing is about combining performance culture with empathy. And that environment needs to work for all people, not just people with certain working styles or characteristics. There is not one thing you can do to score well on this statement, not even a few things. This is about your holistic approach: how you connect with people, the team norms you set, and how you role-model those. Part two of the book covers how to build teams and organizations that are inclusive, and cover other aspects of diversity, equity and inclusion as well.

…Is productive and result-oriented

This statement says something about your ability to set directions and expectations, for instance by setting clear OKRs. It also includes your ability to make sure that all meetings are meaningful and effective. It includes your ability to hold people accountable, yet you also need to balance that accountability with a human approach, and with a care for wellbeing. The score also says something about your personal productivity: are you sufficiently on top of things to provide the team with timely input and feedback, fast decisions and clear direction?

If the lack of input from you slows down the team's progress, you can expect this score to go down.

...Is a good communicator, listening to and sharing information

This statement combines related skills. The more attentive you listen, the better you know what people need to hear, and the fewer words you need to convey the right information to them: both in verbal and in written communications. The process of defining clear OKRs also contributes to the perception of clear communication, and consistency is important: you can't say one thing at one moment and contradict yourself after that, or communicate contradicting facts to different people.

Sharing of information is more than passing on the decks and mails from senior leadership. It's about sharing the relevant bits of information, at relevant moments, with relevant people, while providing a relevant context. It's also about your ability to be transparent whenever you can. That last bit can be tough when you go through periods where certain sensitive information cannot be shared, for instance when a *reorg* is coming up. I've often witnessed managers struggling with this. I think they feared unintentionally sharing things they shouldn't be sharing, and therefore defaulted to sharing very little. I found that there are usually ways to share information, without compromising the need to keep things confidential. Even sharing the fact that there's information you can't share, is already better than nothing.

> *Career conversations and performance conversations are two fundamentally different things, yet they often get mixed up*

...Supports career developments and discusses performance

Career conversations and performance conversations are two fundamentally different things, yet they often get mixed up. Career conversations are future-facing: you try to assess in what direction a person wants to grow, and what path might lead there. Performance conversations are about the past: you assess a person's performance within a defined period in the past, and assign a performance rating (if that is how it works in your organization). You then discuss how you decided this was the right rating. In both conversations you can speak about skills (or a lack of them), and ways to develop new skills, so there is an overlap. Yet I highly recommend keeping career conversations and performance conversations separate. I have written sections on each of these topics, so I won't go any deeper here.

Your scores on this attribute will be high, when your team members feel that you understand their career aspirations, and make an effort to help them develop in the desired direction. For performance management your scores will be high if performance evaluations are perceived as fair and predictable. This implies that you can get positive scores there, even when you have to give people tough ratings. Even tough ratings can be fair and predictable.

…Has a clear vision/strategy for the team

The perception that there is a vision and strategy for the team is not about having some kind of "poetic-vision statement," or an elaborate written strategic plan. It just means that people want to have a sense of meaning and direction: Why does the team exist? Where do we play? Where do we not play? How do we make trade-offs in priorities? How does that translate to my personal role? If you deliver on these questions, you will score high as to this statement, even without writing a vision statement, or without having an extensive plan on paper. Of course, having an inspiring vision and solid plan when writing does help, but it's important to keep in mind that direction and meaning are the things that matter. I know loads of managers who wrote elaborate plans and visions—yet without creating a feeling of direction and meaning for their teams. In part III of the book you will find exercises on creating a vision for your team later on in this book. In the chapter about OKRs, I cover the relation between quarterly results and annual plans.

…Has the key skills to help to advise the team

Management is often seen as a generic transferable skill, but that transferability isn't unlimited. Anyone who believes a good manager can run any type of team, in my eyes doesn't really understand what great management means. A manager doesn't have to be the best or most knowledgeable person in the team, but you do need to have enough understanding of all knowledge domains in your team to connect the dots, to set a meaningful direction, to value the complexity, to know how much work certain accomplishments take, to spot risks, to appreciate what great quality looks like, to know when eighty-percent quality is enough, or when eighty-percent quality is harmful. I've had moments when my team expanded and I became responsible for topics in which my experience and expertise weren't as thorough. The first thing I did was to spend lots of quality time with these teams, to learn about their work, to educate myself, so I could be meaningful, and make the right decisions as a manager. There's also a risk, if you know too much about certain domains your team works on: micromanagement. But that risk is already assessed in the second behavior of great managers. The other risk is that you demonstrate higher interest in the topics you have more affinity with. As a manager, your interest in the domains in which your team works should be agnostic: it's not good for team dynamics if you noticeably have more affinity and a bigger interest in certain types of work within your team, and less in other types of work that team members do. Every part of your team should equally feel you are invested in their work, and that you value their accomplishments.

> *A manager doesn't have to be the best or most knowledgeable person in the team, but you do need to have enough understanding of all knowledge domains in your team to connect the dots*

...Collaborates across Google

If you use the manager feedback survey in your organization, of course you need to change the name *Google* to the name of your own organization. This behavior applies to large organizations mainly, because those are the ones where managers can make a huge difference preventing teams from working in silos. The problem of silos is the number one challenge that always comes up when I work with large organizations upon organizational transformation challenges. It's an inevitable downside of working in a large organization. Managers are the ones that can bridge the boundaries between teams, by collaborating well with managers from other teams, finding synergies, preventing re-invention of the wheel, or situations where a decision in one team negatively affects another team. They can define joint OKRs between teams, and push for change in the organization together. When managers role-model these behaviors, they create an environment that makes it easy for team members to also cross the boundaries of teams. Opening doors for cross-team collaborations can create huge positive energy within the team, because it's nice to feel connected with other teams and to work upon a common purpose. It also creates benefits for people's career journeys, because it helps them build a network. It enables them to experience at first hand what other teams do, and what their team culture is like. And it is great for the organization as a whole. Silos are one of the biggest sources of waste and lost opportunity in large organizations. They often cause a bad customer experience, and they slow down organizational transformation.

...Is a strong decision maker

This last behavior has a relation with the second "Empowers the team and does not micromanage." When you make too many top-down decisions where you add too little unique value, you'll almost certainly be perceived as a micromanager. The whole idea of Managing Without Power is that you only make top-down decisions in situations where your decision adds a value that your team members can't create from their position. This applies in particular to situations where decisions are complicated. They can be complicated for a variety of reasons: the situation might be political, a trade-off needs to be made, there's high ambiguity, team members aren't getting to an agreement, or a decision has significant resource implications. Moments like these happen all the time, and they are a great opportunity to demonstrate through your actions how you make decisions and why. There's always a risk that you get it wrong, yet you still have to decide. If you find the right balance, making decisive and fast decisions at the right moments, your decisions and leadership will be valued. If the balance is wrong, people will experience hierarchy, micromanagement, lack of autonomy, and possibly even psychological unsafety because their decisions are being overruled.

> *Silos are one of the biggest sources of waste and lost opportunity in large organizations. They often cause a bad customer experience, and they slow down organizational transformation*

A good example of an urgent decision with high ambiguity in my time of leading Google Digital Academy, was the moment when COVID-19 hit the world. It was in February 2020 when the first messages came that sounded worrying. My team at that period was running a few hundred face-to-face workshops a year, with Google's largest customers across Europe, the Middle East and Africa. In March we started to get last minute cancellations from our workshops. It wasn't clear how serious this problem would be, and how long it would last. People asked us to shift the workshops until after summer. We received bits of new information every few days. More cancellations came in. Meanwhile Google's sales teams told us customers weren't interested in running virtual workshops. They preferred to wait and see whether a face-to-face option would be possible later in the year.

At the time we were running about forty types of workshops, each with a different topic. The content was designed to enable face-to-face collaboration and problem solving. It wasn't certain that this format would work in a virtual setting. I knew that reworking the content of all forty workshops would easily take three to four months, and would cost lots of money.

I realized though that *not* making a decision could lead to a situation where we delayed these workshops until the second half of the year, only to discover then that we had to delay them even longer. If we would decide on that moment to start reworking the content to a virtual setting, we'd end up not producing any output as a team that year. For a team of more than twenty people that is unacceptable, and can lead to the team being terminated.

Within about three weeks I convinced our leadership team to make a decision. We'd start working to make all of our workshops virtual.

The only wrong decision is often not to make a decision

We were first out of the gates of all teams, and turned around our entire portfolio in about three months. After these three months we started welcoming the first clients into our interactive workshops again, but now virtually. We achieved the same customer satisfaction scores that we had in the face-to-face workshops. The team was acknowledged by leadership for the fast turnaround, and the team felt proud. I knew this was a high-risk decision, but I know it also earned me lots of credits. It's a decision moment I still feel proud of.

Your decisions don't always have to be right. A wrong decision is often a moment to demonstrate vulnerability to your team by the way you handle your own mistake. If you can set that example, your team members will also find it easier to admit mistakes. They will spend less time on the "blame game" and will find a way forward faster. In my Google Digital Academy team, it could sometimes be hard to know what topics for new workshops to invest in. Sometimes I'd ask the team to build for a new topic, which then turned out to be low in demand. In those cases I'd acknowledge I didn't get it right and stopped the program, or sometimes an adjustment to the idea helped us create a successful new program. Sunsetting programs became a standard part of our development process. Most of the time there are multiple "right" decisions. Many problems can be solved in many ways as long as you systematically keep building within the framework of the strategy you picked, while also course correcting. The only wrong decision is often not to make a decision.

…Managing without power and the ten behaviors of great managers

In the opening of this book I advocated for managers to lean as little as possible on the power that is inevitably connected to their position. What's left when you don't use that power? You can use your sharpened senses to invest in these ten behaviors with fully dialed up situational and personal awareness. The actionability and measurability of these behaviors enables you to awarily use the power that you have to demonstrate behaviors that create real value for your team.

This manager feedback survey is one of the most powerful tools that will help you to become a better manager. It will keep providing you with new insights when you engage with results in the right way. In the next part I will cover how to apply these ten manager behaviors in your work, and how to debrief results with your team to learn from their feedback. A survey frequency of once every six months is nice to keep track of progress, while also allowing enough time to implement changes in your management style. Want to give it a try? The full survey can be found in appendix 1 of this book. You can also find a digital version of the survey on Google's re:Work website (rework.withgoogle.com). When you read through the survey, you might notice there isn't always a one-on-one relation between the questions in the survey and the ten behaviors described in this chapter. This is because people can only answer survey questions accurately if the wording of the question doesn't have any ambiguity in it. For the sake of creating a valid survey, Google's people analytics team isolated manager behaviors more from one another. The survey is based on this Oxygen project though, and it's the same one that was used when I was assessed as a manager. You can use Google Forms or any other survey tool to run the survey. You can change things about the survey, so it works in your organization. It's important that you apply the right settings of the survey tool, so you don't collect email addresses from the people filling in the survey. That allows them to submit feedback anonymously.

If you are a manager of managers, I recommend you to run the survey only amongst the people who report into you directly. The managers working under you could do the same with the people directly reporting into them, so all managers get feedback. It's the combined quality of you and your managers that defines how well the team functions.

...Applying the ten great manager behaviors to your work

The findings of the Oxygen research project are valuable, but it means nothing if you don't apply the knowledge consistently. So, how do you make these behaviors real? First thing to realize is that this list of behaviors is *not* a "to do list" or a "tick-box-exercise." There isn't a single score in this list that you can increase by doing one particular thing. All survey statements are driven by a combination of behaviors. All of the survey statements are interdependent. All of them require situational awareness and the ability to flex your approach to the needs of different people. Many of these survey statements require a balance, so you can never be perfect. Luckily, your team doesn't expect you to be perfect. They expect you to be genuine in your care about them as individuals, your care about the team, and in your efforts to improve yourself over and over again on these ten behaviors of great managers. This book helps you to apply the Oxygen findings in a way that fits in with what your team needs.

> *Your team doesn't expect you to be perfect. They expect you to be genuine in your care about them as individuals, your care about the team, and in your efforts to improve yourself over and over again on these ten behaviors of great managers*

I have coached a lot of managers. Some of them were looking to increase their manager scores for the wrong reasons. When manager feedback is part of your performance evaluation, increasing these scores can be a tool to progress in your own career. But that defeats the purpose, because it's an egoistic motive. The survey is meant to get managers to care about the team's success. I think in most cases it was easy for the team to see which managers were genuine in their intent, and which weren't. If they weren't, the scores wouldn't move.

The number one way you can see the behaviors of a manager are more tick box than genuine intent is by the lack of situational awareness. If their intentions were genuine, they'd put more effort into assessing each situation and person, before deciding what is the best approach. Tick-the-box behavior typically comes in a one-size-fits-all treatment. Below are some examples of behaviors I've observed by managers trying to boost their scores, while lacking genuine intent:

- Trying to tick the box of "sharing information" by forwarding slide decks from senior leadership without any type of context.

- Planning a career conversation two weeks before the manager survey comes out, while failing to demonstrate personal interest in the months before.
- Out of nowhere starting to give people feedback and coaching in the weeks before the manager survey came out.
- Putting a vision on a slide, without any clear connection to OKR setting or prioritization.
- Waving a rainbow flag without demonstrating consistent actions to create a more inclusive team environment.
- Buying people presents, while clearly demonstrating disrespectful behavior on other occasions.

I've seen some managers get away with some of these behaviors some of the time. But typically it doesn't last. Faking it, might give a manager good feedback one or two times maximum. But then the team starts seeing the cracks because words and actions don't align, and scores quickly go down. My observation is that most managers genuinely want to do right by their teams, and those are the ones that will see their manager feedback increase over time, and that run the most effective teams.

…End-to-end discipline is a must

Besides genuine intention, there's one more ingredient you must bring to the table in order to apply these then behaviors successfully: end-to-end discipline. Every manager role comes with annoying admin-tasks: for example approvals and sign-offs for project decisions, expense reports, system access, travel, leave days, sick leave, return from leave, purchase orders, and then all types of input for budget planning, performance management, mandatory trainings, headcount planning, etcetera.

I easily get ten to twenty of these tasks a day, and it becomes a big mess when I don't attend to it for a few days. And then there's the stream of mails and chat messages that never ends. Still, I finish almost every day with an empty inbox and to-do-list. It doesn't mean I ignore and archive messages. Every message gets a reply, even if that's as short as:
- "I read it, and it's noted. Thank you!"
- or "Great that you are on this together. You can take me off the exchange, as I don't think I add more value from here."
- or "I like the idea. Feel free to move forward with it, but check with person X to align on topic Y. Tnx!"

When you are senior enough, an ABP (Administrative Business Partner) or personal assistant can take some of these tasks over from you, but most managers don't have that, and even *with* that support you'll still have a mountain of tasks like these left. I know these are annoying tasks, and find them annoying too. In fact, when people say they want to become a manager, this is one of the things I warn them about. But what you have to realize is that these "annoying admin tasks" are service levels to your team. Being slow at those, slows your team members down, and sends the signals that they don't matter. You keep your team in flow by being responsive. They are more efficient and effective as a result. Seeing their own impact and speed, and feeling the support from you, boosts their motivation. So I always make time for these tasks, most of the time the same day the task arrives.

The principle of senior shortcuts applies here too: would you have been slow in approving an expense report for the boss of your boss? Lack of discipline and lack of timeliness in admin-tasks like these, are the first step of undermining all the principles of/in this book, because all principles build upon one another. Cracks in one area cause cracks in all areas. The only way you can apply the principles of this book with maximum effectiveness, is with an end-to-end discipline based on genuine intent. Again there is an analogy with sports here. At the highest performance levels, all people have talent. The ones that compete at the highest levels, are the ones that do not slack in anything: they step over the things they don't like about being a competitive athlete, and make the investments anyway, because they know it's part of the deal.

When I entered working life after twenty years of competitive martial arts, my biggest disappointment was the lack of discipline I observed in the colleagues around me. Of course you don't need to aim at being a world champion in something, but I know for a fact that the principles for being a great and effective team leader cannot be successfully implemented without end-to-end discipline. I've done it for many years in high-pressure performing organizations, and I do *not* work structural overtime, because I want to set an example for my team and my kids, and because it's important in general. I do work evenings every now and then, when I really want to finish something. That's almost never because of a deadline. If a deadline is the reason for working late, you just haven't prioritized sufficiently enough. Deadlines can almost always be anticipated. Of course there are certain jobs where emergencies are the core of what the job entails: for example when you work at an emergency room, or in a PR job for a large public company. Even in these roles, you plan resources, tasks and time, so there's space for regular emergencies to happen, without causing people to get a burn-out. The best PR managers are the ones that can move into a proactive mode, investing in activities that *prevent* PR-crises from happening, despite the turmoil. When I work late, it's mostly because something needs to be created that demands more mindspace, but that makes my life easier later down the line. It's often in the startup phase of a new job that this happens. Once I'm longer in a job my structures are in place, and most things can be anticipated and planned for.

So discipline is absolutely not about working many hours. It's about commitment to prioritize the right things at the right moments, which implies deprioritizing other things. In fact, if a person makes lots of overtime, that typically means they have a *lack* of discipline and *don't* work as thoughtfully and effectively as they could. It's like a diet. You can choose to slack, but the direct consequence is that the diet is less effective. The critical thing about a diet, is to design it so it fits sustainably into your life, and can be committed to for the rest of your life. People with a lack of discipline don't see enough impact from sustainable healthy diets. They then revert to extreme diets that you cannot sustain for an entire life, and that are often less healthy. The weight goes down and up, down and up, and health is never optimal as a consequence.

You cannot succeed in applying the principles of this book without discipline, but you will find that getting manager feedback from your team is very motivating. Addressing one or two areas of improvement, each around of feedback, will make the steps small and achievable, and the progress tangible and rewarding. You will feel your team's gratitude when they see you acting up/on their feedback. You will see your team perform better, and the team culture will visibly improve. That will give you lots of energy to continue improving yourself. I will cover how I used my manager feedback to improve in small steps.

The principles of Managing Without Power create an environment for you and your team to be highly effective in a sustainable way. When you read through the book, and the recommended actions, and you find yourself doubting whether it's feasible for you to apply certain principles, I encourage you to challenge yourself: why is it that you think you can't apply this consistently? Would you also not have done it, if this were about servicing the boss of your boss? Where can you make sharper trade-offs in work and life, so that you create the space and discipline to do this consistently?

Critical points
- When managers "unlearn" the unaware use of power, they can use their sharpened senses to invest in Google's ten behaviors of great managers with a maximum personal and situational awareness.
- The ten behaviors can only be applied successfully when intent is genuine. Lack of genuine intent typically shows through a lack of personal and situational awareness and damages trust and motivation.
- End-to-end discipline is critical to maximizing your potential as a manager and leader, and also to maximize the potential of your team.

Improving yourself with manager-feedback from your team

So, what is a good manager feedback score? First of all, that requires you to know how to calculate the score in the first place. The survey in appendix 1 works with a five-point Likert scale that goes from "strongly disagree" to "strongly agree." The top-two answers ("agree" and "strongly agree") on that scale are considered positive answers. And the sum of the positive answers defines your manager's feedback score. When all people score you "agree" or "strongly agree" on all questions, you get a 100-percent score.

Let's go through an example:
- Let's assume you have nine people who report directly to you.
- Seven out of those filled out the survey.
- The survey asks people to score you on thirteen quantitative questions, so in total there are a maximum of 91 answers given (7 × 13).
- Important: the survey allows people to skip questions when they feel these are not applicable. You have to subtract them from the total. Let's assume there were nine instances in which people skipped a question. The base for your calculations is then 82 answers (91 − 9).
- Now count the number of questions where people scored you as top two on the scale. Let's assume 71 out of the 82 answers are a top two answer.
- Your score is now "87-percent favorable manager feedback" (71 ÷ 82 × 100%)

So a 100-percent favorable manager feedback score means that all answers from direct reports that have filled out the survey were top-two scores. Is an 87-percent score good? It depends on the situation.

What you do with the results matters more than what the score is. Your manager-score should be the start of a journey of dialogue with your team, in order to improve your manager skills based on their feedback. If you have the dialogue in the right way and demonstrate through your behavior that you act upon feedback, the score will inevitably go up over time.

To get high-quality feedback from your team, you first need to win their trust. Getting manager feedback is somewhat scary for the manager, especially if it's the first time you experience this: What if results are bad? But giving feedback *to* your manager is also scary. Giving honest feedback to your manager, and then discussing it together is by definition a risky business. You might think it's safe for people to give you feedback, but you are the one that has the power. Most people have experienced situations in their career where being honest and saying something to a senior leader (that this person didn't want to hear) backfired. Some people may even have lost career opportunities over this. So people are understandably weary when they have to give a manager feedback. Different people experience different levels of trust and risk, yet in order for you to have a 360-degree view, you need honest feedback from all people.

> *Giving honest feedback to your manager, and then discussing it together is by definition a risky business*

So, the first round of manager feedback that you get is almost certainly not going to be of the highest quality. The way you engage with the team on the feedback, and the way you act on it, defines the feedback quality that you will get in future surveys. You need to find ways to have an open conversation that helps you to understand what the feedback means, and how you can act upon it. If you then demonstrate through your actions that you take the feedback seriously, you will enter an upward spiral with your team: higher trust, sharper feedback, more opportunities to act upon the feedback, higher trust, sharper feedback... etcetera.

I used the four steps in figure 3 to improve myself, based on the manager feedback from my team, and in doing so to win the trust of the team.

Step 1 was analyzing the results and reflecting upon them. I checked on which statements I scored highest, and on which lower. The comments people wrote, about what went well and what I could improve upon, were the richest source of information. Particularly that part of the feedback becomes a richer source of information when you build more trust. The open comments in those surveys are most risky for people to fill in, because as a manager you can often recognize whom a comment comes from—based on the language they use or the situations they describe. The worst thing you can do to damage trust within your team, is to use something people wrote in these comments, and to confront them with it in a way that might feel threatening to them. Even the feeling of mild pressure based on a comment in the survey is already enough to damage trust. It doesn't

Figure 3 *Improving yourself through the feedback from your team is more important than what your manager-score is: four steps for entering an ongoing dialogue and improvement journey with your team.*

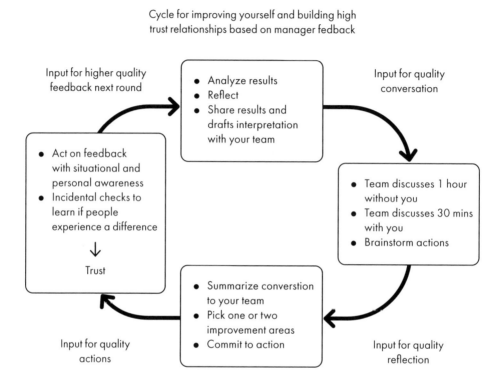

mean you cannot discuss comments with individual people. It just depends on *how* you use the information. A curious mindset is key. No matter what people write about you, they are never wrong. Not even if you disagree fiercely. Your objective is not to be right. Your objective is to find out how your management style makes people feel, so your team members can't be wrong.

When I felt I had a good basic understanding of what the feedback meant, I summarized it on slides. I'd provide a quick overview of the quantitative results, showing which items scored highest and which ones lowest. Then I'd summarize in a few bullet points what I thought the feedback meant. I'd list things I thought people were happy with, and I'd list things I thought people were less happy with. Next I'd write down features I intended to keep doing, or dial up more of them. I'd also list new things I'd like to try, and things I wanted to avoid. Finally I'd phrase questions about things I didn't feel certain about. Why is score X lower than the other scores? The score on statement A seems to conflict with the score on statement B: what do you think this means? I noticed several people commented about… I tried dealing with this issue by doing…, but it seems like that didn't work. Why do you think it didn't work? And what other options should I think of in order to improve this?

> *No matter what people write about you, they are never wrong. Not even if you disagree fiercely. Your objective is not to be right. Your objective is to find out how your management style makes people feel, so your team members can't be wrong*

I'd share the slides with the team in an email. In the mail I'd thank them for the feedback, ask them to read my analysis as a prep for a meeting I would put on the calendar, where we could discuss it. One of the phrases I'd often use was: "This is my personal interpretation, but you are the ones that wrote the feedback, so you know better what it means. I'd like to use the meeting to learn to what extent my understanding is correct."

Step 2 was a ninety-minute meeting with a special format. All my direct reports were invited, because these are the ones that provided the feedback. In the first hour of the meeting, the team would discuss the results, my interpretation and my questions, without me being present. That gave them a safe space to discuss the feedback, without worrying what my reaction would be. In the last half hour someone would send me a chat message, when the group was ready for me to join. Typically, by then one person would have taken the role of "moderator" of the discussion. This person would be the one who debriefed the main discussion outcomes to me. The moderator was a person who felt safe expressing the feedback to me. Through this aggregated summary, the people who might have felt less safe in expressing the feedback directly to me, could still convey their thoughts without having to step forward. The moderator would ask the group whether the summary reflected the discussion accurately. People would then often fill in some blanks, or a personal nuancing they wanted to add. From there I'd ask some questions and suggest the actions I might take.

These conversations were a good experience, and also it was a bonding experience for the team to have this hour of candid discussion without me in the room. Because my team was distributed across various countries, these conversations happened as remote meetings. Some people would sit in a small group in a meeting room. Others, including me, would join individually from a different country.

Step 3 was a debriefing email I had sent the team: I had written a short debriefing of the additional things I had learned from the conversation. I'd pick one or two improvement areas, and would commit to actions. Sticking to a small amount of improvement areas and actions at each feedback round, is a great mechanism in order to find the discipline for applying the behaviors of great managers. Every time you change one thing, and you see the positive impact upon the team, you feel their gratitude, and see a score go up that gives you the energy to tackle the next improvement area in your subsequent feedback round. I always asked people to let me know if it works or not. In some cases I'd still have a conversation with individuals in our regular one-on-one meeting about a theme that was clearly important to them.

All of the above ideally happens within a time frame of about three weeks after the survey results appear. The longer you wait, the more it feels to your team that you're not taking their feedback seriously. On top of that, over time people forget what scores they gave you, what they wrote and why. So the quality of their reflections descends the longer you wait. The only reason to delay this meeting could be that the team is going through a period of high workload, and you don't want to put another meeting on their plate. If that's the case, I recommend being explicit about it and ask what their preference would be: doing it now, knowing it's an extra meeting at a busy period, or doing it a few weeks later?

Step 4 is the genuine journey: you have to demonstrate through your actions that you do things differently. Most of the time you don't have to be explicit if you act upon a feedback. You need to allow your actions to speak for themselves. If you do that with great situational awareness, people will notice the difference. You could pick a few moments to communicate more explicitly what your efforts are to act upon the feedback. For instance, you could ask people in one-on-one meetings whether they notice a difference. Or you could use the next manager feedback-cycle to summarize the things you tried. If you do this consistently—with genuine intent, attentive listening and situational awareness—you will experience a bond of trust developing between you and the team. One that allows you to set high performance standards for yourself and for them, while still connecting at a human level. You will also see that this same connection and mindset is shaped *between* your team members. By going through this cycle over and over again, you set the most powerful role model you can.

Is 100 percent a feasible score?

My track record of twelve consecutive performance cycles, with 100-percent score, is rare for several reasons. It's only partly because of the effort I put into it. There were also elements of luck in how my team came about. When I joined Google Digital Academy, I originally inherited a small team of three people. But soon after I joined, there was a reorg. There was a new team structure, and all people, including myself, needed to apply to the jobs in the new team structure. In that process, I became a manager of a larger team of six people, which was a result of merging two existing teams. Nine team members applied for these six positions. Because I had already worked with these people, I had experienced at first hand which of them were the more powerful performers, with the best attitudes. That's a luxury position to be in as a manager, because in a normal job application you have to assess with a lot less of information which person is the best candidate for a role. The odds of getting it wrong are much worser then. In this particular case, it meant I could select six persons that I already knew were great people who could perform well. And that was the start of my team.

After that, in a relatively short space of time, two more reorgs happened. Meanwhile I had built up a positive reputation as a manager, so the same thing happened again in these reorgs. High performers from the teams that were reorganized landed in my team. Because of the way I managed the team, I retained almost all the people whom I hired, or that were moved under my management. Only one person left my team in a period of six years, and that's a someone we kept working in a freelance capacity.

In my first two cycles of manager feedback, I was completely new to management. So the 100-percent score definitely didn't reflect the fact that I had mastered all aspects of being a manager. I believe it actually reflected that my team saw the unusual and genuine effort I had put into getting to know them, and to building trusted relationships. You can't get twelve consecutive 100-percent scores that way, though. I believe the fact that I retained the high scores after that, was a result of relentlessly working to improve myself as a manager, making a conscious use of the feedback from the team.

When negative feedback appears in your survey, it mostly means you've overlooked several instances in which people gave signals that something was wrong

In most cases I'd notice myself where I could improve, so the feedback never reached the formal manager survey. When negative feedback appears in your survey, it mostly means you've overlooked several instances in which people gave signals that something was wrong. There were many situations where I noticed certain small reactions from people to the things I did, or towards one another, or the things they didn't say. I would reflect on those situations, build a hypothesis about what I might have done wrong, and would try whether a different approach worked better. If I wasn't sure, I would ask a person what their interpretation of the situation was. People saw because of my actions that I was genuinely listening and improving myself, and the more I did so, the more people felt safe to come to me directly with feedback.

The fact was the luck that I acquired my team through the process of these re-orgs, filtering out the strongest people. Although the reality is also that these people still chose to apply to the roles in my team, because they wanted to be in my team. They might have also chosen to apply to roles in different teams. The fact that I retained all the strong people for such a long period was a result of hard work, listening attentively and acting upon feedback.

The team situation could have been very different: imagine you inherit a team of ten people, out of which five are low performers or people with a bad attitude. It's almost certain that this will have a negative impact upon the culture of the team. You're going to have to turn these people around, or usher them out. Either way, you'll have to hold them accountable, and give them difficult feedback. When you have a team with high-performing people and great team dynamics, difficult feedback doesn't harm your scores if you land it in a thoughtful way. It can even increase your scores. But in the context of working with low performers, it's likely that, giving difficult feedback and managing people out, will backfire in your manager's feedback scores. That process can easily take several months or up to a year, so you have to mentally prepare yourself to accept lower scores during that time.

Consistently scoring 100 percent isn't a realistic goal, while scoring lower doesn't by definition mean you're not managing well. When you systematically improve yourself, based on the feedback from your team, and act diligently if people aren't performing, you can achieve scores between 80 and 95 percent under normal circumstances.

Are you being too nice to your team when you score 100 percent?
People often told me that getting a 100-percent score perhaps isn't a good thing, because it probably means you are being too kind to your team. I know this is untrue. It is possible to achieve a 100-percent score once or twice by just being kind to your team, or maybe by making promises about promotion or other kinds of rewards. But the reality is that, at some point, you do need to deliver on these promises. Every manager in an organization has to work within similar boundaries. There might be a certain distribution of scores you must stay close to, or for instance a maximum budget for reward and promotion. So you can't sustainably promise more than other managers can promise. A high score for one person typically means a lower score for another, and only a few people can get promoted. Yet all people need to score you 100 percent in order for you to get a 100-percent favorable manager feedback.

There are also lots of trade-offs between the dimensions that you are scored on as a manager. Too much of one thing leads to a lower score on something else. For instance, if your primary strategy is to try to get your team members to like you and to please them; at some point you're going to get low scores on the statement "is productive and results oriented," because you'll fail to hold people accountable. The statement "is a strong decision maker" will also suffer: for scores on this statement are primarily based on your decisions that require tough trade-offs. These are the types of decisions where there's no way to make all people happy. So a manager who is too nice to the team, cannot score well on those statements. It shows you how good this piece of research actually is. You can get a 100-percent score once or twice at the max, by faking or charming, but there is no way you can achieve a consistent track record of 100-percent scores (or even scores above eighty percent), without a genuine and balanced investment in the behaviors of great managers.

> *Consistently scoring 100 percent isn't a realistic goal, while scoring lower doesn't by definition mean you're not managing well*

Critical points
- What you do with the manager-feedback that the team gives you, is more important than the actual score.
- Pick one or two improvement areas every feedback round, in order to lower the barrier for yourself to create a real change, and use the manager feedback-survey to track the progress.
- When you consistently do this, it should be possible to score between 80 and 95 percent.
- Trust intrinsic motivation, and then improved team dynamics and effectiveness are the real reward.
- It can be scary to receive manager-feedback, but giving feedback to your manager is even more scary: for, when trust increases the quality of feedback goes up.
- It's impossible to consistently score high through faking or charming.

Five Brilliant Basics for great managers

Managing Without Power is about realness. Realness starts with the Brilliant Basics in figure 4. These are effective vehicles to help apply consistently to Google's ten behaviors of great managers. These are also the things that every manager must succeed at before thinking about anything else. If you fail at Brilliant Basics, there are few things left that you still can do well.

Figure 4 *The five Brilliant Basics for great managers.*

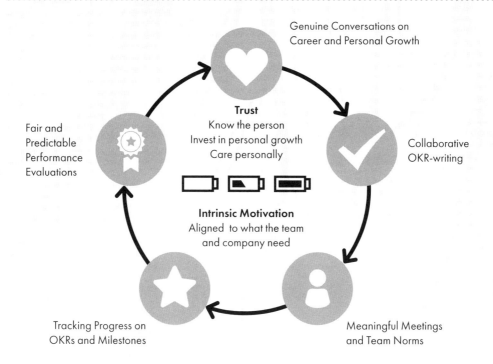

The following five Brilliant Basics will help you to build a strong foundation for your team: a team that is effective and that has a good team culture. The Basics build upon one another. That also means they will lean upon one another, so one weak link can break up the whole chain:
1 *Genuine conversations about career and personal growth* help you to understand who your team members are, what drives them, what drains their energy,

what they are good at and bad at, where they want to grow, what they want to learn, and more.
2. *OKR-writing* is the process where you align the intrinsic motivations from people to the things that the team and organization need from them. OKRs help you to a set direction and clear expectations.
3. *Meaningful meetings and team norms* will help you execute projects in order to achieve OKRs effectively and respectfully. They connect the right people at the right moment in order to agree upon the right actions and decisions. They keep people connected along the journey, so that communication doesn't fall between the cracks. Finally, they keep the manager connected to the team in order to connect the dots, coach, nudge, prioritize, give feedback and more.
4. *Tracking of progress on OKRs and milestones* will help you to correct the course where needed, hold people accountable, and identify the people who are delivering the most impact.
5. *Fair and predictable performance evaluations* help you to reward people who have delivered meaningful impact, and it also helps you deal with those that didn't.

> *If you fail at Brilliant Basics, there are few things left that you still can do well*

These five Basics are a circle that starts over and over again. When you implement the Brilliant Basics consistently, you build strong relationships of trust, and so you increase the intrinsic motivation of your team members:
- You build trust between yourself as a manager and your team members.
- Team members build trust amongst one another.
- You increase intrinsic motivation from team members, in order to make contributions that are valuable to the team and organization, and in order to learn and grow.

When high-trust relationships and intrinsic motivation grow, they become a source of energy, like a battery that is charged: this energy helps the team to perform, and it fuels the team's culture too. Unfortunately, this battery can also run out—that's what happens when you don't apply the Brilliant Basics consistently, because that almost inevitably leads to situations where, as a manager, you disappoint your team because your words and actions are out of tune. If you apply the Brilliant Basics systematically, you will see this reflected in higher manager-feedback scores. But more importantly, you'll see your team become more effective, and you'll see the team's culture improve.

It all starts with trust

The single most important thing you need to do when you start managing a team, or when new people enter your team, is to establish high-trust relationships. This is about the relationship between you and the team members, but it's also critical to nurture an environment that will lead to increased levels of trust *between* your team members. *Harvard Business Review* published an article titled "The Neuroscience of Trust" by Paul J. Zak, which is about trust. They combined the results from three types of studies in order to assess the "return on trust," and found some powerful proof points—compared with people in low-trust companies, people in high-trust companies report: 74 percent less stress, 106 percent more energy at work, 50 percent higher productivity, 13 percent fewer sick days, 76 percent more engagement, 29 percent more satisfaction in their lives, and 4 percent less burnout. Those are a lot of reasons to invest in high-trust relationships.

Trust means different things to different people. It's worth reflecting upon what trust means to you. Think about people in your life and at work whom you deeply trust. Why do you trust them? What behavior did they demonstrate to achieve this level of trust, and how do they retain it? And think about people in your life and work that you distrust. What did these people do that reduced the trust you had in them? Or did you never trust them in the first place? What behaviors confirm you that these people still can't be trusted? Are there any behaviors that would be a reason for you to revise your opinion about these people? What are behaviors which people can demonstrate that would earn them points on your "trust scale"? And which behaviors would make them lose points? To what extent are lost points reversible? What's the level of trust you typically extend to people when you meet them for the first time and still know very little about them?

The trust equation

A useful tool that came up in several of the manager trainings I had, is the "trust equation" you see in figure 5.

Figure 5 *The trust equation from* The Trusted Advisor *by David Maister.*

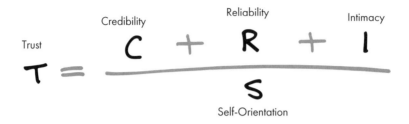

The trust equation was first introduced in 2000 by David Maister in his book *The Trusted Advisor*. The trust equation breaks down the "feeling of trust" into four dimensions. The three dimensions that build trust are credibility, reliability and intimacy. The dimension that reduces trust is self-orientation. Let's look at each in more detail.

Credibility: "I can trust what you say about…"
Credibility is "do people know what they are talking about?" We trust people like doctors and lawyers, because they are trained professionals. They've had to pass exams and have been tested to make sure they are credible, and that they have a level of knowledge to advise people. At work people assess one another in similar ways. What work experience does a person have? What companies and organizations has the person worked for? What roles were they in? What projects did they work on? What knowledge do they have? Of course those experiences and the knowledge only add to the trust levels if they are sufficiently relevant to the job the person is doing now.

Reliability: "I can trust you to…"
Reliability is about delivering on their promises, about alignment between words and actions. Do these persons deliver on their commitments, or do they consistently fail in this regard? Repeated failures to do what you say, undermine trust. Consistently being late for meetings, not meeting deadlines, or not meeting the agreed quality bar all are things that erode trust. There's a point with people where a part of you already suspects they might not deliver what they say they will deliver. That's a sign of eroded trust. Reliability doesn't mean the person always does what you want them to do. In fact, a person who always says yes is often less reliable. Some people say yes so often that they become overloaded to the point that they can't deliver on any of their promises. Reliability relates to clear communication and the management of expectations: if a person

knows when to say no, it also means they're more likely to deliver within agreed deadlines when they say yes.

Intimacy: "I feel safe discussing this with you..."
Intimacy has to do with how secure people feel in entrusting someone with personal information, particularly about doubts and insecurities. As a manager, it's the level of emotional security around you, including your level of empathy. If people feel they understand who you are, it increases their levels of trust in you. Sharing our vulnerability with people is an important driver of trust there. This explains why so many of my team members positively commented on the moments where I shared that I was going through difficult periods and situations. We can increase the level of intimacy that we have with others by opening up about who we are. We can share details of our personal lives, share our thoughts, feelings and doubts. The more you share about yourself, the more people share back to you, and then you need to listen with empathy and demonstrate that they can trust you to keep the confidential things confidential.

Self-orientation: "I can trust you care about..."
Self-orientation is the only dimension in the equation that reduces trust. It questions: Where does this person's focus lie? Do they have my best interests at heart, or are they doing this for themselves? Are they helping me, or are they simply doing this to get something out of it? If people sense that you care more about your needs and objectives than theirs, they trust you less. So to increase trust, you need to lower your self-orientation. Here's where the insight that trust is situational is helpful: by aligning mutual goals you can create situations where a person's self-interest aligns with your interests, so that you don't have to worry about their self-orientation and they don't have to worry about yours. Stephen Covey uses a nice phrase for this in his book *The 7 Habits of Highly Effective People*: the phrase is "Win-win or no deal." It encourages people to only enter partnerships and collaborations where there's something to gain for both sides. If you work hard enough to find common ground, you will see that this gets you there most of the time.

I like the clean and intuitive structure of the model. You can easily walk through different people in your mind, put yourself in their shoes, and assess how they might look at you on these four dimensions of trust. Or the other way around: you could visualize these people in your mind, analyze how they make *you* feel on these dimensions, and thereby understand better why you do or don't trust them. The model makes the concept of trust more tangible.

Exercise: Assess trust levels between team members and yourself
An exercise I recommend is to make two tables for yourself. Each of them looks like the one in figure 6, with the four dimensions of trust in the column on the left, summed up by a total trust score in the last row, and then the names of your team members at the top of each column.

Figure 6 *Exercise to assess trust levels between you and your team members.*

	Name 1	Name 2	Name 3	Name 4	Name X
Credibility	+ +	– –	+ +	+	+ +
Reliability	+	+	–	+ +	+
Intimacy	+	+ +	–	+ +	+
Self orientation	–	+ +	– –	+	+ +
Trust	7	6	4	8	8

In the first table, go through your team members one by one, visualize their faces as vividly as you can. This works better with your eyes closed in a quiet space. And then put yourself in their shoes while you remember conversations you had with them, things you said to them and how you might have come across. Think about situations they might have observed you in, or heard about you through others, decisions you made and how they might have interpreted those. Then try to assess how each person might feel about you on each dimension. Don't try to score too precisely, because you're working based on assumptions anyway. One or two pluses and minuses are sufficiently precise. In the bottom row you can sum up for each person in a score from one to ten what you believe their trust levels in you are. Remember that self-orientation works in reverse: more self-orientation means lower trust.

Look at the end result for each person, and then reflect: as to which of these people do I believe I need to work harder to win their trust? What dimensions do I need to dial up? What behaviors would help me to do that? What conversations would I need to have? Perhaps there are people for whom you know making more effort to win their trust just isn't going to work. For instance, they might lack the will to build up a trusted relationship with you. That could be a sign that your team isn't the right one for them.

Now do the same at your second table, but the other way 'round. Think about your experiences with each team member: things they said or didn't say, things they did or didn't do, how you've seen them work on projects, how they interacted with the people around them—or maybe feedback you heard about them. Score them with pluses and minuses on each of the trust dimensions, based on how you feel about them. Sum the scores up again in a score from one to ten.

Look at the end result and reflect: In which of these people do I have a low trust? What dimensions are causing that low trust? What behaviors or situations led to that low trust? Is my low trust a consequence of my own biases? Would I feel the same about this person if he or she had a different gender, skin color, ethnicity, sexual orientation, or if they were more like me? Would I feel different about this person if they were co-located with me, instead of working in a different country? If yes to any of the unbiasing questions, what can I do to unbias myself, and connect with this person at a deeper level? If you feel confident your low trust is not a result of bias: did I give them feedback about this already? If not, what do they need to hear from me so that they become aware of the impact their behavior has on my trust in them? Is it likely that I can turn their behavior around? What would that take? If it's not likely that my trust in this person can be turned around, or if it would take an unacceptable amount of effort, should I manage them out?

It's also nice to reflect on the people if you feel high levels of trust. What dimensions are contributing to the trust I have in this person? What behaviors or situations increased my trust? Is the fact that I trust this person more than others related to any biases I might have? Would I feel the same about this person if they had different gender, skin color, ethnicity, sexual orientation, or if they were less like me? Would I feel different about this person if they were working in a different country, instead of being co-located with me? If yes to any of the unbiasing questions, what can I do to connect to the people in my team where biases may have influenced the fact that I have a lower trust in them? If you feel confident your high trust is not a result of bias: Did I give them feedback about this already? Did I thank them for being so reliable, for their expertise, for their humaneness or for their consistent high-quality work, or the value they bring to team culture? If not, what do they need to hear from me, so they see how much trust I have in them and why? Have I rewarded this person enough through acknowledgement, pay, promotion, career opportunity, high-profile projects, connections or endorsement?

Actions that build up trust

Now that you have assessed how strong your trust relationships are with your team members, it is good to think about what behaviors would help build trust where it is needed. A book that helps with that is *The Speed of Trust* by Stephen Covey. The book lists thirteen behaviors that build trust:

1. *Talk straight*: Be honest. Tell the truth. Let people know where you stand.
2. *Demonstrate respect*: Care for others and show it. Treat everyone with respect, especially those who can't do anything for you.
3. *Create transparency*: Tell the truth, be real, genuine, open and authentic.
4. *Right wrongs*: Admit when you're wrong, apologize quickly, show humility, don't let pride get in the way of doing the right thing.
5. *Show loyalty*: Give credit to others, speak about people as if they're present and represent others who aren't there.
6. *Deliver results*: Establish a track record of getting the right things done. Make things happen, on-time and within budget. As Yoda says: "Do or do not, there is no try."
7. *Get better*: Continuously improve. Increase your capabilities. Be a constant learner. Don't consider yourself above feedback.
8. *Confront reality*: Tackle all issues head-on, even the "undiscussables." Address the tough stuff directly. Confront the reality, not the person.
9. *Clarify expectation*: Disclose, reveal and validate expectations. Don't assume they're clear or shared. Renegotiate if needed/possible.
10. *Practice accountability*: Hold yourself accountable first, others second. Take responsibility. Be clear on how you'll communicate how you're doing and how others are doing. Don't blame.
11. *Listen first*: Listen before speaking. Understand, diagnose, listen with ears, eyes and heart.
12. *Keep commitments*: Say what you'll do, then do it. Make commitments carefully and keep them at all costs. Don't break confidentiality.
13. *Extend trust*: Extend trust abundantly to those who've earned it, conditionally to those who are still earning it.

I find this list of behaviors highly practical and intuitive. The next exercise helps you reflect upon how to use these behaviors to build trust with your team members.

Exercise: Actions to increase trust between you and your team members

When you are thinking about ways to increase your trust levels with your team members, you can do a similar exercise to the previous one: building two tables that look like the one in figure 7. Put all actions in the first column, and the names of your team members on top of the other columns. In this case you can limit your first table only to the people where you think you have to build more trust, and your second to those that you trust less.

Figure 7 *Exercise to identify possible actions to increase trust between you and your team members.*

	Name 1	Name 2	Name 3	Name 4	Name X
Talk straight		+			
Demonstrate respect	+	+ +			
Create transparancy					
Right wrongs	+ + +				+ + +
Show loyalty	+ +				
Deliver results			+ +		
Get better			+ +		
Confront reality					
Clarify expectation					
Practice accountability		+ + +			
Listen first	+				
Keep commitments	+ +	+ +			
Extend trust					

Start with the people you want to build trust with. One by one visualize them. Remember why you think they might have a low trust score in you (based on the previous exercise). Go through the behaviors one by one, and reflect how much you believe these behaviors would help you increase trust with this person. If you believe there will be a low or neutral impact, cross out this field. You don't want to end up with a long list. If you think a particular behavior would help build trust with this person, assess with pluses how strong you think the impact of this behavior would be. When you finish the list for one person, pick a maximum of three behaviors, and agree with yourself how and when you will apply them to this person.

Next, do the same for the people where you have low trust in them (and are confident that this is not because of your own biases). Visualize these people one by one, and remember why you scored your trust levels low in the previous exercise. Then for each person walk through the trust-building behaviors one by one. Try to imagine whether your trust levels in this person would go up if they demonstrated these behaviors or not. If not, cross out the field. If you think demonstrating a particular behavior would give you higher levels of trust in this person, estimate with plusses how much positive impact that behavior would have on your perception of this person. When you finish the list for one person, pick a maximum of three behaviors that you hope this person would demonstrate more. Then think about how and when you are going to land that feedback with them. How will you explain to them what behaviors led to you having low trust in them? What behaviors would bring them back on track? Which projects or circumstances would be great opportunities for the person to demonstrate those behaviors? What do you think barriers might be? Can you do anything to make it easier to overcome those? Or is it better if you allow the person to take full responsibility? Commit yourself to a moment to deliver the feedback, and do the same for the other people on the list.

Despite the best intentions, trust can erode
Even when you do everything within your power to build and retain trust, it's worth acknowledging that situations can occur where trust is harmed in a way that's out of your control. Below are some examples that most managers will experience when they are long enough in the job:

- *Top down decisions beyond your control or visibility.* Sometimes your senior leadership makes decisions that you don't agree with, and that could even go against your values. Yet you may still need to enforce those decisions as a manager, and you can't always afford an attitude of openly disagreeing with senior leadership. In some cases those decisions might even be communicated without you getting a warning first, taking people by surprise. Moments like these can cause situations where you made promises that are being overruled. When you work in an organization where ratings and promotions are decided by committee, it's inevitable that there will be occasions where you need to give team members a rating that you don't agree with, or someone you think deserves a promotion might get declined. I've had many of these situations. The difficulty is that you can't just blame senior leadership, because that undermines people's trust in the leadership of the organization. That isn't good for anyone. But you don't want to end up lying to your team members either. I made my assessments case by case, to land whatever I needed to land in the most thoughtful way. It helped when I managed people's expectations in advance by explaining how "the system" works. For instance I would explain clearly where the limitations of my influence are in performance evaluations. When I received feedback about team members that I didn't agree with, I'd still explain to them what that feedback was, what the perception about them was, and I would empower them to influence that perception. Sometimes I explained that issues like these happen in any company, and that they'd better learn to deal with it. That way I could instill a sense of realism in people, acknowledging that things aren't ideal all the time. I could never completely avoid moments of disappointment, but on balance I think I made it work.

- *Moments of high impact for your team that require confidentiality.* Sometimes you know a high-impact decision is coming that will have a serious impact on your team, but you aren't allowed to communicate about it. An upcoming reorg is the most common example. In a reorg people could lose their jobs, or they could see colleagues they consider to be friends lose their jobs. And you haven't given them any warning! You can explain afterwards that you weren't allowed to share the information, you can coach people to deal with the situation, help them find new jobs, give them positive endorsement—yet some people might still resent you for never giving a sign that you knew this was coming. A mechanism I had to deal with this problem was to always make people aware that it's not a given fact that our team exists. Every team that exists is an investment of resources from an organization, and it's the job of that team to demonstrate it is still a good investment, by doing impactful work. There's a risk if you overdo it with this type of communication: people might start to feel unsafe about the existence of their jobs. Yet I still feel it's good if people take responsibility for the fact that the organization chooses to invest in them and in the team. In career conversations I would sometimes even bring up scenarios: if the team were reorganized out six months from now, what would you do? I also included the positive scenario: if a reorg happens and our team gets more resources and managers' positions would open, would you be interested in those positions? Going through scenarios like these prepares people mentally for moments of unexpected decisions. It needs to be clear these are hypothetical scenarios. That works best if you have conversations like these when there are no immediate plans for a reorg.
- *Information falling between the cracks.* Your communication consists of countless moments, one-on-one, in team meetings, mails, chat messages, career conversations, performance conversations, etcetera. In all of those channels you try to bring clarity of direction and expectations, but your team members also get information thrown at them from all sides, so not everything will always land and be understood in the way intended. Sometimes you

might have forgotten to clarify things, because you never expected them to be unclear. Sometimes people hear what they want to hear as a result of wishful thinking, or because they consistently have unrealistic expectations. This can, for instance, create situations where people think they will get a promotion or a certain rating, despite the fact that you actively managed their expectations. No matter what the reason is, bits of information will fall between the cracks, and sometimes that leads to disappointments. You can reduce how often it happens, but you can never eliminate it. When it happens, try to avoid assigning blame if you can. Just focus on figuring out what information fell through the cracks and clarify things moving forward. When you feel you could have done more to land certain information, you can apologize for the fact that information didn't land as intended.

Some team members will understand your position when you explain it, some won't and that may not always feel fair. I'm pretty certain there have been moments where some of my team members felt I made unfair decisions, even though those were out of my control. It's the reality you need to deal with as a manager. This is where manager forums are valuable: you can exchange experiences with peers about situations like these, learn how others deal with it, and see that you aren't the only one. Realistically you're never going to be perfect. But you can still try, over and over again, using the results of your manager feedback. Your team will see that and appreciate it, and most of them won't expect you to be perfect.

> *It is under pressure that you have the biggest opportunity to build trust with people, or a risk to lose it*

One thing is critical when it comes to building trust: it is particularly when you are under pressure that you can demonstrate to your people that they can trust you. It is under pressure when your values come out the strongest. It is under pressure that you have the biggest opportunity to build trust with people, or a risk to lose it. For example, if a top-down push from senior leadership would result in actions that are bad for culture, and you choose to challenge that, you send a powerful signal about the importance of a healthy organizational culture. So try to look at situations of pressure as an opportunity to stick to values, norms, agreements and promises, rather than an excuse not to.

Trust is powerful and it's the number one foundation of the effectiveness and culture of your team, but you miss the point when you look at trust as a "management tool." It's not something you tactically plan. It needs to be genuine, and tuned in at individual people and situations. Trust is not something you build once. It's largely built and maintained through consistent behavior over time. The five Brilliant Basics provide you with a framework to consistently invest in trust, building behaviors across all things you do as a manager. The higher the trust levels between you and your team, and between your team members, the more and the faster people will admit mistakes, learn from them and find a way forward. High trust means you as a manager are allowed to make mistakes too, without it instantly damaging relationships or it backfiring in your manager feedback. You can give people difficult feedback or tough performance ratings, and make painful decisions without demotivating people. High trust helps you bring your team along fast with organizational changes. I navigated my team through three reorgs in six years. In each reorg people lost jobs, and the periods before the reorgs got announced were full of tension and uncertainty. It was the trust we had between people, that helped me navigate the team through so much change in such a short amount of time. I imagine this is why Stephen Covey titled his book *Speed of Trust*: for when trust levels are high, everything you and your team do goes faster.

> **Critical points**
> - Trust is the foundation of every successful team: trust between the manager and the team, and for team members amongst one another.
> - Credibility, reliability and intimacy increase trust. Self-orientation reduces it.
> - The job of a manager comes with many situations, where trust can erode despite genuine intentions.
> - You can't be perfect, but most people don't expect you to be.
> - When trust levels are high, everything you and your team do goes faster.
> - The five Brilliant Basics help you make consistent investments that build high-trust relationships over time.

Intrinsic motivation

Besides trust, I have placed intrinsic motivation at the heart of the Managing Without Power model. Or to be more precise: intrinsic motivation, applied to what the team and organization needs. Having an intrinsic motivation to play the drums isn't exactly relevant if you are trying to build a career in finance.

Intrinsic motivation to me means people have an always-on will to add relevant value, to learn and grow. It doesn't require anyone to tell them what to do before they do anything. They seek ways to add value and improve, even when no one is watching. Team members that *lack* intrinsic motivation, or whose intrinsic motivations are too far removed from what the team and organization need from them, are the ones you always have to push and hold accountable. Even when you push them and hold them accountable, you don't get the same quality work, ideas and team contributions like you get from the intrinsically motivated team members.

> *The number one thing that kills intrinsic motivation in people who have lots of it, is top-down management or even worse, micro-management*

Intrinsic motivation is often seen as something people either have, or don't have. But as a manager you can easily destroy people's intrinsic motivation, and it requires an aware cultivation to maximize the intrinsic motivation that exists in people. When people have lots of intrinsic motivation, it doesn't automatically mean they will perform well. It requires a particular type of manager to create an environment in which these people thrive: a manager that can manage without power. The number one thing that kills intrinsic motivation in people who have lots of it, is top-down management or even worse, micro-management. It doesn't mean they can do whatever they want. In fact it's even critical that you as a manager set the right structure and direction so people can align their personal motivations to team goals and organizational goals. You just need to do it at the right moments, on the right level and with the right situational awareness. The ten behaviors of great managers already have this balance in them. People score you on the balance between empowerment (not micro-managing), but also on your ability to have a clear vision and strategy, and your ability to set clear structure and direction. The managing without power principles help you strike this balance, so that people deliver maximum impact based on the intrinsic motivations they have.

It's important that team members have intrinsic motivation in at least three aspects of their work:
1 *Internal drive and fascination for a variety of topics.* Drive and fascination in an individual manifest themselves in many ways. People are eager to learn about a topic, to try new things, create things or maybe even teach others

about the topic they care about. They seek new information, identify problems, design and test solutions in the areas of their fascinations, without being told to do so. Areas of fascination can be narrow or broad. People can have a small amount of fascinations or many of them. How much this matters depends on the role you need people to play. A specialist could for instance have a smaller set of fascinations than for instance a generalist project manager. Although you could argue that a fascination with project management is also a specialist skill. It just happens to be one that is easily transferred to many topics. Some flexibility and breadth in people's fascinations is critical though, regardless of the job they are in. Every organization changes over time, and the rate of change accelerates. So people need to be willing and able to develop new fascinations, in order for your team and organization to transform fast enough. Besides that, people need to have a certain tolerance for working on things that fascinate them less, because every job always comes with elements connected to it that aren't at the core of your fascination—yet you still need to find a way to do them with the right amount of care and attention.

2 *The will to align to strategy and guidelines from the team and organization.* The fact that people have drive and a fascination with relevant topics isn't enough in itself. You want people to apply their fascination in a way that is relevant for the organization. For example, two of my team members at Google Digital Academy had an extreme fascination with everything that has to do with organizational change and innovation. They were among the best that I met in this field. Yet I needed them to develop a point of view about organizational change that was unique to Google, and where Google had a right to speak. My team members did have the intrinsic motivation to align to strategy, so we built great programs together that leveraged the energy, creativity and expertise of the individuals, but that were still unique to Google. Team members need to be willing to apply their fascinations in ways that maximize their impact for the team and organization.

3 *Openness to connect to others and seek synergies.* Finally, in most jobs you don't build success on your own. People often need to work with peers or suppliers who have complementary skill sets in order to produce work that has maximum quality and impact. For most types of work you need to digest feedback from stakeholders, and use this to optimize your work and make it more relevant. For example, a person who designs processes needs to do so in a way that is workable and helpful for the people who use the processes. This means you need to be open to connect with people, share information, listen attentively to their opinions, thoughts and ideas, co-create, respect

their expertise, etcetera. A person who lacks the will to do these things is unlikely to achieve a maximum impact for your team and organization.

> *Team members need to be willing to apply their fascinations in ways that maximize their impact for the team and organization*

In the chapter about managing low performers, I will discuss how to deal with people who lack one or more of these three types of intrinsic motivation. But we will first start with the Brilliant Basics. These Brilliant Basics help you to maximize trust over time, and they help you understand people's intrinsic motivations, align them to the team and company goals, and cultivate them. The next chapter, the first Brilliant Basic, shows how to use career conversations to align people's intrinsic motivation with team goals and organizational goals, and also what to do when you see that this alignment becomes more difficult over time.

Critical points
- The number one thing that kills intrinsic motivation in people who have lots of it, is top-down management, or even worse: micro-management.
- Intrinsic motivation is critical in three areas:
    - Internal drive and a fascination for a variety of topics
    - Will to align to the strategy and guidelines from the team and organization
    - Openness to connect to others and find synergies
- Managers need to take action if one of these three is missing. What action that is, will depend on the person and situation.
- The five Brilliant Basics help you understand people's intrinsic motivations, align them to goals, and cultivate them.

Basic 1 Genuine conversations about career and personal growth

When I became a manager for the first time, I wanted to deeply understand each person in my team: who they are as a person, where they get energy from, what drains their energy, what they are good at, bad at, what they want to learn, what inspires them, what annoys them, what brought them to where they are now,

Figure 8 *The first Brilliant Basic is "Genuine Conversations on Career & Personal Growth".*

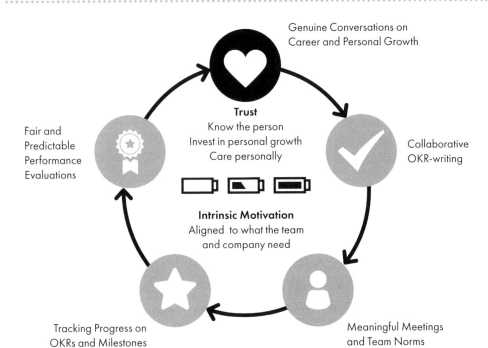

and where they want to go next. You can't know all of these things if you limit your interest to people's professional lives. People have more fascinations than their work, and these fascinations can help you understand how people tick. People's aspirations for work are typically influenced by what they aspire for in their private lives.

I was a remote manager for all of my team members throughout my entire time running the Google Digital Academy team. I was the only team member based in the Netherlands. The others lived and worked in six countries distributed across Europe, the Middle-East and Africa. When you are co-located, you learn a lot about people's lives during informal coffee chats, over lunch, and in the small chats you have before and after meetings. You don't have those things when you work remotely. I knew it would be harder to set the direction in a way that motivates people, if I didn't understand their motivations. I knew it would be harder to give the right projects to the right people, if I didn't understand people's skills and the ones they wanted to develop. I knew there was no way that I could manage remotely with a top-down management style, and I didn't want to be that kind of a manager in the first place. Running a distributed team remotely is impossible if your primary tendency is to manage top-down. You can't see all the time what people do and don't do. You can't control them all the time. On the contrary, I wanted people to work based on their own intrinsic motivation, and in addition I knew that you get more out of intrinsically motivated people if you give them more autonomy and flexibility.

In-depth career conversations helped me to genuinely understand people's aspirations for their career and personal growth. That helped me as a manager to create a situation in which they worked based on intrinsic motivation, so I could manage them effectively while being remote. For that reason, I drew out a lot of time for these conversations, and always flew to meet with my team members face-to-face for that purpose.

Separating performance and career conversations

I want to mention again that career conversations are fundamentally different from performance conversations. Career conversations are future-facing: you try to assess in what direction a person wants to grow, and what path could lead there. That conversation includes the near future when this person is still working in your team. But it extends beyond the time your team member works in your team, and could even cover scenarios when this person doesn't work for your organization anymore. Performance conversations are about the past: you assess a person's performance in a defined period within the past and assign a performance rating. Even if your organization doesn't have such a thing as formal performance ratings, you are still evaluating a person's performance. There's an element of "casting judgment" in that conversation. Feedback can be given by both types of conversations. In performance conversations you give feedback to explain how you arrived at your assessment of the person, and what they can do to grow further. In career conversations you give feedback to help people explore what it would take for them to achieve the career path they have in mind for themselves.

Because there is overlap between performance and career conversations, theoretically you could start with a performance evaluation, and then transition to a career conversation. Many managers do this, but it isn't ideal. This is because the mindset required by you and your team members to run these conversations—with the right depth and quality—is fundamentally different in one type of conversation versus the other. Because a career conversation is future-facing, it is an expansive conversation. It requires imagination to wander into all the areas your team member's career and life could develop into. An expansive conversation requires an expansive mindset, both by the manager and the team member. A performance conversation is by definition somewhat unsafe, because you are casting judgment on someone. If you do a great job building trusted relations with your team members, giving them ongoing feedback and managing their expectations, you can avoid negative surprises and make performance conversations a lot less unsafe. But there's always at least some element of unsafety in them. Unsafety leads to a reductive mindset, and it's very hard to shift from a reductive to an expansive mindset within one conversation if that reductiveness is caused by unsafety.

My career conversations were the primary instrument that helped me to develop a deep understanding of my team members. That knowledge aided me to assign the right projects to them: the ones where their intrinsic motivation matched what the team and organization needed, and the ones that helped them grow in the desired direction. As a result they'd proceed upon these projects with more energy and creativity. They came up with solutions I didn't think of, and they progressed fast, even when I wasn't watching. Often they would overdeliver versus the objectives we discussed.

What makes a good, or bad, career conversation?

At one point in my career I did a small survey, asking people to describe in their own words what their best and their worst career conversation looked like. For the best career conversations people said things like:

- The conversation explored career and life holistically
- It was genuine, open and honest
- It was aspirational
- It was actionable
- It was structured
- Lots of questions were asked
- It was non-judgmental
- It felt supportive, personal and empowering

For the worst career conversations people said things like:
- It was short-term focused
- My manager was disengaged
- It felt unpersonal
- Wasn't actionable
- It was vague and overwhelming

- There was a lack of trust
- My manager was directive and selfish
- It felt like a box-ticking-exercise
- The conversation never happened

I think these answers paint a vivid picture of what "good" and "bad" looks like. Apart from that, it's worth addressing the main objectives of a good career conversation:

- Knowing your team member, as a professional and a person.
- Your team member getting to know *you*, as a professional and a person (but please remember this conversation is not about you, so don't take over the conversation with your own stories).
- Understanding what gives people energy and what drains it, so you can design for the right balance of energies in their work.
- Understanding where people want to grow: in the near future, medium-term future and longer-term future, inside their current role, outside of their current role, outside of your team, or even outside of your organization.
- Understanding all the other things people hope for in life, so you can create an environment that helps them to design a work-life in a way that is compatible with their private lives.

If you achieve all of the above, and you follow up to make outcomes of career conversations actionable, these conversations become a strong driver of high-trust relationships.

Running a full day career conversation

A lot of my career conversations were full-day conversations, and I often had these talks while walking together in nature. But this certainly wasn't always the case. It isn't advisable to go for a full day of conversations for everyone all the time, and you don't always have to visit nature to have a good conversation. I always changed the length and format of the conversation, depending on the person and situation. For new joiners the conversations would be different than for people who had already been in my team for several years, and with whom I already had many career conversations. In my manager- feedback, people often commented positively about how these conversations kept bringing up slight new angles and insights over time, despite the fact that you don't cover completely new ground anymore. People would be grateful when we managed to find ways (big or small) to change their projects, or even their role in order to move closer to their desired career paths, one step at a time.

The COVID-pandemic forced me to change my approach significantly. I no longer had the option to visit people in their home countries. I didn't see any of my team members in person for a period of three years. I still retained the habit of running these conversations, but only differently and briefer. I will cover in this chapter how to adapt career conversations to a virtual setting, though I still recommend doing it face-to-face whenever you can. Let me start by walking you through how I ran my full-day career conversations, and from there I will explain how you can adapt this format depending on the person and situation.

> *Career conversations should feel structured, and you should prepare them, but ideally your team members don't notice that you're walking them through a structure*

In figure 9 you see the conversation framework I used. I rarely used the whole framework end to end. I also didn't bring it with me. That would make the conversation feel like you're trying to tick off a list. That would make the conversation less organic, less expansive, less genuine and less personal. Even though I didn't bring a list, I did prepare myself based on this framework. I'd have this framework at the back of my mind, to guide the conversation. I had hunches on what parts I wanted to zoom in on, to learn more. I personalized the questions to their specific situations and personalities. I think people felt there was a certain structure to it, but they mostly didn't realize how structured it was in my head. Career conversations should feel structured, and you should prepare them, but ideally your team members don't notice that you're walking them through a structure.

The four middle parts of the framework are the core conversation: focus, expand, imagine and bring back to the now. The first and last part of the framework are like "ease in" and "ease out", before and after an exercise. If you run a full-day conversation you can spend lots of time in these two stages. If the conversation is shorter, you'd probably spend ten to fifteen minutes max on each of those two. I will walk you through an example career conversation, to bring to life how the framework works in reality.

Ease in
I'd often meet a team member at the airport in their home country. From there we'd for instance travel to a nice lake in the neighborhood with beautiful forest

Figure 9 *Conversation framework for genuine conversations about career and personal growth.*

	Goal	Exemplary questions
Ease in	Tune in Build trust Prime for the conversation	How was your week? How are you doing? How are you feeling? What's happening in your work? What's happening in your life? How do you think the team is doing?
Focus	Assess the now Understand progress versus last career conversation	Are you still enjoying your work? What things give you energy? Which things we talked about last time worked out well, which didn't? Which things do you want to keep, drop, or want more of? Which skills do you want to use more? Which skills are you missing for your current role?
Expand	Explore • stretch in current role • next steps within the team • next steps outside team within the organization • next steps outside of the organization	How could we stretch your role to help you expand your skill set? How long do you think we can stretch the role enough? If we reached the limits of stretching, what could be the next steps in the team? If those steps don't work out, what options do you see within the organization? What options outside of the organization would you consider after this role?
Imagine	Explore • more senior or different roles to aspire to • future perspectives in work and life	Which person would you like to become or not like to become? Why or why not? (point out to example seniors or peers in different jobs) What would you do if money were no object? What does your ideal future life look like?
Bring back to the now	Seeds to plant • Skills to develop • Network to build • Projects to work on • Personal brand to create	What skills would help you qualify for the future scenarios you have in mind? What people would you need to work with to get on the radar and discover openings? What projects would support building the network and the skills? Could these projects be core work? If not, are you still in the right role? Given the skills you have and where you want to go, how should you position yourself so that others understand the roles you might play?
Ease out	Deepen personal understanding Go deeper on sensitive topics Relax	If you establish deep trust in previous parts of the conversation, natural opportunities will emerge to learn deeper things about the person (e.g. how they were raised and what shaped their world views), or you could cover topics for which regular meetings wouldn't offer the right psychological safety. This is also a perfect moment to relax (e.g. talk about music and what people enjoy in life).

around it. Ahead of these conversations, I'd always ask team members to pick a place that makes them feel relaxed. It brought me to many nice places. We did the same thing the other way around when they would visit my home country. I would bring them to nice places in the Netherlands. A relaxing space helps setting the expansive mindset required for this type of conversation, the same way it does when you run a team offsite in nature.

The conversation starts pretty much immediately. You talk while you travel to the location. How are you doing? How are things at work? At home? Automatically you cover the "ease in"-stage. If you can afford the time, you can wait until the conversation organically moves to the focus stage. In a full day's conversation that would typically happen by the time we started a walk in nature, or sometimes the "ease in"-stage would last until we'd sit down for lunch somewhere. The lunch would always be a good moment to pivot to the focus stage, if that hadn't happened organically already. If your time budget is shorter, you can steer towards the focus stage through the questions you ask. If needed you can explicitly move to that stage by saying something like "let's talk about your career reflections".

Focus
In the days before the conversation I would always send some stimulus to help people reflecting ahead of the conversation. It's easier for people to do that in their own time. It encourages them to prepare for the conversation, which adds to the depth. I don't force anyone to prep though, and I certainly don't ask them to put anything in writing. This allows everyone to prepare their own way. Later in this chapter, I will share an example of stimulus material you can share in order to prime people. Some people would come with sketches of visuals they used to organize for themselves, some would just come with thoughts. That's all okay. The fact was that people had done at least some thinking, before the conversation allowed me to open the "focus stage" with a phrase like: "So I imagine you've done some reflecting on your career. Can you tell me more about that?" I'd let them open the floor and then kept asking, using versions of the questions listed at the focus stage. I'd make those questions more specific by referring to specific projects they worked on. If we already had career conversations before, and we'd tested working on new projects, I'd ask whether that worked out as expected or not. The fact that you refer back to things discussed in the previous conversation six months ago, and that you remind them of the fact that you acted on it together, increases trust levels so that you can take things to the next level in this new conversation.

Given the amount of time between those conversations, you have to take notes so you don't forget these things. I prefer not to take those notes during the conversation, because it makes it less organic. I always take my notes directly after the conversation when I'm back home.

Expand

When you look at the example questions in the focus and expand stage, you might notice that I start in the here-and-now, and then move towards the future, step-by-step. From the projects people work on now, to the new projects they could do within their current role, to new roles within the team, potential roles outside of the team, and even a future outside of the organization. Some managers run career conversations the other way 'round. They would for instance start with the question "Where do you want to be five years from now?" This may work for some people, but I find that many people struggle to come up with an answer if that is your first question. When you start in the here-and-now, and take people into future scenarios step by step through your guiding questions, many people will find it easier to give you answers about their longer-term future.

What you might also notice in these questions, is that they are exploring possibilities to stretch people's roles in order to fit their career aspirations. Yet the questions also acknowledge that there could be scenarios in which people's personal objectives may no longer match with what the team needs from them. This honesty is an important part of career conversations, and it is why you also have to explore scenarios outside of the team and the organization. When you can build trusted relationships with people who allow you to have conversations about futures beyond your team, you can prevent situations where people are no longer happy in their jobs, and then spiral down. This can prevent situations of low performance.

If the trust between you and your team member isn't big enough, people may not give you full transparency about the things they don't like about their current role, or the scenarios outside of your team that they might consider. They might fear a backfire in an upcoming performance evaluation. If a manager knows a team member might leave the team soon, is that manager still going to advocate a high rating? Or a promotion? Or would the manager then prefer to give the higher rating and promotion to team members who are more likely to stay on longer with the team? It's easy to see why people may want to keep information from you, and how high your integrity as a manager needs to be in order for these conversations to reach the full depth that they may go.

Imagine
At the "imagine stage," we discuss the scenarios that might be away out in the future five to ten years from now. The further out you go, the more scenarios there might be, and the vaguer these scenarios may become. I therefore prefer to throw in specific examples. Instead of asking "where do you see yourself?", I prefer to point to some examples of people who are a few years ahead in their careers. That could mean pointing to people two or three layers up in the organization, vertically or diagonally. "Would you see yourself in the role of this person? Or that person? Why? Or why not? What parts of that person's job appeal to you? What part doesn't? And what if you would have their job and would be able to run it your own way? Which of your skills would make you successful in that job? What do you think you need to learn?" I often point to people in different parts of the organization, or to different companies or organizations of which I suspect they could match a person's aspirations. Sometimes I deliberately point to people who are on a similar job level, but work in different fields that might be interesting. This opens scenarios where the career growth doesn't necessarily have to go upwards. Horizontal moves can be a great source of growth and energy for people across various stages of their careers. Going through examples like these helps people articulate far more precisely which scenarios are desirable and which ones less so.

The question "what if money were no object?" is an important one to move into the most expansive state you can be in. And once you are in that state, after having brought your team member there step by step, the last question "What does your ideal future life look like?" becomes a lot easier to answer. This question expands the conversation beyond work, which is something you should also consider at the other conversation stages. At the "ease in"-stage people may have shared things about their life. In the other stages you can awarily refer back to those things, and ask people how certain work-related things would fit in with their personal lives.

Bring back to the now
So you have now expanded into a variety of future scenarios in the short, medium and longer-term future. If you'd leave it there, the conversation would end up being vague, and it wouldn't be very actionable (although it may still have

been a great experience). This stage is where you explore opportunities to take real steps, big or small ones, that help your team member to increase the odds that one or more of the desired scenarios will actually happen.

At this point many managers start talking about courses people might do, or about joining a mentorship program. At Google you have a concept called "twenty-percent projects." These are projects where people are allowed to spend twenty percent of their time upon a passion area. It's easy to suggest that a team member should jump onto a twenty-percent project, as an action following a career conversation. Yet it's better if you can achieve it in the core role. In my experience you can mostly facilitate career ambitions by putting people on the right projects that stretch their core role, connecting them to new teams, and helping them build new skills. It just requires some creativity. When ambitions discussed in the career conversations cannot be enacted within the core role, that's a sign to me to have a conversation about how long this role will stay sufficiently interesting for the team member.

Sometimes you need to allow the ambitions of your team members to shape part of your strategy. For instance, I referred earlier in the book to two team members in my Google Digital Academy team, with a fascination for organizational change and innovation. Around that time the *Google Cloud Business* was growing fast. Organizational transformation is a topic high upon the list of Cloud customers, so we increasingly got a demand for creating programs about organizational change for the highest management level: the C-suite (CEO, COO, CFO, etcetera). The fact that there was demand, and that I had team members with talent and fascination for the topic, had made me decide to start investing in these workshops. If either of the two hadn't been true, I would not have decided this. It wouldn't have made sense to do this, if personal ambitions didn't align to business needs. So don't overdo it when adjusting strategy to the ambitions of your team members. If personal ambitions of individual team members would push the team too far off the strategy, it's better to have an honest conversation about the limits of what is possible within the team. At the end of this conversational phase, you'd discuss how ideas translate into specific projects and OKRs. You can take these into account in the future cycles, when you are writing OKRs for the team and individuals (OKR-writing is the second Brilliant Basic that I will cover next). Trainings and mentorship can also be part of the action plan. This action-oriented phase in the conversation largely determines how these conversations help you to strengthen trust-relationships and the intrinsic motivation among your team members. If these conversations lead to concrete actions that help your team members to grow, then both trust and intrinsic motivation will grow. On the other hand, if these conversations do not lead to concrete actions, then that will lower trust and motivation. So make sure you formulate clear actions—*and* that you implement them as well.

Ease out

The "ease out"-stage is a moment of relaxing. If your time budget is short, this is just a casual conversation to close down the session. If you are in a full-day career conversation, and the right levels of depth and trust have been achieved, this is a moment when all kinds of things can crop up that are on people's minds. These might be sensitive topics that you wouldn't normally discuss within a meeting. But this may also be a perfect moment to talk about music, sports, art, food, or whatever topic comes to mind. That is when you can add more color to your understanding of the people in your team.

Preparing for career conversations and following-up

I mentioned earlier that I always send people a stimulus ahead of career conversations. The material I use most often as a stimulus are the "Pivot questions" in figure 10.

Figure 10 *Pivot questions from the book* Pivot, the only move that matters *by Jenny Blake.*

Plant Know yourself	Scan Brainstorm skills, people & opportunities	Pilot Run experiments	Launch Take a smart risk
• What is most important to me? • What are my top strengths? • What is my ideal day? • For what do people come to me for advice? • What do I enjoy most about my current role? • What impact do I want to have in the next year? • What does success look like over the next year? • How do I want to feel one year from now?	• Who do I admire? • Who do I want to build a relationship with? • Who is doing something that excites me? • What skills do I want to learn or to grow? • What skills of mine are in demand? • What challenges excite me most?	• What experiments can I try? • What experiments have I tried that I could build upon? • What next action can improve my skills? • How can I expand within my current role? • What opportunities exist (twenty-percent projects, volunteer activities, job shadowing, etc.)? • How can I track the results of my pilots? • Which of my next steps comes first?	• What have I learned from my pilots? • What is one goal I've got for the next year? • What larger moves or projects would I want to tackle in the next year? • In what direction do I want to move?

Pivot is a book about careers I highly recommend. It was written by Jenny Blake. The book describes how tangible experiments can help you to prepare for career pivots. She defines four stages that help to realize the next step in your career. "Plant" is the moment where you stop and ground yourself: "who are you, and where do you want to go?" "Scan" is where you look at your environment in order to explore options. "Pilot" is where you define tangible experiments that allow you to take the first steps on your journey that could lead to a career pivot over time. A career pivot is a methodical shift into a new, related direction, based on a foundation of your strengths and on what is already working.

The questions are very suitable as a reflection tool, ahead of the conversation. The people I shared this with as a primer, always responded positively to it – and came prepared with meaningful reflections as a result. It's even possible to use the same set of questions to prime for several career conversations with the same person over time. Each new moment leads to new reflections, even if the questions don't change. I don't recommend though to use these questions to structure your conversation. They don't work well as a conversation framework, which is why I created my own structure for career conversations.

After closing the career conversation I always write down the things I heard and understood in a short email to my team member. I also add the agreed actions to that mail. I then ask my team member whether this was an accurate reflection of the conversation or not. Sometimes people reply with some additional nuances. I would then combine my own mail and their reply to store it, within a document in order to remember what we discussed. I revert back to this document whenever we write OKRs for the team, so I can consider people's career ambitions when writing OKRs, and I also revert back to this document in my preparations for the next career conversation with this person. Finally, I often refer back to career conversations in one-on-one meetings to verify how well we're progressing with the actions we agreed on. That might help discover opportunities to correct the course. If you keep coming back on meaningful moments to what was discussed, this is what builds most trust with people to go a level deeper in next conversations.

I never force people to write their career plan down. I prefer giving them the autonomy to decide how to best store their ideas and plans. It's their career, so they will own it in the end. After the career conversation, I put a reminder on my calendar about five months later, to ask team members whether they feel it's a nice moment for their next career conversation. I don't force any fixed frequency on anyone, but typically twice a year is nice. Long enough to progress with agreed actions, but short enough to stay in tune. For some individuals there could be reasons to run extra career conversations, and for others to skip one. Als long as people feel the door is open, that's all OK.

Running career conversations with varying lengths

I've mentioned that I tend to adapt length and format to specific people and situations. In a full day's conversation. The "ease in"- and "ease out"-stages can easily take two hours each, and the other four stages combined might take about three hours. It's also possible however to run an effective career conversation within a total of three hours, or even within ninety minutes. This is particularly true, once you have established a number of high-trust relationships. A shorter conversation will inevitably be more transactional. A longer conversation leaves more room to deepen and enrich the connection between you and your team member—that is, if your team member will let you.

If the conversation lasts three hours. Then I'd spend about thirty minutes on "ease in" and again thirty on "ease out". The other stages combined would then take about two hours. You'll need to become more focused in moving the conversation on by asking the right questions. But three hours is a decent amount of time. And then conversation won't feel rushed at all.

If the career conversation is ninety minutes, I would decide in advance on which of the stages I want to zoom in most. This is why it tends to work well with people about whom you already know more on the basis of previous conversations. You could skip certain stages of the conversation framework by summarizing what you remember from any previous conversations (by using your notes). You might ask whether something in that respect has changed or not. This will gets you there much faster, so that you are able to explore only the reflections that are new.

You can also disperse different parts of the conversation over separate conversations. This is what I mostly do if a person is new in my team. I will then know less about them, while levels of trust may not be there yet, though this person is then also in the intensive process of onboarding. That last bit means that the headspace for a long career conversation might not yet be there. It's also hard to articulate answers to some of the questions, if you are completely new to the job. You will need to change the framing of some of the questions. For instance, when a person is about two months into the job, I would plan a conversation using elements from the "focus stage". Yet instead of asking "What parts of the job give you energy?", I might ask "What parts of the job are what you hoped they would be?" And "What parts do you feel less certain about?" Questions like these bring you similar information, but they also help you be of more support during the onboarding of your new team member.

At the four-month mark, I might plan another conversation. By that time the spirit would be more like the "expanding" stage. Again I'd reframe the questions. "You seem to have landed well in the job—is it still sufficiently challenging for you?" and "Are there any projects you'd love to work on more?" If the person is a high performer you might give projects of a higher complexity or of more autonomy. Should the person be happy the way things are, that's also good to know. If the person is struggling, you can see whether more guidance might be given, perhaps workload could be reduced, or whether a different type of project would prove a better fit to the skillset of this person.

At the six month's mark, it would be a good moment to plan "a full career conversation'. But the previous two conversations may already have provided you with a lot of understanding of this person, so you might zoom into specific parts of the career conversation much sooner.

Running career conversations remotely
I mentioned that you might ideally run career conversations face-to-face, but preferably not in the office and not at a video-conference. Yet, sometimes you have no other choice but to hold these conversations remotely. I did this for three years with my team members during the COVID-pandemic, so I know it's possible, though slightly less powerful than a real face-to-face conversation. The principles stay the same in a remote setting. If you can do so, I would still recommend visiting an environment that is relaxing. The main difference is that you can't do it together. Yet it still makes a big difference if both people walk or sit in a forest, versus sitting at their desk, staring at a screen. It fundamentally changes the dynamics of the conversation, and one isn't disturbed by emails and chat messages.

I bought a pair of wireless noise-canceling headphones especially for this purpose. I would highly recommend that. It allows you to sit or walk around in a relaxed way, while talking. You won't be able to see each other. But if both of you are in a quiet space somewhere in nature with only each other's voice, you'd feel as if you were close together.

When you run the conversation this way, the maximum length is about ninety minutes. I typically ended-up using something between sixty and ninety. In order for the conversation not to feel rushed, you need to prepare well, and choose carefully what parts of the conversation you want to zoom in on most. The earlier section "Running career conversations with varying lengths" will help you with that. I was positively surprised how well this still worked, and how much connection could be retained after three years of not seeing each other. I hope you don't have to spend that much time without seeing your team members, but I certainly know these remote-conversations are a good way to stay connected, and to keep building trusted relationships despite being in a remote situation.

Difficult career conversations
Finally, some career conversations can be difficult, or feel awkward. The most common reason why a career conversation can be difficult is when the trust between you and your team member is not serious enough. It may also be that a team member is not quite sure what they themselves want. That might result in you getting short answers to all of your questions, which makes it hard to understand what your team member's desires are. If that is the case, you ought to consider what the best strategy is. Don't try to force it into a long conversation. Instead, start with small steps. Start with a conversation of maximum ninety minutes. It's usually best to do that face-to-face if you can, and outside of the office.

Ask open questions with genuine intent, just like you would do with any other team member. Don't try to reach out too far in the future during the conversation. Focus on the short- term future, and on the tangible things you can do now in order to work on projects that help to build skills and to provide more energy. Try to find at least one or two tangible actions that would help your team member to grow. If you found those, that would be a big win! It would allow you to demonstrate by your actions that your intentions with these conversations are true—and how these conversations can make a positive difference for your team member. If your team member sees how you use information that was shared to give them opportunities helping them grow, the next conversation might be a bit easier. This means you'll find more actionable insights, and can demonstrate again how that could lead to more growth etcetera.

If a person keeps being closed and passive in career conversations, despite your going through efforts like these, then at some point I'd start using less effort myself. In the end people will have to own their own career. Whether or not this should lead to conversations of leaving the team, might depend upon their level of performance. If they're happy and performing well in their current job, there's no reason to force them into career conversations and career paths. If you reach the point where you feel like you want to invest less time and effort in a person's career conversations and -aspirations due to their lack of initiative, I would definitely mention that honestly. It could be that this is a feedback they need to "wake up," or it could be that this is just fine for them. Either way, they will realize that the ball is in their court.

> **Critical points**
> - Performance-evaluation conversations and career conversations should be kept separate: the first is looking at the past, the second at the future.
> - Career conversations cover the current role in your team, future roles in your team, and also roles outside your team or organization.
> - The conversation should be structured, but should feel organic too.
> - It starts within "the here and now", and expands step by step into the future. And finally, you need to bring it back to "the here and now", in order to make future scenarios actionable.
> - Duration can vary from ninety minutes to a full day. Face-to-face is best, but remote is possible: not in the office though, and not at a video conference.
> - During OKR-writing, career ambitions must be considered.

Basic 2 Collaborative OKR-writing, setting direction and expectations

The second Brilliant Basic helps you set direction and clear expectations for your team: collaborative OKR-writing. OKRs stands for Objectives and Key Results. The concept became known through the book *High Output Management* by former Intel-CEO Andy Grove. Many Silicon-Valley-companies use OKRs, but the use is also widely spread beyond those companies. I personally value the use of OKRs so much that I would try to implement a version of it wherever my career takes me. I added the word *collaborative* because the use of OKRs is only impactful if you write OKRs *with* your team, not just *for* them. By the way, you can of course choose to use a different system than OKRs for setting directions and expectations, just as long as it helps you to establish similar principles to the ones described in this chapter.

Figure 11 *The second Brilliant Basic is "Collaborative OKR-writing".*

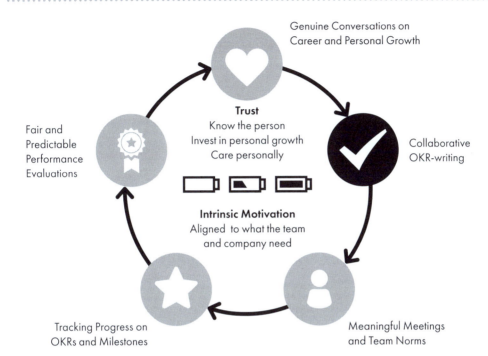

There are two questions to be answered when writing OKRs:
- *Where do I want to go?* This answer provides the *objective*.
- *How will I pace myself to get there?* This answer provides the *milestones*, or *key results*.

> *OKRs work at an organizational level, team level and individual level, so it's a powerful tool for vertical as well as horizontal alignment*

OKRs work at an organizational level, team level and individual level, so it's a powerful tool for vertical as well as horizontal alignment. OKRs have three main functions for managers and their teams:
1 *Creating clarity of direction and expectations*:
   a What should team members spend their time on?
   b How is success defined?
   c When should they deliver milestones?
   d Which of *their deliverables* are critical enablers of someone else's deliverables?

2 *Prioritization*:
   a   Anticipating workload-issues, and resolving them before they happen.
   b   Fair and healthy distribution of workload.
   c   Providing autonomy to make decisions when priorities compete.
3 *Holding people accountable, and enabling fair and predictable performance evaluations*:
   a   Transparent evaluation of performance based on what people delivered.
   b   Clarity of expectations to avoid negative surprises in performance scores and promotions.
   c   Fair distribution of high-profile work and opportunities.

I always base objectives on the annual plan for my team. That annual team plan is always written in alignment with broader company goals. At the start of each year, I define a maximum of five or six objectives that are the framework for the OKR-writing process for the rest of the year.

> *If there isn't any uncertainty about the feasibility of your annual objectives, they are probably not sufficiently ambitious*

Objectives are ambitious, and may feel somewhat uncomfortable. If there isn't any uncertainty about the feasibility of your annual objectives, they are probably not sufficiently ambitious. Key-results are measurable, and they break down the objectives in feasible steps that you take at a slightly ambitious speed. The reason why Silicon-valley companies typically set objectives which feel somewhat uncomfortable, is that people can often deliver more than they thought if they focus on big bets, also sometimes referred to as "stretch-OKRs." This also means people aren't expected to hit every single one of their OKRs by a 100 percent. Though they do need to hit the most critical ones, and the combined progress needs to demonstrate a clear impact. Priority labels help people to know which OKRs are critical and which ones are considered ambitious.

What makes a good OKR?

Let's have a look at some example OKRs. The examples below aren't real, but they are derived from the kinds of activities I worked on with my team.

Objective
Finish the year with 250 workshops delivered for "top-Tier clients" across EMEA with a portfolio that covers eight out of ten business-priorities of Google's *Ads Business*.
- Key result 1: Deliver ninety workshops in the first quarter (average customer satisfaction of 4.2 out of 5)
- Key result 2: Build a pipeline of 100 interested clients for Q2
- Key result 3: Create 25 customer success stories

Not all objectives and key results can be quantified by numbers. For example, progressing the development of the content of a new learning program is hard to quantify in numbers. In our design process, we therefore defined clear development milestones. These could be stages like:
- Draft content
- Alpha test stage
- Beta test stage
- Production ready
- Full production

Achieving a particular design stage in the journey became a measurable outcome by using names for these stages. We also agreed desired quality standards for each stage. For instance at the alpha-stage customer satisfaction scores would be around four out of five, while full production programs consistently scored higher than 4.

An OKR could look something like this:

Objective
Launch our new portfolio of workshops to support C-suites with organizational transformation
- Key result 1: reach "Full Production" stage for Design Thinking workshop (deliver five workshops in first quarter with customer satisfaction of 4.3 or higher);
- Key result 2: get the vision-/mission-workshop to a "Production Ready"-stage (achieve delivery capacity of fifty workshops a year);
- Key result 3: run two alpha tests for Culture of Innovation workshop (customer satisfaction at least 4 or higher).

Below are some criteria you can keep in mind to evaluate the quality of OKRs:
- Objectives should last about six to twelve months, key results are written per quarter.
- Key results are measurable milestones that set a path in order to achieve the objectives.
- Aim for about five objectives, and about three key results per objective.
- Key results should describe outcomes, not activities.
- Good OKRs make the team's vision/mission actionable, and thereby should provide a sense of direction and purpose.
- Good OKRs feel at least somewhat like an uncomfortable stretch goal.

Who writes OKRs?
When you see the concept of OKRs in action for the first time, you could perceive it as a form of micro-management. Can't you just trust your people to do the right things? OKRs can indeed result in feelings of micro-management. I've seen many teams where people perceived them as annoying "tick-the-box"-admin. Those are signs that leadership doesn't deploy OKRs the right way.

> *OKRs can give people the power to prioritize their own workload, while knowing they are still aligned with you as a manager*

When done well, OKRs are empowering for your team. They provide a sense of direction, clarity and security. They ensure there's dependability between team members, and OKRs can give people the power to prioritize their own workload, while knowing they are still aligned with you as a manager.

OKR-writing is a combination of a top-down and bottom-up process. It's best to run that process once per quarter. It takes several steps across a time window of about three weeks. It's easiest to explain this process using the example of my former team Google Digital Academy. This team consisted of 23 people. These people were split between three sub-teams. Each sub-team had their own responsibilities, but they were also dependent on each other. One team focused on the creation of programs for the C-suite audience about organizational change. The second team focused on the creation of digital-marketing transformation programs. And the third "Ecosystem and Operations Team" built the processes and systems that helped to scale these programs to about 1000 workshops across EMEA a year. Decisions made in one team often had an impact on another as well. For instance, the team that scaled our workshops to 1000 a year, worked with an external pool of about fifty workshop-facilitators. If one of the other teams decided to change some of our content, these trainers needed to be trained in the new content. If the Exec Programs team launched too many programs at the same time as the Digital Marketing Transformation Programs team, the Ecosystem and Operations Team would quickly get overloaded. For our team to hit our objectives, without burning people out, it was important to have the right alignment between teams.

Each team had their own manager. The managers reported to me. Each quarter we'd write OKRs, approximately with the following steps:

1 *Draft-team objectives and key results*. I wrote a high-level overview of objectives and key results, that we needed to deliver as a team. This overview was a summary of the work of all sub-teams. High-level enough to see how all things connect together. Detailed enough, so that each team could see anchors for their own OKR-writing. Because the objectives were derived from our annual plan, they were roughly the same all quarters of the year. Only the key results would change each quarter, based on achieved milestones and the scoring of OKRs in the previous quarter, combined with the pace needed to hit the annual plan. Tracking progress on milestones and scoring OKRs are covered in the fourth Brilliant Basic.

2 *Fine tuning draft OKRs by the next level of managers*. I'd share my first draft summary with the managers who reported to me directly, and we'd have a brainstorm about it a few days after. That meeting would take about one and a half hours. In the days ahead of the meeting, the managers commented in the document about critical things I might have overlooked. It could be that they saw an interdependency I wasn't aware of. They might have discovered that a particular project is more work than originally thought. Or perhaps several priorities would land on the desk of one and the same person. Maybe they worked with a critical stakeholder who needed us to hit a particular deadline. By tagging me and one another in comments they'd resolve many of the issues ahead of the meeting. They'd agree which key results were reasonable, and which people would work on each of the projects.

3 *Final agreement about team level OKRs and priorities*. In the meeting we'd discuss the challenges that were too complicated to solve in comments. We'd agree which projects were the "must-deliver"-projects and which project groups needed to have certain meeting cadences in order to deliver on the OKRs. This discussion could lead to a deprioritization of one or more

projects, if it became clear my original draft was too ambitious. It also sometimes surfaced new projects.

4 *Translating team OKRs to individual OKRs.* The managers then went through the same process with their teams to translate team OKRs into individual OKRs, for all people. These individual OKRs would be more detailed than my team overview. When team members wrote their individual OKRs they often raised thoughts and issues our manager group didn't anticipate. My managers would then let me know, and we'd adjust team level-OKRs if needed. Each individual would publish their individual OKRs on a platform where anyone at Google could see what they are working on. I did the same. My personal OKRs were typically a shortened summary of the team OKRs, plus some critical manager tasks, like filling open roles, or for example work on next year's business plan. My personal OKRs would also include personal side-projects, like the trainings I ran for peer managers, or work I did with working groups on diversity and inclusion.

5 *Final confirmation to the team about OKRs (and sometimes final tweaks).* As a final check and confirmation, each sub-team would present in our bi-weekly team meeting what the main OKRs for their team would be that quarter. Everyone in the Google Digital Academy team thereby had the opportunity to see the overview of the work of all subteams. Sometimes this still triggered a discovery of an interdependency we overlooked, or a situation where more workload landed on one person than anticipated. This was also my opportunity to raise people's attention for things I knew they'd need to be extra sharp. I would also emphasize situations when I wanted one part of the team to support another part of the team. This was the final moment where we could change things. After that, everyone would know what was expected from them, what they could expect from people they depended on, while no one would be overloaded.

I hope you see that this sequence of steps enables team members to co-create OKRs at all stages of the process. Of course, not everything always goes as planned. During each quarter, people might hit unexpected barriers delaying work, or someone might get sick. Sometimes unexpected projects come up during a quarter. Two mechanisms help you course-correct in the right moments:

1 Priority labels that were applied during OKR-writing and that gave people the autonomy to make priority calls to manage their workload. I will cover those in the next section.

2. Meaningful meetings to keep an eye on progress and to ensure continuous alignment between the right people. Meaningful meetings are covered in the next chapter.

Through these two mechanisms, changes in OKRs can happen during a quarter, while minimizing risk of misalignment.

Applying priority labels to OKRs: P0, P1 and P2

It's important that you apply priority labels to each OKR. I always use three types of priority labels:

- *P0*: This is a key-result that *must* be delivered this quarter, typically because a critical milestone depends on it. It's often because other people have a problem if that milestone isn't achieved. It could be that there's interdependency between your team members, or it could be that a stakeholder elsewhere in the organization or a customer depends on your deliverable. If a P0 OKR is at risk of not being achieved, you need to instantly escalate the problem to the relevant people. Most of the time a barrier can be unblocked through deprioritization of P2 or P1 projects, or through escalation to the right senior executives. Not achieving a P0 OKR is a problem. It's only acceptable if it was unavoidable, if escalations happened in time, and if expectations with all stakeholders have been managed through clear and timely communication. If a P0 wasn't achieved and there wasn't a timely escalation and communication, this is something that should be taken into account when evaluating the responsible person during performance evaluations. Appropriate in-the-moment feedback also needs to be given. I dedicated a chapter in part II of this book, on how to do this without undermining psychological safety.
- *P1*: This is often a key result that is an investment which sets you up for success in the quarter after the current one. In the first OKR-example I wrote a P1-key result to build a pipeline of customers for Q2 (second quarter of the year). By succeeding at this in Q1, the team will enter Q2 with a good foundation of warm leads, which makes it easier to succeed in Q2. If it looks like a P1 OKR isn't going to be achieved, it's important to communicate about it in time. The team can then make a conscious trade-off. Can we afford to invest harder, in order to still achieve the P1 OKR? For instance by deprioritizing some P2 OKRs? A team member should never compromise a P0 OKRs in order to achieve a P1 OKR. In many cases team members can make the trade-offs themselves, as long as they communicate clearly about it with all relevant stakeholders.

- *P2*: This is typically a key result that is an investment in a longer-term bet, with high ambiguity. For projects like these, it is wise to invest time early in the journey, to solve some of the ambiguity in the project. The project can then be planned with more certainty, by the time it needs to be delivered. For instance, you can already start doing a needs analysis amongst certain stakeholders, or it could be that you need to build a network of people you know you will need to succeed on the OKR. Or maybe you need to explore what suppliers with relevant knowledge exist in the market. Not delivering on a P2 OKR is generally not an instant problem. It's still good if a team member communicates about it if they choose to deprioritize it. That way all relevant people, including the manager, are informed of the decision- made. If a P2 OKR gets delayed several times, eventually it will become a P1 OKR. This means other things will start to get deprioritized in favor of the achievement of this OKR. The twenty-percent projects (side projects) that people are sometimes involved in and that I mentioned earlier, are also often P2 OKRs.

Below, I have added priority labels to my previously mentioned OKR-example:

Objective
Launch our new portfolio of workshops to support C-suites with organizational transformation
- Key result 1: reach "Full Production"-stage for Design Thinking-workshop (deliver five workshops in first quarter with customer satisfaction of 4.3 or higher) – *P0*
- Key result 2: get the vision/mission-workshop to a "Production Ready"-stage (achieve delivery capacity of fifty workshops a year) – *P1*
- Key result 3: run two alpha tests for Culture of Innovation workshop (customer satisfaction at least 4 or higher) – *P2*

In this case, the Design Thinking-workshop in Key Result 1 has a P0-label, because it is already going to be run with many clients, and promises have already been made to clients. You then just can't afford to have the content finished a little later. The Vision/Mission- workshop in Key Result 2 is at an earlier stage of production, where we were preparing production-capacity in order to be able to invite more customers. In case of an emergency, achieving this Key Result can also be delivered a few weeks later without causing problems. This is why the priority label is P1. The Innovation Workshop in Key Result 3 is in the earliest stage of development. There are no strong dependencies on achieving this Key

Result yet. The priority label-P2 indicates that in case of an emergency, it is fine to push this Key Result forward one quarter.

When you've gone through a few rounds of OKR-writing with your team, your team members will develop their own informed opinion about what is P0, P1 or P2. It's great if you can allow them to set priority-labels for their own individual OKRs. It helps you to see how much of your strategic guidance they have understood. Do they understand what deliverables are the most critical? Do they understand which projects have interdependencies? Do they understand which stakeholders have dependencies on the team and on their work? Individual OKRs always get signed off by managers. The priority-labels are an important opportunity for an alignment conversation between manager and direct report.

Once OKRs are written and priority labels are assigned and signed off by the manager, team members have a framework that provides them with autonomy to make their own planning and prioritization decisions. In any given week, they can choose what they prefer to work on, as long as they stay on track with the agreed deliverables. They can make these decisions without fearing what the consequences are, because it's very clear what's acceptable and what isn't, when you need to escalate and when not. This clarity takes away noise that otherwise would undermine productivity. Because people can make their own decisions, it avoids most situations of work overload.
There's one situation where that can still go wrong: if a person has too many P0's in their personal OKR-list. If you see an individual has seventy percent or more P0 OKRs on their list, it means they have few P1 and P2 OKRs they can use to make priority trade-offs. If a P0-project turns out to be harder or more time-consuming than anticipated, people can soon find themselves with their back against the wall, because there's no other work they can drop. If you check for this risk in the process of OKR-writing, you can anticipate workload-issues and prevent them from happening. For example you could distribute P0's better across people, or make sharper prioritization trade-offs as a leadership team.

Finally, the clarity of OKRs, including priority labels, prevents negative surprises in performance evaluations. I already mentioned the example where there are consequences if a person doesn't deliver on a P0 OKR, and hasn't escalated it or communicated about it in time. Imagine having the same situation if OKRs had *not* been aligned in advance. Not delivering on the project would then probably have the same consequences for the person's performance evaluation, yet it's likely that they didn't see it coming because the expectations were never set properly. In that context, getting a bad performance score is far more damaging than in a context where the expectations were clear beyond any doubt.

Common OKR mistakes

The most common mistake that I've seen people make with OKRs is that they spend too much time focusing on how to write OKRs in line with the "official rules" of OKR-writing. You should never forget that OKR-writing is not a goal in itself. OKR-writing is a tool that helps to create clarity of direction and expectations, it helps with prioritization and with holding people accountable. OKR-writing is an alignment-exercise, not an admin or language exercise.

Of course the quality of the wording used in OKRs helps make the process stronger, but quality-*conversations* are more important. If you spend too much time on "wordsmithing," the quality of the alignment conversations always suffers. If that balance goes wrong consistently, people start looking at OKRs as an annoying admin-exercise, because it takes them too much time compared to the value it creates for their needs.

> *OKR-writing is an alignment-exercise, not an admin or language exercise*

So when I write OKRs with a team, these are the things I pay attention to:
- Do people understand what the main priorities of the team are? And when these need to be delivered?
- Do they understand which ones are the must-deliverables (P0) and why?
- Do they understand who works on what?
- Do they know who to reach out to, in order to align work with one another?
- Do they understand how team priorities translate to their personal priorities?
- Do they understand which people depend on their work?
- Do they know how to make the right prioritization trade-offs, and when to escalate and communicate?

If I see that all of the above things are working, I don't get hung up too much about the exact wording of the OKRs. When you have the right quality conversations, and you go through the OKR-writing process several times, the quality of people's OKR-writing goes up automatically, even if you don't focus on the details of the wordsmithing.

> *Setting ambitious OKRs makes it more likely that people deliver high impact and get good performance scores, even if that means they don't hit all of their OKRs*

The next most common mistake is that people think of OKRs as a checklist of things to do, in order to get a good performance evaluation. If that's how they look at OKRs, they get a tendency for what we often called "sandbagging". This means people deliberately set safe OKRs, so they are confident they can achieve all of them. The outcome is they don't set ambitious goals for themselves, and they deliver less impact as a result. Impact is however what defines people's performance scores, not how many OKRs they've ticked off. Setting ambitious OKRs makes it more likely that people deliver high impact and get good performance scores, even if that means they don't hit all of their OKRs.

So managers need to make team members aware that OKR-writing is the moment where you set yourself up for success, by being proactive in setting ambitious goals, by aligning your goals to strategy and to the people around you, and by agreeing about prioritization. People need to understand that they aren't expected to deliver on all OKRs. They are expected to deliver *impact* within the rules of engagement set by the priority labels.

Distribution of work: the easy way or the growth way

For managers there's one common mistake (or opportunity) that I want to pay special attention to. OKR-writing is the critical moment where you distribute work among team members. In an organization where pay and promotions are defined based on people's performance, distribution of work is the moment when you have a strong influence on equity of opportunity and reward. The projects you assign to people define heavily what their opportunity to perform is.

The easiest way to assign work to people is to do it based on whom already did it successfully in the past. That's the safest bet, but it's mostly not the best one for the long-term success of your team. The person that already did it successfully several times before, gets the smallest growth-curve from doing another project of the same type. That person might benefit more, and get energized more, by a slightly different project. What kind of project that is, ideally is something you have discovered by having one or more meaningful career conversations. And the project that was less interesting for this person, could be a career opportunity for another person (informed by information from career conversations with that person).

> *When you assign OKRs to people, do so from a growth mindset: what distribution of projects helps individuals and the team as a whole, to grow and increasingly perform better?*

Of course, you don't want to create risks for your team's deliverables by assigning projects to people who aren't fully equipped to run them, but most of the time that isn't the case. If you and other managers in your team are sufficiently in tune with people's skills and ambitions, you should be able to assess what projects are a stretch to them that's as yet still feasible. And you could also consider making people who worked on similar projects in the past, a coach for people who do it for the first time. That coach role could be in line with career ambitions that these people might have. I had many people on my team that wanted to become a manager, yet there weren't enough manager roles. Becoming a guide for a more junior team of members can then be a good intermediate step.

So when you assign OKRs to people, do so from a growth mindset: what distribution of projects helps individuals and the team as a whole, to grow and increasingly perform better? Every now and then a project is so critical that you have to be pragmatic and need to prioritize certainty and security, so that you know the project will be delivered successfully and on time. But whenever you can, prioritize growth over certainty—and you will get more out of your team.

There are many other methods for setting directions and expectations. OKRs are just one way of doing it. What I like about OKRs is that it's a relatively light instrument: you can create structure without asking people to spend lots of time writing elaborate plans. If your team or organization has a different method for setting direction and expectations, and that works well for you, that's perfectly fine. It might still be useful to check whether your method hits all the principles discussed in this chapter. I created a checklist to help you do so. You can find that checklist in appendix two. It might help you spot opportunities in order to improve on your current method.

Critical points
- OKRs are a powerful tool to set direction, and manage expectations about desired output.
- P0, P1 and P2 priority labels help people prioritize work, and deal with situations where stretch goals can trigger moments of high workload.
- Objectives are set for a year in alignment to your annual plan. Key results set the pace per quarter.
- OKR-writing is an alignment-exercise, not an admin-exercise: having the right conversations is more important than wordsmithing.
- OKR-writing is a combination of top down, bottom up and horizontal alignment.
- OKR-writing is the critical moment when you can help your team members to grow, by establishing fair distribution of high-profile work in line with people's career ambitions.
- If you use a different tool than OKRs to set direction and expectations, that's also OK, as long as it supports similar principles and outcomes.

Basic 3   Meaningful meetings and team norms

The third Brilliant Basic is: "Meaningful Meetings & Team Norms." "Meaningful meetings" refers to setting up the right meeting-cadences between the right people, and to making sure that each meeting is effective. Team norms are the rules of engagement in and between meetings. They are like "service-level agreements" between team members: when do we believe a meeting is relevant and effective? When should I accept a meeting? When should I decline one? The fact that it is even OK to decline a meeting under certain circumstances, is a team norm in itself. Team norms also cover communications in and between meetings: how do we debate when we disagree? What's a reasonable response-time to emails? And to chat messages? What's a reasonable time window to follow up on the actions agreed on at a meeting?

One of the most common problems in organizations is a lack of effective meetings. In fact, Larry Page made this his first action-item at Google when he took over as a CEO from Eric Schmidt in 2006. He sent a company-wide email about

Figure 12 *The third Brilliant Basic is "Meaningful Meetings & Team Norms".*

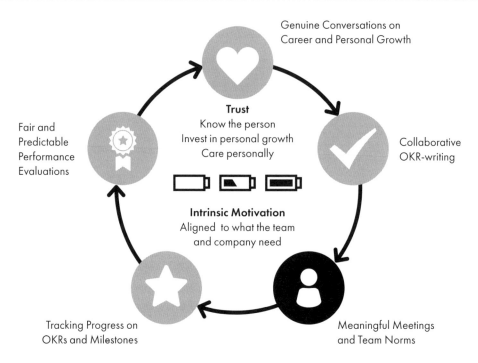

the importance of effective meetings, and he stated what he thought made meetings effective:

- Every meeting needs a single, clear decider.
- You can debate topics with strong opinions in a meeting, but when a decision is made, you act upon that decision as if it was your own.
- Every meeting needs a purpose and structure. This means setting and circulating an agenda ahead of the meeting.
- If you are invited to a meeting and there isn't an agenda, you should always ask for it—and if there still isn't an agenda, or the agenda isn't relevant to you, you can refuse the meeting.
- If you choose to be in a meeting, you need to be "fully present." This means closed laptops and no smartphones open. I remember Larry raised some research about humans being unable to multitask effectively. If you think you can multitask in a meeting, that means the meeting isn't important enough for you to be there at all.
- Not more than eight participants, but widely circulated notes afterwards.

- And adhere to the time constraints. At Google many meetings only take about thirty minutes, and that does the job for many topics. It forces you to focus on the agenda and make decisions. Meetings rarely exceed an hour, except when groups are discussing a long-term strategy, or for instance if performance scores are discussed.

I fully subscribe to these guidelines, and I've used them to provide my team with guidance about meetings ever since. I discovered some additional nuances though.

The rule of thumb I use for most group meetings is that the smallest group of people who has the collective knowledge and decision power should be in the meeting, and let the rest know what they decided. Most companies I worked with struggle with large amounts of meetings, and most professionals complain how a meeting load keeps them from the work they should be doing. If you establish this rule as one of your team norms, it can prevent lots of meetings for many people.

> *The smallest group of people who has the collective knowledge and decision power should be in the meeting, and let the rest know what they decided*

As to meeting notes, I believe it's important not to overdo it. Mostly, a maximum of half a sheet of paper is sufficient. They should repeat the agenda of topics discussed, the key decisions made, and the actions with their owners. If slides are presented, links to the slides (or attachments) should be included. If meetings aren't confidential and have a slightly larger audience (larger than five), it's worth recording the meetings so that people who couldn't make it still can watch the recording. In the teams I ran, there were always people dialing in remotely. This makes recording easy: it's just one tick of the button in the video-conference software. Meeting notes should ideally be distributed on the same day as the meeting, so that people immediately can start following the actions. A slow distribution of meeting notes typically slows down the work of several people. If too much time passes, people's minds turn to different topics and actions start getting procrastinated.

If meeting notes are longer than half a sheet of paper, they are often too detailed. Too protracted meeting-notes result in *admin* for the person that has to write them, and they take time for the people who need to read them. Critical decisions and actions can get lost if notes are too long. Most professionals are buried in emails every single day. The best way to get your information ingrained in people's minds is by being brief.

The exception to this rule is when you work for an organization in which the meeting notes are a mandatory archive of everything that was discussed. Many governmental institutions have fixed rules for how the information that was discussed between people should be stored. In most organizations though, the most critical things about meetings are the decisions taken and the actions agreed. Once all actions have been decided on, the notes no longer serve a meaningful purpose.

The way you run meetings and how you distribute notes present examples of team norms. There are a number of themes, as to which each team should formulate team norms. Presenting team norms is best done in dialogue with your team members. This allows you to get a sense of what is important to people. Sometimes things surface that you didn't expect. Most of the time, people collectively come up with all reasonable rules that anyone might want to live by. The fact that they came up with these themselves makes it more likely that people will adhere to the rules, because it becomes an agreement between the members of the group. Let's have a look at the most important themes in which agreeing on team norms is important.

Norms for communication
The first critical domain for which team norms are created, is "communication." This stretches across all channels people use in order to communicate with one another. It's about setting rules of engagement, for the interactions between people in and around meetings. Like: How do we debate? How do we solve indifferences? How do we communicate if someone isn't delivering what had been promised? Under what circumstances may you escalate? And how do we make sure all people get heard?

At Google we often used catch phrases to remind people of the communication norms in meetings. The nice thing about these phrases is that they are memorable: they become like a language that is part of the organization's culture. They also make it possible to set rules in a way that feels playful. This reduces any resistance to these rules. An example of such a phrase is "share the air"—this phrase encourages people to be aware about the amount of time they spend talking versus listening. It encourages people to allow others to speak before them, should they themselves already have had an opportunity to speak earlier during the meeting. It can even lead to someone saying something like: "We haven't heard person X speak during this meeting. What do you think about that?" If you hear people in your team say such things that's a great signal of positive working norms and team culture.

At virtual meetings the "hand-raising"-functionality is a useful one, in order to make sure people share the air. In particular it helps more introverted people, who might find it hard to step into an on-going conversation, to ask for speaking time. The hand-raise function is also critical within a context where some people sit with a large group within an office room, while others remotely join from various locations. In that context it is a lot easier for the people in the room where the majority is, to jump in and start talking. If you have clear norms about the use of the hand-raising function, then people from elsewhere will have an equal opportunity to contribute to the meeting. Whoever is the Chair of the meeting should pay attention to the hands people raise, and in general to whether all people are being heard. If you make this a team-wide norm for people to live by, you will see that not only the Chair will pay attention. You will regularly have folk in the meeting drawing attention to someone raising their hand for a while. This will happen more, if one as a team lead would role-model that behavior. It's good for the sense of belonging for all people in your team, but it also ensures that all important perspectives are being heard, so that better decisions are being made.

Two other catchy phrases that were used a lot are "debate the topic, not the person" and "disagree respectfully." These phrases underline the importance of people not shying away from debate, yet at the same time they are clearly not damaging one another and their relationships while debating.

There's a related one that I really like. One of my former team members—who was a thought leader in innovation and organizational change—used it a lot: "strong opinions, loosely held." This phrase invites people to be as open as they can be, expressing ideas or opinions about ideas, while also being able to let them go. It encourages people to keep a balance between advocating ideas, and digesting those of others. Organizational change requires innovation to be the "default state" of your culture. So this phrase, that originates from innovation workshops, is a highly valuable one to have as part of your communication norms.

Norms for email and chat

E-mail and chat are the next important topics for team norms: the continuous stream of mails and chat-messages is a source of stress to many professionals. Some people find their way to deal with it, and choose their own moments to answer messages with discipline, while consciously planning other moments when they do focused work. Other people never get on top of their inbox, and may even decide that it's OK if many messages stay unanswered. But that means other team members and stakeholders can't depend on them. If you allow this attitude in your team, work will slow down, and the service levels from your team towards stakeholders will be unacceptably low. Information will keep falling through the cracks, causing mistakes, delays and balls that are dropped.

Seeing messages pop into your inbox outside of working hours is an important source of stress for many people. Some people don't mind working late hours, yet others do. Some people find it easy to ignore messages in the evening, but others feel an obligation to respond—particularly when the message comes from a person that is more senior to them. For all of these reasons, you have to set team norms that enable people to be on top of their inboxes, while also managing stress levels, and allowing space for moments of focused work. Without such norms, it's pretty much a guarantee that the effectiveness, wellbeing and culture of your team might be harmed. In the teams I worked with, the rules about email typically were something like this:

- Keep your emails and chat messages short and structured (and consider whether the message is important enough to be sent at all).
- Be conscious about the amount of people you CC in a message, and about the use of "reply all." Every person you mail is a resource cost for the organization.
- Acceptable response time for mails is mostly 48 hours, but it's better if you can do it faster.
- If you need an answer faster from the receiver, clearly state this in the header of your mail, or use a chat.
- Don't send emails and chat messages outside of work time. If you do, use "schedule send"—so it arrives during the working hours of the receiver.

If time-zones make it impossible to schedule mails so that everyone receives them within working hours, then the agreement is that the receiver should always feel free to ignore the message until the next working day.

This list is not complete, but you'll get the idea. Try to work with your team members to get the list that works best for them.

Norms as to calendar, work time and location

Another area where team norms are valuable is the use of people's calendars. Calendars are a good way for people to signal when they are available and when not. If you aren't proactive about it, people assume that you are available at all moments when you don't have meetings. But that might lead to meeting an overload, fragmentation of work time, and meetings happening outside of people's official or preferred working hours. The first rule that is critical is that calendars should always be up to date, and visible for all stakeholders. If that basically isn't in place, the planning of meetings causes way too much communication and noise.

Two concepts that are valuable are:
1. *Flexible boundaries*: these are preferred boundaries, but they can be flexible when they need to. It means a person has to ask, before planning anything on these time-slots.
2. *Hard boundaries*: these should be respected at all times.

The combination of these types of boundaries allows people to protect their working time without becoming inflexible. An example of a hard boundary for me is *no meetings at weekends*. If you are working part time, it's wise to put your working hours on your calendar (signaling hard boundaries) outside those hours, and the same is true if you work in a different time zone than most of the people you work with.

An example of a permeable boundary for me is *preferably no meetings between at 5 p.m. and 6 p.m*. When I travel home around that time, I can still eat dinner with my family. If I travel later I can't. So if possible, I'd like to keep that time free. But if a meeting with a large group can only be held at that moment, I will allow meetings on these time-slots. Sometimes time zone-differences are so large that you have to allow for some permeable boundaries outside of normal working hours. There are parts of the world where working days might only overlap with your time zone for one hour, or there might not be an overlap at all. If you don't allow flexing in those cases, you force other people to cross *their* working-hour boundaries. In those cases it's often a matter of sharing the load:

people can take turns organizing the meeting outside of their working hours, so no one has to absorb this problem every week. If you don't like this causing meetings outside working hours for you, you shouldn't be working in an international situation. Another example of a permeable boundary could be putting blocks in your calendar with the title *Focus time: please ask before scheduling*. Putting boundaries like these on your calendar helps people to be thoughtful as to one another's balance between focused work and meetings.

> *If there are people in your team as to whom you need to worry about what they do when you don't see them, you may have hired the wrong people*

Without norms like these, people have a tendency to keep an eye on the boss and how that figure works. If this person regularly works late hours, many people will think this is expected from them as well. Sometimes that will be true, but I know many leaders who work long hours themselves without expecting it from their staff. If you are one of those leaders, better make sure you set team norms explicitly. People will otherwise, often unawarily, put pressure on one another, based on the example you set. And even if you do set team norms encouraging people to work within working hours, it's still worth thinking about the role model you set. If you say you "don't expect people to work overtime," but you do it yourself consistently, it creates a situation where your words and actions don't come across as aligned. This is why I always communicate explicitly to my team that I often do some emails in the evening to create flexibility for myself in order to arrive later in the mornings, so I can bring my kids to school. And I explain explicitly to people that I use "schedule send", so they don't receive my mails in the evening. This way I can work evenings if that's important for my work's life balance, without creating a culture where people feel a pressure to do overtime.

Norms for remote work
Since COVID, the working location has become an important topic in many organizations. A question many leaders struggle with is whether they will force people to come to the office for a certain amount of days or not. There's value in people connecting with one another face-to-face with a certain frequency, and an office makes it more likely that people make surprising connections with the teams around one. I think some managers and leaders fear they have less control over what people do, and how hard they work, if they don't go to the office. In my view, if there are people in your team as to whom you need to worry about what they do when you don't see them, you may have hired the wrong people.

If you hire the right people and manage them well, they will work based on intrinsic motivation. If people work based on intrinsic motivation, more flexibility means that you get more out of them, because you're providing them with a sign of trust. They'll appreciate that, and they can work in a way that makes them most productive. I ran my Google Digital Academy team from a distance for six years, and team members were distributed across many countries. No one was forced to come into an office, and it was never a problem.

Instead of pushing people to go to the office, I'd rather create reasons for them to *want* to enter the office: you could for instance pick one day a week for co-located team members to have a joint lunch with extra nice food, and another day where there are some drinks at the end of the day. Other than weekly moments for face-to-face connections, I use offsites, career conversations, brainstorm meetings and kick-off meetings for large projects as instruments to bring people together face-to-face. If you establish the right depth of connection at these moments, I find it sticks for a while when people work remotely. The glue created by the right frequency of face-to-face connections can prevent moments of friction between team members while working remotely, because their human connection is stronger.

> *The glue created by the right frequency of face-to-face connections can prevent moments of friction between team members while working remotely, because their human connection is stronger*

That glue can last particularly long if you add cultural team habits that keep people connected while being remote. For example, my team had a "water cooler-chat": this was a chatroom where people would post informal things about work and life. I kickstarted this chatroom myself (based on a suggestion by a peer manager) and I actively contributed to it. From there, it started leading its own life: it became part of team culture. It helped people feel connected while being remote. You'll be surprised how much team culture you can create despite people working remotely, when you establish the right norms and meeting cadences.

Given that people in most organizations nowadays have at least a few days a week in which they work from home, it's useful to have a team norm to indicate on your calendar what your working location at any given day is. Most calendars nowadays have a functionality that allows you to do this. It's a pity if you come to the office hoping to meet someone in person, only to discover that this person decided to work from home that day.

Exercise: Co-creating team norms with your team

I highly recommend planning some time with your team in order to discuss and co-create team norms. You can do this at team meetings or at team offsites. People are generally engaged and enjoy brainstorming on this topic. The exercise flow below, supported by the worksheet in figure 13, can help you to run your own workshops in order to set your team norms with your team. If you do this as part of a longer offsite, you can probably afford to cover all types of team norms in one big session—of one and a half hours or so. If it's one of several topics in a team meeting, I'd recommend focusing on one type of team norms at a time. The steps below help you to open the dialogue with your team, and brainstorm about team norms.

Open the floor

As a team lead, open the floor sharing some examples of norms you prefer to live by, and that you know are important for the team. Perhaps point to examples where you've seen healthy team norms in action within the team already. Also raise some examples of behavior that you see as the consequences of a lack of team norms. In this case, it's best to use generic examples that don't point to any specific person in or around your team. This should take a maximum of ten minutes.

Provide each person with a worksheet

Share the team norms' worksheet from figure 13 with people, or the parts of it that are relevant to the team norms you want to discuss. The questions in the sheet are a stimulus for people to reflect upon behaviors in the team, and how team norms could make a positive difference. In your preparation for the session, you can add additional questions, or change some of the examples I wrote. There could be more areas or channels than the ones mentioned where team norms could be useful. For example if your team makes intensive use of internal social platforms to communicate, you could consider norms that moderate what is OK to post and what not. Meetings, email, chat, calendar, working hours, working location and communication norms are the topics that I think every team should have team norms for.

Reflect in small groups

Give people about fifteen minutes time to reflect on the questions in the document, and to come up with three types of behaviors. First, behaviors the team should stop doing, because they aren't healthy for the team's culture and effectiveness. Second, behaviors that would be healthy for team's culture and effectiveness, but that aren't happening yet: things that the team should start doing. Third, healthy behaviors that the team is already demonstrating and should continue doing. It's best if people reflect on these behaviors in a dialogue with one or two other persons, so that they can look beyond their own personal perspective. Depending on the size of your team, you can therefore split up people into groups of two to five people for this reflection. Ask them to write down their observations in the worksheet.

Debrief reflections and brainstorm on team norms

Spend about thirty minutes debriefing the reflections of the groups: ask each group what came up in their conversations, and what behaviors they wrote down for "stop, start and continue." You can use each group's debriefing to ask other groups whether they covered similar topics, or whether other groups had a different perspective as to the same topics. Thereby you use the debriefs to open a dialogue. Make sure you keep an eye on the time and structure of the conversation. Some people might be more vocal than others. Make sure all people are heard. Allow all perspectives to be brought to the table, and then move the conversation on. There are situations where people can get emotional about topics. If that happens, acknowledge the emotion, and underline that this is why you are having this dialogue, and why you want to create healthy team norms. Every now and then you can ask the group: "If we'd phrased a team norm in order to solve this, how would you formulate that team norm?" Ask people to build upon one-another's proposals.

Summarize, commit and close

Summarize what you heard and what team norms you think would be valuable for the team. Ask the team whether your summary was accurate and complete. Ask them whether these are team norms they could live by, and whether these would solve observed challenges. Ask them what could get in the way of living by these team norms, and how barriers can be removed. Iterate on your summary and your proposed norms, until most people seem to be behind your initial proposal and seem to be confident that they can live by them. Explain to the team how you intend to "role-model" these norms. Ask people to hold you and each other accountable. This part should in total take a maximum of about thirty minutes.

> *When you are too passive in cultivating team norms, you will gradually see your team culture slide, because norms and culture are inseparable*

Plan a moment at a future team meeting to evaluate how it's going, and to discuss whether further iterations to team norms need to be made. Thank them for their open and honest contributions and their personal care. It helps if you write down your summary, and send it to the team after the session.

Figure 13 Worksheet for running a team norms exercise with your team.

	Stop	Start	Continue
Meaningful meetings • Are the right people at the right meetings? • Are all people fully present? • Is the length and frequency of the meetings right? • When is it OK to decline a meeting? • Who sets the agenda? • Who chairs it? • Who takes notes? • When should we circulate recordings? • Are notes and recordings circulated to the right people? • How do we make decisions? • Are we hitting agenda items effectively? • Are people timely in following up on decisions and actions from the meeting? • Is leadership role-modeling healthy meeting habits? …			
Communication norms • Are people "sharing the air"? • Are debates held respectfully? • Are all opinions being heard? • Do we communicate respectfully in all channels? • Can remote people participate and contribute to meetings as easily as anyone else? • Can remote people participate in informal communication as easily as anyone else? …			

Stop   Start   Continue

Norms for email and chat
- At what times do we send each other messages?
- Are all messages sufficiently relevant for the receivers?
- What's an acceptable response time?
- Is the content of messages clear and succinct?
- Are email headers clear and succinct?
- Are people replying to messages? If not, why not?
- Are people sufficiently careful with the "reply all" button?
...

Calendar norms
- Is it clear what people's hard and permeable boundaries are?
- Are people's working hours and locations clearly visible?
- Are people respecting each other's boundaries?
- Do people's calendars allow for sufficient flexibility to plan meetings?
- Are calendars always up-to-date and visible for the right people?
...

Work location norms
- How often do we feel people should be in the office? And why?
- How often do we feel people should be able to work from another location? And why?
- What are critical moments when face-to-face connections make a positive difference?
- How often and when should these moments occur?
- What habits would help create the right level of connection between people (at a personal and work-related level)?
- Do all people have equal opportunity to connect to the rest of the team?
...

Cultivating of norms and culture

In the period after the session, do what you promised and hold people accountable, though you don't want to end up policing people. Team norms can only be established effectively if people adhere to team norms based on intrinsic motivation. That way you know they will also live by these norms when you aren't watching, for instance at project-group meetings when you aren't present. Instead of policing team norms you should *cultivate* them: this is active work. When you are too passive in cultivating team norms, you will gradually see your team culture slide, because norms and culture are inseparable. I've seen managers try to create team culture by organizing team building activities. There's nothing wrong with team building activities, but you should not forget that most of the culture of a team or organization is established through every-day behavior: living by agreed team norms. In fact, it's often the practical behaviors of people who shape team culture. On a cultural level you can for instance agree that you believe people should be able to rely on one another, but when people systematically fail to live by agreed response-times for email and chat, that cultural agreement will never be lived by. So, practical and cultural team norms are inseparable. Figure 14 illustrates what it takes to cultivate agreed and lived team norms.

Figure 14 *Cultivating agreed and lived team norms.*

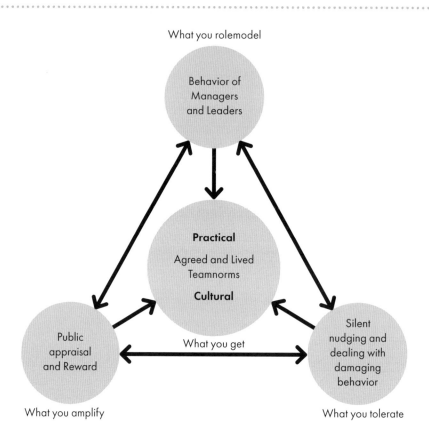

It starts with the role-modeling of managers and leaders: you can't underestimate how important role-modeling is for cultivating team norms. In fact, if you would *not* discuss team norms at all, and you would *not* run a workshop the way I described, you can still cultivate almost all healthy team norms purely based on how you role-model them, and how you nudge people. It works both ways: you can create healthy team norms and culture through your personal example, you can create toxic team norms and culture through your personal example, and anything in between. Establishing team norms is about shaping habits. Shaping habits for yourself is hard. And it's even harder for a team. The consistency by which leaders and managers cultivate team norms defines the time it takes for the team to adopt healthy habits. When you are a manager or leader, and when it comes to organizational or team norms, what you live is what you get!

> *When you are a manager or leader, and when it comes to organizational or team norms, what you live is what you get!*

Another principle that works well for cultivating team norms is "public group appraisal, silent individual nudging." Compliment people openly when you see them acting by these norms. It's most powerful if you can compliment groups of people living by these norms together. When you compliment individuals too often in an open forum, you risk creating the perception of having favorites. Individual people might start demonstrating behaviors in order to please you as a leader. Instead, you want them to do it because it's the right thing to do among one another. Public group appraisal can be given in a "reply-all"-email, or for instance during your digest in the first ten minutes of your team meeting. Individual silent compliments can easily be given by sending people a quick chat-message: "Thank you for calling that out" or "Thank you for noticing that the opinion of person X wasn't being heard". Simple chat-messages like that hardly cost you any time, but they are a strong encouragement for people to keep doing the right things. People will feel valued and seen. The only thing it requires from you is the willingness to notice the big *as well as* small things people do to contribute to positive team norms. It is important that formal reward is aligned to what you want to amplify. When you for instance encourage team norms for a healthy work-life balance, but then primarily reward and promote people who work full-time and that regularly work overtime, no public appraisal can ever make up for that.

If you see people *not* living by team norms, try to nudge them gently in a way that doesn't expose them negatively in front of their peers. Preferably you do so by planning some one-on-one time. If you nudge people through a chat or mail, you can't see how your comment lands with them. Some people tend to over-react quickly when a senior person nudges them about something that isn't quite right. A quick personal conversation is almost always better. When done well, that conversation can even bring you closer to a person. In most cases you won't have to plan some one-on-one-time in order to correct people. Positive endorsement combined with your personal role-modeling will solve ninety percent of all issues. There are sometimes severe cases where people demonstrate damaging behavior. In those cases, silent nudging may not be enough. When people are damaging towards colleagues, and they don't respond to nudging, you need to do whatever it takes to stop them from further damaging people. This can mean you need to fire the person. When you fail to nudge if people demonstrate small behaviors that aren't aligned to team norms, or when you fail to do what it takes when people systematically damage colleagues, your culture will become toxic. Then your culture is what you tolerate.

Finally, role-modeling, amplifying and nudging heavily depend on one another. This is why the three outer circles in figure 14 are connected by arrows. When you don't consistently role-model, you won't be credible when nudging people, or even complimenting them. People are likely to politely nod—and then ignore you, because they know words and reality don't match. When you publicly compliment people on positive behaviors, but consistently fail to act on negative behaviors, your encouragement can trigger cynical reactions. Reversely, when you consistently act on negative behaviors, yet don't consistently compliment people for positive behaviors, your actions start to feel like policing. Culture is not what you say it is: it is what you role-model, what you amplify and what you tolerate, so that agreed norms are lived by...

> *Culture is not what you say it is: it is what you role-model, what you amplify and what you tolerate, so that agreed norms are lived by...*

In addition to the importance of effective meetings and living by agreed team norms, it is important to consciously schedule the right meetings, at the right frequency, between the right people. Which meetings create the optimal frequency of contacts between people depends on the size of your team. I will cover the most important meeting types, and will show how to adjust the nature and frequency of meetings for different team sizes.

One-on-one meetings with direct reports

The one-on-one meetings you run with your direct reports are one of the most important and most underestimated types of meetings that you can have. It is in these meetings where you develop a trusted relationship step by step, stay in tune with how people progress on their OKRs, where they need support and where they don't. They are the platform for people to raise ideas or concerns with you; and for you to give people feedback in the moment, so they can act upon your feedback, and don't end up being surprised during formal performance evaluations.

> *The one-on-one meetings you run with your direct reports are one of the most important and most underestimated types of meetings that you can have*

For your one-on-one meetings to play all of these roles, they need to be longer than thirty minutes though. I had managers that planned a maximum of thirty minutes for their direct reports per week, or sometimes every two weeks. This meant those meetings were very transactional, and these managers rarely developed the depth of understanding about me as a person, or the projects I worked on, to be able to come with any meaningful guidance and feedback.

I typically plan weekly one-on-one meetings with all of my direct reports. It doesn't mean we use all of them, and we don't always use the full hour, but I want to give the signal that I am available. I rarely cancel or shorten these meetings, yet I always remind people *they* are allowed to cancel, shift or shorten these meetings—if they feel there aren't enough relevant topics to cover, or if they have a busy week. The signal of being available extends beyond one-on-one-meetings. I also deliberately respond to the mails and chat-messages of my team members fast, often within minutes and almost always the same day. And if people need more time from me, I will always try to create it the same or the next day. Those signals lower the barrier for people to come to you, when they've something on their mind. It prevents people from getting stuck on things too long, or from running out of sync with OKRs and team goals. When you are a manager, your calendar is generally busy—so it will always feel like you can't afford the time. But when you are a manager, the biggest impact you can achieve is the impact your team achieves. If you are not sufficiently accessible, and people get stuck on challenges, or they start to put less effort into raising challenges with you, then everything you achieve as a team becomes slower. There's nothing that you can do individually as a manager, that is faster than what your team can do collectively, so making time for your people almost always pays off.

> *There's nothing that you can do individually as a manager, that is faster than what your team can do collectively, so making time for your people almost always pays off*

I always come to one-on-one meetings mentally prepared with an agenda, and almost always read the material which people share with me before meetings. That means they don't have to spend time presenting material to me in the meeting. It allows us to use all time to discuss topics that require brainstorming or decisions, and we keep enough time to discuss how the person is doing and feeling. For agenda-setting I use a loose mechanism that allows both parties to suggest agenda topics in the period between meetings. I open a Google-docs page that allows for joint editing. As the week progresses both parties park topics they want to discuss in the document. At the start of the meeting, we walk through the items that were parked there, and agree upon an order to go through them. I vary by person how directive I am in suggesting topics on the agenda. Some people have a level of proficiency and proactivity in their work that results in them always suggesting a relevant and complete agenda. If I see that, I allow them to set most of the agenda, while only adding nuances here and there. This level of proactivity is something I will certainly consider when assigning performance ratings, and that people will hear positive feedback about.

If you and your team are disciplined in writing OKRs, every one-on-one is essentially a mini check-in about OKR-progress. You can skip OKRs, or touch upon them only lightly, when you already know the status of the work. You only zoom in on OKRs that require discussion.

I always open my one-on-one meetings with the question "How was your week?" This has many benefits over "How are you doing?" First of all, people give you more specific answers. The question makes them reflect about the past few days and what happens. From there, they are free to choose whether they answer the question based upon work-related topics or based on personal topics. This helps you see what is most top of mind for people. When you don't plan enough time for one-on-one conversations, people share less personal things. Meetings will become mostly work-related. If that happens across a period of a few months, the relation between you and your team-member will become more transactional than trusted.

In the last five minutes of each one-on-one meeting, I always summarize actions. I follow up on my actions the same day about ninety percent of the time. This again signals personal care. It shows you deliver on promises, and it avoids situations where team members slow down work because they're waiting for you. If I can't follow up on the action the same day, I will let the team member know *when* I will follow up on the action, and I'll stick to that.

The approach described—with one hour one-on-one time every week with each direct report—only works if you have about three to six direct reports as a manager. To me this is the optimal amount of direct reports, where you have enough scope as a manager, and at the same time can give every person the time and attention to be meaningful for them. Therefore, when designing teams and organizations, I would always ensure that there are not many more than six people reporting directly to managers. However, exceptions to this are possible if managers run teams in which people's jobs are very similar, for example, when you run a call-center team. Then it is quite possible to understand people's work, and provide meaningful guidance if you have as many as ten or twenty people reporting to you.

Managing at increasing scale

When you grow as a manager and leader, your team may grow in size too. You might become a manager of managers, or perhaps you already are. Your team might consist of a hundred people, a few hundred, a thousand, or even several thousands of people. No matter what size your team is, you still want to connect with your people, communicate with them, feel "in tune" with your organization, and be meaningful and inspirational to them. All of the above gets harder, the larger your team is. Above a certain size, you can no longer connect to all people, and communicate to all people through regular meetings. Even with a size of several hundreds of people, most information that originates from you arrives at individual people as second-hand information: through their manager, who got it from *their* manager etcetera. Or they might hear stories through peers. Information will be distorted and lost in the process of passing it on.

Team members might observe things in the organization that look wrong to them, and attribute these to things you as a leader do or say, even if you had nothing to do with it, or even if you are working really hard to solve these problems in the organization. Many individuals look at senior leaders as powerful people who can do with an organization whatever they want. So if something is wrong with the organization, it must be because of the leaders. Not all people realize that an organization is a living organism, and therefore that no leader can ever make it function exactly the way they want it to function.

> *Not all people realize that an organization is a living organism, and therefore that no leader can ever make it function exactly the way they want it to function*

If your team is large, most people will rarely have the opportunity to meet you in person. And even if they do have that opportunity, they mostly won't have the opportunity to interact with you enough to know who you are as a person. They won't know on the basis of first hand interactions what your values are, what makes your heart tick, what your skills and passions are, or what your flaws, doubts and fears are. So they fill it in based on the bits of information they gather over time. They will almost certainly be wrong, because of the inevitable gaps and distortions in that information. That could be favorable, if they make you more intelligent, honorable and heroic than you really are. But it could also be unfavorable, if people don't see the heart you bring to the job, the hard work, and the tough decisions you need to make. People often don't see the bad things you *prevent* happening. They only see the ones that *do* happen. They might even make a villain out of you in their head. Most of the time that won't be fair.

So as a leader of a large team, you have to consciously design mechanisms and channels for you to stay connected and be heard. Staying connected is probably harder than being heard. When you run an organization of hundreds or thousands of people, somehow you need to find ways to engage with people in all layers of the organization, often enough to understand their challenges and their sentiment. That works best if you are a leader who grew up in the organization, having moved up the ranks step by step, while seeing the mechanics of various types of jobs. It is much harder if you are a leader that entered the organization at a senior level. And even if you have the luxury of having seen many parts of the organization in past roles, it takes a conscious effort to keep your connection with all layers of the organization alive over time. People in the organization see the difference between a leader that is in tune with the organization, and one that isn't. In the most favorable scenario, a leader that isn't in tune sounds a bit too generic, not so relevant, and rather patronizing. That scenario means people just don't feel as engaged, heard and seen as they could. At its worst it makes people angry, because it looks like the leader makes decisions that are bad for the organization, and doesn't show any signs of a learning curve.

There's one person I have always admired for his ability to lead upon a grand scale, while staying in tune with the organization. This is Philipp Schindler, currently the global leader of Google's Global Business Operations. During my time in the company this was an organization of more than 10,000 people. Philipp Schindler joined Google in 2005. After his first few years, he became a global leader, in a few steps that came relatively fast after one another. His journey gave Philipp the chance to see many parts of the company, but it was also his attitude that made a difference there. He built a reputation for always being curious about the details of people's work. He'd walked through the office, looked at someone's screen, and asked with curiosity what they were working on, what problems they were solving, what made it hard etcetera. In the years when he was a global lead you could clearly see how this paid off. Despite the enormous scale of his organization, his communication in all meetings would always feel personal and relevant. When he spoke about business strategy or challenges, he'd always illustrate it with specific examples he'd observed in various countries. He could make each individual feel he understood what they bump into in their jobs. I've seen him give clear and transparent answers to the most difficult questions. Most leaders in that context would come with generic answers that feel like the corporate script. Philipp's answers rarely felt like that.

It made me realize he still must have mechanisms to meet people in all layers of the company. He kept prioritizing listening to them, asking questions about their work, and about how they felt at the company. If I ever get a role of that magnitude, I hope I can demonstrate that skill in the same way.

The table in figure 15 gives you an idea about the mechanisms, meetings and forums that could help you establish the right levels of connection and communication at various team sizes.

Figure 15 *Meeting and communication mechanisms at different team sizes.*

	3 to 10	11 to 25	26 to 100	100+
One-on-one meetings with direct reports	Weekly			
Project group meetings	Defined by project group			
Project progress check-ins	Monthly for each project		Monthly/quarterly for select amount of projects that you are a sponsor of	
Meetings with entire team	Bi-weekly		x	
All-hands	x		Quarterly	
Skip-level meetings	x	Quarterly		
Office hours	x	x	x	Weekly
Leadership meetings	x	Bi-weekly	Weekly	Weekly
Manager forums	x		Monthly	Quarterly
Small group Q&A sessions	x		At least quarterly	
Team offsites	About twice a year		Once per year or less	
Leadership offsites	x	About twice a year		
Email updates	Based on personal choice		Monthly and on special occasions (including personal video message)	
OKR-writing meetings	Quarterly writing between manager and direct reports Team OKRs to be shared with entire team			
OKR scoring meetings	Quarterly scoring between manager and direct reports Light mid-quarter check-ins Scores on team OKRs to be shared with entire team			

Teams up to 25 people

Up to about nine people you can easily meet all of your team members one-on-one once a week, you can be part of most project-meetings, and you can bring your entire team together bi-weekly. That creates most of the connection points you need. Between 9 and 25 several things change. Most likely you will become a manager of managers, and at transition stages you might end up with a few too many direct reports. In that scenario you will start visiting project-meetings more selectively: the project groups will keep meeting without you, and you will join them about once a month to get an update on progress. For people who report to your managers, you might run "skip-level"-meetings: these are meetings with folk that work two layers under you in the organization. I always tried to make sure I spoke to each individual at least once per quarter, in order to see how they are doing and for them to have the opportunity to tell me about their work, or to raise observations about the team. For these skip-level meetings it's important to realize that you are not the manager of these people, so you cannot ask them to work on certain projects, and you cannot promise them anything without talking to their manager first. If you do those things, you'll end up undermining the role of the managers working under you. It's good practice to debrief with the manager what was discussed in these skip-level meetings, but always let the individual know that you are doing this, and never share anything that could be confidential or harm the individual team member. When you have more than one manager, you'll need to establish a recurring leadership-meeting between you and your managers. Bi-weekly is a nice frequency for this. When it comes to email communication, at this team size, you can do it mostly intuitively: your mails won't be part of some kind of orchestrated communication plan.

Teams larger than 25 people
When your team size exceeds 25 people, more things change. You won't be able to be connected to all projects anymore, so you need to pick a selective amount of projects that you sponsor. The larger your team, the less projects you can sponsor. As a senior sponsor you might join project-meetings monthly or quarterly, depending on your level of involvement. You can help the group make the right decisions, connect them to the right people in the wider organization, support them with resources, and support them by removing barriers. You being a sponsor is also good for morale: it underlines the importance of the project, and gives project members personal visibility towards you as a leader.

Bringing your entire team together in a bi-weekly meeting won't make sense anymore at this size. A quarterly all-hands format makes more sense from this size onwards. These are large-scale meetings in which senior leadership communicates with the broader organization. If people work in the same country, these may be face-to-face meetings. In international organizations, these types of meetings are usually streamed to all countries by video. During these meetings you can still cover topics related to team and culture, do organizational updates, personal updates, project updates etcetera. The format is just more scalable and thereby slightly less interactive. You can still make an effort to come up with engaging formats, do quizzes, throw in bits of entertainment, etcetera. When a leader runs a team of several hundreds or thousands, an all hands-meeting typically justifies professional support. Many companies have a dedicated internal communications person, or even a team. Such a function can support the orchestration and programming of all-hands meetings. At the size of thousands, there might even be a production-company supporting these sessions.

Teams of hundreds or thousands of people
At team sizes of hundreds or thousands, you can still do skip-level meetings with people who report into your direct reports. But below those levels, the amount of people quickly becomes too large for the skip-level meeting-format. Office-hours are then a good mechanism. Instead of you planning one-on-one meetings, people can come to you for snappy ten-minute conversations about a topic that's important to them. Most leaders of large teams I know dedicate about two hours every week to office hours. The process for booking slots in these meetings is typically supported by a person or process. Based on how many of these slots get booked, you will know whether two hours a week is too little or more than enough.

As your team grows in size, leadership meetings will be held only with the managers that report directly into you. And there might be guests coming at these meetings that lead important projects. A larger org means more strategic decisions, and more project leads wanting to speak to senior leadership. So it's likely that your leadership-meeting needs to move from bi-weekly to weekly. When you have several layers of managers working under you, there will also be a need for these managers to come together as a group. Up to twenty managers or so, you can do this in a monthly manager-forum. You can appoint a few of your best managers to run this forum. They will bring the managers together once a month, and will gather opinions amongst the managers (and from you) in order to set an agenda for these sessions. An hourly online meeting works perfectly for this group size. Topics that are likely to come up are pretty much all the topics discussed in this book: performance management, coaching, OKRs, agreeing organizational norms about remote work, best practice sharing on difficult situations, etcetera.

If you have many more than twenty managers working under you, an online meeting reduces the depth of the exchanges managers can have. It makes more sense then to bring managers together face-to-face once per quarter for half a day or even a full day. You could use part of that time to discuss similar topics you'd cover in the online monthly-sessions, but you can also use this moment to train people as to management and leadership skills. In one quarter you could train all managers on coaching skills, the next could be about performance management, or about career conversations. The experience of meeting each other face-to-face as a group of managers and going through learning experiences together, can create a sense of bonding between managers that connects parts of your organization. The personal connections between these managers can reduce the friction between teams—it helps them to spot connections, makes career journeys between teams easier, besides it helps people break through silos and more.

Meetings for OKR-writing and scoring ideally happen in all layers of the organization on a quarterly basis. The writing and scoring of individual OKRs is always done between managers and their direct reports. Each manager aligns OKRs to the wider team they are part of, and translates these to OKRs for the teams and people who work for them. It's a good habit to post individual OKRs at forums where anyone can see them and the team OKRs and scores should always be communicated to the entire team.

> *In large organizations, managing your personal communication and how people perceive you, becomes similar to managing a brand*

When it comes to email communication: if you get to team sizes of well beyond a hundred people, you won't send mails based on personal intuition anymore. Your mails and most things you communicate to your organization will be part of a communication plan. That communication plan might have a monthly recurring personal-update, containing a video-message, but it will also include critical communications moments on organizational topics. The plan will include all communication channels and forums at your disposal, so each gets used for the right purpose at the right moment. In large organizations, managing your personal communication and how people perceive you, becomes similar to managing a brand: you want to cut through the noise with messages that are genuine and clear, and that help people see who you are, and what you believe is important.

Team offsites at varying team sizes
Offsites are important moments to bring members of your team together, but the role they play varies largely with the team's size. At a team size up to 25 people, twice per year is a nice frequency for most teams. You'd then spend one or two

days together. Many of the exercises in this book are suitable for these offsites. When your team gets much larger than 25 people, leadership-offsites start to make more sense than bringing the entire team together, at least from the perspective of strategic decision-making. The larger your team, the less often you will bring the entire team together. A larger team means that an offsite is more costly, while at the same time having lower relevance to all of the attendees. In addition: if every layer in the organization decides to bring together their entire team twice a year, in a large organization you end up with people being in offsites every month. So if the organization decides to bring people together at the highest level, some of the mid-level offsites will need to be canceled. Hence I've written in the table that offsites with the entire team would typically happen once a year, or less if your team is very large. When you bring people together at that scale, you can always create opportunities for smaller teams to connect in breakouts at the same moment as well. That brings you the best of both worlds.

Critical points
- For a team to be effective, all meetings need to be effective.
- Besides meeting norms, teams need to have norms for at least the following topics: communication, email, chat, calendar, working times and work location.
- It's most powerful when you set norms together with your team members.
- Establishing team norms is about changing habits.
- You have to cultivate team norms by setting an example yourself, by amplifying desired behavior through public appraisal and reward, and you have to correct undesired behavior through silent nudging.
- If people continue to exhibit damaging behavior despite nudging, you must do what it takes to stop it.
- Your culture is the sum of the example you set, the behaviors you amplify, and the behaviors you tolerate.
- The principles of this chapter change depending on the size of your team.

Basic 4   Tracking progress on OKRs and milestones

The fourth Brilliant Basic is tracking progress on OKRs and milestones. Tracking progress is important for a variety of reasons:

Figure 16 *The fourth Brilliant Basic is "Tracking Progress on OKRs & Milestones".*

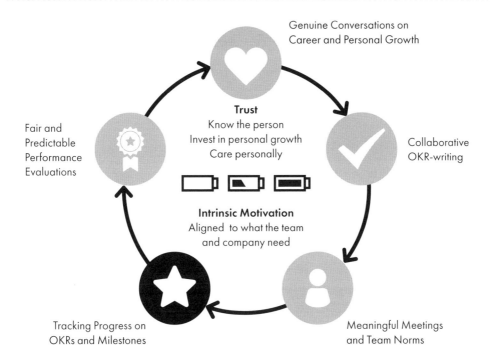

- *Identifying early when team members get stuck and need support*: This could be because of lack of knowledge, complexity of a decision, a blocker they encountered, a conflict that came up, and many other reasons. With the right mechanisms to track progress, you can make sure people always keep moving at the right speed.
- *Identifying early when team members go off brief*: Even when you write clear OKRs and when you brief people clearly, it doesn't mean they will stick to that briefing. In some cases that's good, because they may have come up with better ideas to solve the same challenges, but sometimes they move off brief in a way that isn't good for the project. This could be because the brief wasn't understood as well as you thought. Often people get pressured by stakeholders to change things about a project, and they might not realize that a particular change makes it less likely that they will hit the project's objective. With the right mechanisms to track progress, you can spot early on when things are moving in the wrong direction—and use those moments as an opportunity to clarify the brief.

- *Coordinating projects with cross-functional dependencies*: Sometimes multiple projects are dependent upon each other, and you are the one that oversees all projects. People in one project group might make decisions that affect another project group without knowing it. Or they might come up with an idea that would be beneficial for another project group without knowing it. With the right mechanisms to track progress you can spot risks and opportunities, and connect the right people at the right moments.
- *Providing a sense of encouragement*: If people progress well within their projects, it's nice for them to show you what they did. In particular when people have a high sense of autonomy and an ability to come up with creative solutions, they will be proud to show you the solutions they came up with. They may want to brainstorm with you about what more is possible as a result of these solutions. With the right mechanisms for tracking progress, people can always connect to you in order to showcase critical new ideas, solutions and milestones they achieved.
- *Evaluating people's performance and providing in the moment feedback*: Great managers don't wait with evaluating people's performance and giving feedback until the performance evaluation. They do it all the time. By evaluating performance and providing feedback all the time, you give people a chance to learn and grow, and you set them up for maximum success. And if they did not do well, despite you keeping a close eye and providing in the moment feedback, then it's clear why a performance rating is lower and you avoid surprises. More about that in the next chapter about performance evaluations.
- *Writing next quarter's OKRs*: Tracking of progress on OKRs and milestones of the *previous* quarter, is the input you need for writing OKRs for the *next* quarter. With the right mechanisms in place, you will know which projects went slower than expected, and which ones faster. You might spot milestones that were achieved, or solutions found that open new doors for projects in the next quarter. All of that input will go into OKR-writing for the next quarter. If it's near the end of the year, it will also be an input for next year's annual plan.

The good news is: if you apply the principles from the previous chapter about meaningful meetings, you've already done eighty percent of the work when it comes to tracking progress. Your one-on-one meetings were platforms where you could check in with individuals on the progress on their OKRs, challenges they faced, ideas they had, etcetera. You will have had many opportunities of giving them honest and actionable feedback. You've been able to encourage them and compliment them, or nudge them into a different direction.

Through your presence at project meetings you've been able to see how people in the project group collaborate, how they make decisions and make progress. You've been able to support them at moments where they got stuck, or needed a decision, or resource, or something else. You've been able to keep the work of different project groups aligned. There have been moments where project groups could share their progress with you, and with the entire team in the project's deep dives at the team's meeting. All of these things combined mean that you've ticked almost all of the boxes for tracking progress.

The only thing still missing is formal scoring of OKRs. I recommend doing this twice per quarter. First as a mid-quarter check-in. This makes you and team members conscious of critical projects that could be at risk, so that you can collectively prioritize and focus efforts in the second half of the quarter in order to hit the most critical milestones. The second time you score OKRs is about two weeks before the end of the quarter. That's also the kick-off for the next quarter's OKR-writing process. There are four steps in the process of scoring OKRs:

1 Team members score their individual OKRs.
2 They discuss scores with their manager, correct them if needed and the manager signs off.
3 The team lead aggregates all scores by scoring team OKRs.
4 Actions and implications are discussed.
    a For mid-quarter scoring, decisions are made to prioritize and focus efforts. It could be that expectation management needs to be done with stakeholders when a certain output cannot be delivered.
    b For end-quarter scoring, decisions are made to set OKRs for next quarter.

The OKR-scores and achievements are also an important input for performance evaluations. I will cover that in more detail in the next chapter about performance management. Let's first have a look at how OKR-scores work.

OKR-scoring
The scoring of OKRs is done by applying a number between 0 and 1. You'd think that a score of 1 indicates the OKR was achieved—but that's not how most Silicon Valley companies do it. A score of 0.6 or 0.7 is typically considered "on target." A score of 1 indicates you have strongly over-achieved on an OKR. Anything below 0.6 means the OKR has not been completely achieved. A score of 0 means there was no progress at all. Key results are scored first. Objective scores are the average of the scores of the key results under the objective. You can choose to weigh some key results heavier than others if you believe they are

more important. The example OKRs Scorecard in figure 17 is from Google's re: Work website. This site also explains Google's philosophy on OKR-scoring.

Figure 17 *OKRs Scorecard from rework.withgoogle.com.*

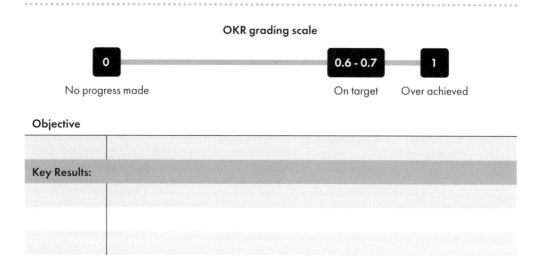

The scoring definitions relate to the way goals are set. Google often sets goals that are just beyond the threshold of what seems possible, sometimes referred to as *stretch goals*. Creating stretch goals is tricky, as it could be seen as setting a team up for failure. However, such goals can tend to attract the best people, and create the most exciting work environments. Moreover, when aiming high, even failed goals tend to result in substantial advancements.

The key is clearly communicating the nature of stretch goals and what are the thresholds for success. Google likes to set OKRs so that success means achieving seventy percent of the objectives, while fully reaching them is considered an extraordinary exception. When a sequence of seventy percent achievements on stretch goals adds up across many quarters, the combined achievement will be much more remarkable than what people would have achieved if you had set goals you already knew were feasible in advance. This way of thinking, setting and scoring goals keeps people on their toes: Larry Page calls that "uncomfortably excited."

This only works if you as a manager ensure that people understand this philosophy. And you must combine it with a clear sense of prioritization using P0,

P1 and P2 labels the way I described when covering the fourth Brilliant Basic about OKR-writing. If you don't apply the principle of priority labels well, setting stretch goals almost inevitably leads to workload issues and stress. It's also critical that you create high levels of psychological safety in your team. It's hard for people to accept stretch goals when they don't feel safe. Psychological safety is covered in part II of the book about high-performing teams.

So it's expected that, on average, team members end up scoring their OKRs 0.7. In this model, if a team member scores all of their OKRs 1, that would be a signal that the manager and that team member haven't set sufficiently challenging goals. What is a good score also depends on the priority label of the OKR. A 0.3 score on a P2 OKR is never a problem. A 0.3 score on a P0 OKR is a big problem, because P0 OKRs are the must-deliver OKRs. It's particularly a problem if a P0 OKR scores too low, if there haven't been any escalations about this that could have prevented the low score from happening. Both the manager and the team member should have intervened at a moment when course correcting was still possible if they saw that this P0 OKR was at risk. The only scenario where scoring low on a P0 OKR is acceptable is if all people have escalated to the right channels, and had still ended up hitting barriers that couldn't be overcome. In that scenario they must instantly manage the expectations of all stakeholders. If they did all of that, the low score on the P0 OKR is not a surprise and not a problem.

> *A range of high scores of your OKRs doesn't automatically mean you get a favorable performance evaluation. It's the impact of the OKRs that makes the difference. Not the score*

One implication of the above is that OKR-scores are not synonymous to your performance evaluation. A range of high scores of your OKRs doesn't automatically mean you get a favorable performance evaluation. It's the impact of the OKRs that makes the difference. Not the score. An 0.6-score on a stretch OKR can mean a team member delivered more impact than another team member which had a score 1 for an OKR that was easily achievable. When team members don't understand that their performance score is *not* a sum of their OKR-scores, some might start playing around with OKR-scores to look better, and the quality of your information for decisions about next quarter's OKRs will go down.

You can choose to deviate from this way of scoring if you think it doesn't fit the way of working or the culture in your organization. You might choose to make 1 the score that indicates "on target." Whatever scoring method you choose, make sure all people understand it and apply it consistently. Otherwise you cannot consistently interpret the results. You can even choose to use a completely different method than OKRs for setting goals and priorities. That's all OK, as long as you have at least some mechanism that helps people understand what is expected from them, how to prioritize their work, and how progress will be tracked and evaluated.

Critical points
- Ongoing tracking of progress, including scoring of OKRs, is critical to avoid people getting stuck, to identify when they go off brief, to spot cross-functional risks or opportunities, to provide in the moment feedback, and to course correct in time.
- It's important that all people use the same definitions when scoring OKRs, and that they understand their performance evaluation is defined by their impact, not by the OKR-scores.

Basic 5   Fair and predictable performance evaluations

The fifth and last Brilliant Basic is "Fair & Predictable Performance Evaluations." When you applied all previous Brilliant Basics structurally and with genuine intent, delivering on this last Brilliant Basic is much easier. In the most favorable scenario, the performance evaluation is a predictable summary: of accomplishments that were agreed and delivered, and of feedback that had already been given, resulting in a rating and reward that were in line with expectations of your team members.

Unfortunately, this isn't always reality. In less favorable scenarios, people may experience moments where their manager has unrealistic expectations of them, or gives them unexpected, unclear, inactionable or unfair feedback and evaluations. When elements of performance evaluations are perceived as unfair or unpredictable, it damages all Brilliant Basics you've established. It's your job as a manager to manage people's perception. If you don't get it right, trust and intrinsic motivation will erode as a result. A performance evaluation is the mo-

Figure 18 *The fifth Brilliant Basic is "Fair & Predictable Performance Evaluations".*

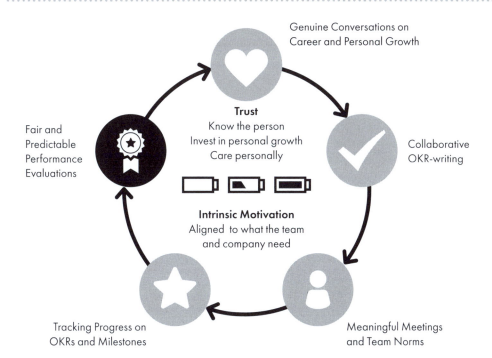

ment when people can see whether "your money is where your mouth is." It's relatively easy to give people encouraging words about their impact and performance. But it's extremely hard to do this in a way that manages expectations within the boundaries of the performance evaluation and the reward-system in your organization.

In the most favorable scenario, the performance evaluation is a predictable summary: of accomplishments that were agreed and delivered, and of feedback that had already been given, resulting in a rating and reward that were in line with expectations of your team members

When things go wrong during people's performance evaluations, most of the time lack of investment in the *other* four Brilliant Basics is actually the root cause. For example, it's hard to have aligned expectations about output, if you haven't invested enough quality time in the process of writing OKRs and tracking progress. And without the right cadence and quality of meetings, it's easy for expectations to gradually grow out of sync without noticing, or you might notice it too late for team members to still demonstrate a turnaround. Without the right frequency and depth of career conversations, it's hard to develop the depth of understanding of team members that is needed to align projects and OKRs to their intrinsic motivations. People will run projects with less energy as a result, which will have consequences in performance evaluation that might have been avoided. If you don't spend enough quality time with people at one-on-one meetings, or if levels of trust in the relationship aren't high enough, it can be hard to give people the in-the-moment feedback they need in order to avoid surprises in performance evaluations. Finally, the largest part of people's feeling of being valued and rewarded comes from being seen and appreciated by their manager and leadership. With the right level of personal care, people in lower paid jobs can feel highly rewarded, while lack of personal care can make highly paid people feel undervalued.

> *With the right level of personal care, people in lower paid jobs can feel highly rewarded, while lack of personal care can make highly paid people feel undervalued*

'Fair and predictable' doesn't mean scores and rewards always need to be high. It doesn't mean you always need to give people what they want. In fact, in my Google Digital Academy team I went through six years with almost no churn: only one person left the team. The rest meanwhile grew their skills and experience. That created a luxury problem. There wasn't a lot of scope for promotions in my team, and the distribution of ratings I needed to hold people to didn't change along with people's professional development. I gradually needed to increase the bar in performance evaluations: getting the same level of ratings gradually got harder for people. And because scores are linked to pay, achieving high financial reward also got harder. Despite all that, my manager scores remained positive.

There was still some sentiment of unfairness here and there, when people felt it was easier to get rewarded and promoted in other teams. But people trusted that I applied performance-evaluation principles in a fair and predictable way within the boundaries of our team. I also honestly shared with people that future growth-opportunities within the team were limited. That meant people could consciously choose whether or not to stay with the team, knowing what the consequences would be. People don't score you favorable as a manager because you always give them what they want. They score you favorable when they believe you understand who they are and what value they bring, and when they believe you do the right things to manage them as well as the team effectively.

> *People don't score you favorable as a manager because you always give them what they want*

How much influence do you have on the performance system?
Depending on what organization you are part of, as a manager you may or may not have a lot of influence on the performance system. Your organization's performance system might be tight and prescriptive, or maybe there isn't a performance system at all. Whatever your situation, as a manager you always have at least some influence over what a performance system feels like for your team.
Even in the tightest systems, there's always some room for personal interpretation as to how you apply processes and rules, and there's room for interpretation when explaining the rules of the system to your team. For example, if your organization is prescriptive when it comes to the distribution of the scores you allocate, you are still the one that decides where on the spectrum of that distribution you put each of your team members. You are the one that explains to individual team members what the boundaries are within which you evaluated them, where on the spectrum you have placed them and why. The quality of your explanations, combined with your trusted relationship and personal care define people's experience of the performance system, more than the system itself does.

If you work in an organization that has no performance system at all, you might have an opportunity to create one based on your own preferences. That may sound daunting, until you realize how small a performance system can be. I will illustrate that with an example. In one of my teams we had six event-manager roles that were occupied by temporary workers. The maximum tenure of these workers was two years. After the first year we'd need to make a decision whether or not to prolong the contract for a year. Some of the event managers used that moment to ask for a raise, others didn't. Some event managers even asked for a raise earlier than the end of the first year.

The quality of your explanations, combined with your trusted relationship and personal care define people's experience of the performance system, more than the system itself does

Based upon the principle of equity of reward, I didn't like the fact that an absence of rules could result in the most vocal people getting higher pay, even if those weren't always the best people. I pulled my managers together and agreed on a simple set of rules that would help us define, based upon objective criteria, who gets a raise and who doesn't. It looked something like this:
- At the one year-mark we'd evaluate for every individual whether they should get a raise or not.
- When we were happy with their service, and they started contributing to the design and improvement of our event-management processes, rather than just executing them, we'd give them a raise.
- The percentage raise was the same for all individuals that qualified.

And that's it: very simple, but it is actually a mini-performance system. With these three rules we took the bias out of the system. If a person was vocal, yet wasn't delivering quality work, that person wouldn't get a raise. If a person asked for nothing, yet delivered high-quality work and contributed to evolving our event-management processes, they would get a raise without asking for it. So a performance system can be very small, and you can create one yourself if your organization doesn't have formal processes in place.

No matter what situation you are in as a manager, whether your organization has a bit too much structure in performance evaluations or none at all: you always have influence upon how your team experiences the performance-evaluation system. You can choose to go big or small, but whatever you do, make sure you do it consistently so you avoid undesirable biases.

Why is a performance system important?
If you work for an organization that has an established performance-evaluation system, you'll need to apply it whether you want it or not, at least to some extent. It's still relevant to reflect on why performance-evaluation systems exist in the first place. People in large organizations typically don't like the performance-evaluation system, because it's easy to see all the things that are annoying about it. It's harder to see what the organization would be like in the complete absence of such a system.

In my opinion there are three main reasons why having a performance-evaluation system is preferred to not having one:

1 *Recognizing, rewarding and retaining the people who bring most value to the team and the organization.* You can talk forever about how you define exactly what "most value" means. But the reality is that the difference between your highest and your lowest performer is likely to be large in almost any team. Even at a group size of about ten people, your highest performer can easily have three times more impact than your lowest performer. It doesn't require precise calculation to see that. When you can roughly divide your team into low, medium and high performers, you've already done a pretty good job of evaluating performance. If people do a great job, a good performance system helps rewarding them for their impact.

2 *Dealing with your lowest performers.* Some people don't meet the bar of what is an acceptable performance. There can be a variety of reasons why such a situation occurs. Sometimes they're not in the right role, sometimes there's lack of will, sometimes they lose faith, sometimes they are actively damaging people—and many other reasons can exist. In most cases, the same person can perform fine in a different role, team or organization. I have a dedicated section on dealing with low performers later in this chapter. The one thing I want to say now is this: if you allow people who don't meet the bar to get away with it for too long, it drags the team down. Peers can't rely on these people, which causes frustrations and often people spiral down if you don't act. It can be demoralizing for a team to see a person slacking over and over again, while not being dealt with. It often feels harsh to give people bad performance ratings, but if you do it at the right moments in the right way, it has high value for the health of your team.

3 *Creating equity of reward and opportunity.* In my simple example of creating a set of criteria to decide about pay-increases for temporary workers you could already see how the absence of such criteria leads to a bias in favor of the loudest people. This problem lies at the heart of many challenges that relate to diversity, equity and inclusion. For instance, there's a lot of research showing that women find it harder to negotiate as to salary than men, which is one of several reasons for the significant pay gaps that exist. There's also a lot of research that demonstrates leaders, in the absence of a consistent set of criteria, often make decisions in favor of people who are like themselves, or that happen to be closest to them. This is why it's so important to unbias rules and processes for hiring or assigning performance ratings, reward and promotions. It's almost inevitable that you create situations of unfair distribution of reward and opportunity if those rules and processes don't exist.

> *As a manager you can consciously minimize the negative aspects of the performance system, while maximizing the value it brings*

Yes, I know that there are a lot of downsides to having a performance-evaluation system. For a start, in many organizations it comes with a lot of admin. And if the system is on the harsh side of the spectrum, it can create tension and competition in the organization. But as a manager you can consciously minimize the negative aspects of the performance system, while maximizing the value it brings. If you do that successfully, I am of the opinion that having a performance-evaluation system is always preferred to not having one. The guidance in this chapter hopefully supports you in your efforts to minimize damage while maximizing value.

Evaluating the "what" and the "how"

So how do you maximize the value of the performance system you use? First of all by applying it on the basis of consistent criteria. There are two types of criteria to consider:

- *What* people do: this is the impact they achieved by delivering on the OKRs that you have defined and scored together.
- *How* they do it: what you assess here is typically articulated in a set of statements that phrase which behaviors you want to amplify in your team or organization. Some of these statements could be like skills or competences that people need to be successful in their job. For instance how people approach stakeholders, how they communicate, how they solve problems etcetera. But there can also be references to the culture you want to set. For instance, you could have statements that say something about how a person deals with conflict or change, and how they treat their colleagues and customers. You can also articulate which behaviors from people help the organization create value for the world and society. The media is full of examples where organizations ended up doing damaging things as a result of people achieving their goals without considering negative side effects. Well-articulated "how statements" help making sure that people do the right things for people, planet and profit.

Let's have a look at a specific example of a "how statement" about project management. As an example I will formulate the statement on three different job grades or levels.

- *Job level or grade 1.* Provides support to projects within clear guidelines from a senior supervisor. Performs routine project tasks and activities.
- *Job level or grade 2.* Autonomously performs project activities, being responsible for specific deliverables agreed with the supervisor. May lead less complex projects within bigger projects.
- *Job level or grade 3.* Manages defined projects with moderate risk and business impact. Guides less experienced colleagues on the execution of project tasks and activities.

> *Well-articulated "how statements" help making sure that people do the right things for people, planet and profit*

Whether jobs actually start at the example levels I described, depends very much on the seniority of your organization. And project management may not be a relevant attribute for jobs in your team. I mainly picked it as an example, because it translates to many job types. I'm using the example to illustrate that "how statements" like these help you define expectations on each level or grade in your organization. This is important so managers apply consistent criteria in performance evaluations, and it is important to create clarity of expectations for your team members. Without a solid set of "how statements" it's pretty much impossible to run a fair and predictable performance-evaluation system.

As job grades go up, the "how statements" will articulate a variety of ways in which jobs, responsibilities and skills become more complex. For example:
- *Proactiveness and ownership increases with seniority.* On one level employees assist based on instructions from a more senior colleague. On the next level they run a light project autonomously, and after that they might assist more junior team members. From there, more senior people might set the future roadmap, and create roles and responsibilities for project team members, etcetera.
- *The level of complexity and ambiguity goes up as employees grow more senior.* First they might run fixed and defined processes, next they help improve processes, and eventually they might define processes and projects from scratch. In even more senior roles, people might set the strategy for entering completely uncharted territory for the organization.
- *The seniority and complexity of stakeholder management typically goes up.* In junior roles, the main stakeholder for a person is often their supervisor. On

the next level, they might need to coordinate with several team members that work on the same project. Another level higher, they might be the face of the project towards stakeholders in the execution phase of a project. On an even higher level, people might have to align with senior leadership for setting strategy and making decisions. More senior roles typically require you to interact with more senior stakeholders, which requires a different level of thinking and acting.

Addressing both the "what" and the "how", with clear expectations by job grade or level, is critical if you want to run fair and predictable performance evaluations, and create a healthy performance culture. A balance between the "what" and the "how" avoids situations where a person achieves goals at the cost of other things that are equally or more important. For instance, a sales representative that achieved a target at the cost of customer satisfaction, could still get a lower bonus. Or a team member that achieved a deadline by pushing peers or more junior team members into overwork and unnecessary stress, could still end up getting a bad performance rating. Or the other way around: someone that worked on a project with high complexity, could be saved from a low performance score if they did everything within their power to overcome difficult obstacles. You can reward people for the value they contribute to the culture of your team and organization, and thereby get your team to perform highly in a way that is sustainable. When you define a performance-evaluation system, or when you assess how to apply it, you can choose how much weight you want to put on the "what" versus the "how." I'd recommend applying roughly equal weight to both.

> *Addressing both the "what" and the "how", with clear expectations by job grade or level, is critical if you want to run fair and predictable performance evaluations, and create a healthy performance culture*

Whatever rules, processes, criteria or statements you define, it's always important to leave a level of discretion to cater for nuances of different situations, people and roles. For example, once "how statements" have been written for a variety of roles, dimensions and job grades or levels, there's a tendency to start applying them as fixed rules. But the people who define these statements on behalf of the organization find themselves tasked with the impossible job of coming up with a consistent set of statements that somehow covers all types of jobs and levels in the entire organization. There's no way that this is possible, so they end up making choices. They pick the set of statements that does the job in about seventy percent of all situations. Trying to cater for the last thirty percent would result in a monstrous set of statements that's impossible to use for managers. So as a manager and leader, when you apply the statements available to you, you must be aware that there will always be people in your team who do not fit the mold. If you fail to recognize that, these people will always end up being evaluated unfairly. When you work together with managers to agree how to apply the rules of the evaluation system, it's therefore always important to actively look for the outliers, and to agree how to best evaluate these people. Sometimes it's just a matter of writing tailored statements or criteria yourself. Those don't have to be perfect. Having something is always better than nothing.

Critical ingredients for an unbiased performance system

So having a performance-evaluation system is preferred to not having it. And whatever you do, no matter how big or small-the system is, you need to make conscious choices to maximize the value of the system and minimize the damage. In this chapter, let's have a look at some critical ingredients of a performance-evaluation system that you could consider. I already mentioned two of them:

- Quality OKR-writing and -scoring to address the "what" in evaluations.
- A consistent set of statements by job grade or level to define expectations on the "how."

Below is a summary table of ingredients in a performance-evaluation system. It isn't complete, but these are the most common elements you will find in most organizations. It will vary by organization to what extent systems and rules have been defined, and how consistently people apply them.

Because I already covered OKRs and "how-statements" I will only dive into the other elements. For each, I will cover ways they can create value, and risks that could cause damage if you don't pay attention. As you read, it's worth reflecting upon your own organization. To what extent does your organization or team have these elements, and how are they being applied? Do the systems work well in practice? Or do they need refinement? Are there any gaps? Can you fill some of those gaps yourself, by how you apply principles or by defining some of your own criteria and processes? Can you work together with peer managers, leadership or HR to make improvements? The exercise below helps you reflect.

Figure 19 *Exercise to brainstorm about healthy ingredients for a performance-management system.*

	Stop or avoid	Start	Amplify
OKR system for evaluating the "what" ☐ OKR-writing ☐ OKR-scoring			
'How attributes' by job grade and level ☐ To align with managers on consistent criteria ☐ To set clear expectations with team members			
360-degree feedback ☐ From peers and stakeholders ☐ From managers ☐ From leadership ☐ From customers and partners			
Assessment ☐ Self-assessment ☐ Manager assessment			
Rating scale ☐ Rating definitions ☐ Distribution guidance ☐ Discretion			
Agreement and guidance to run fair and unbiased performance evaluations ☐ Leadership guidance ☐ Manager forums ☐ Calibration sessions ☐ HR guidance ☐ Training (e.g. about the system, or unbiasing) ☐ Objective data checks			
Performance based reward ☐ Monetary (e.g. base salary, bonus or equity) ☐ Non monetary (e.g. coaching, senior acknowledgement or high-profile projects)			
Performance based progression ☐ Promotion ☐ Access to job roles with expanded scope ☐ Access to talent resources or programs			

Exercise: Defining your ideal Performance-Management system

The table in figure 19 helps you reflect: Which behaviors, systems or processes do you consider damaging and should be *stopped or avoided*? Which things are not used in your team or organization, but would add value when you'd *start* doing them? And which things are already happening that could be *amplified* more because of the value they create? You can complete this table on your own, reflecting on your own team. You can also do it with a leadership team or a group of peer managers, reflecting together on what is right for your organization.

360-degree feedback

The term *360-degree feedback* is widely used across organizations. A lot has been written and said about it. I will not try to repeat all that. The goal of this chapter is mostly to summarize the role it plays in performance evaluations, and to help you avoid some pitfalls. Most large organizations have some kind of system that allows people to give each other feedback during performance-evaluation cycles. Even if your organization doesn't have any of those systems, you can still gather feedback from various sides to inform performance evaluations—and it is wise to do so.

There are three audiences for whom it is important to gather feedback:
1 Peers that work on the same project or in the same team as your team member: these people can comment on the quality of work, collaborativeness and dependability of a person. They can tell you what it's like to work with this colleague of theirs.
2 Peers or stakeholders outside of your team that your team member serves or needs to collaborate with. These people can comment on deliverables, quality of communication and alignment, reliability and also collaborativeness.
3 Senior sponsors with an interest in the work of your team member, and that have sufficient visibility upon the work. That last bit is important. It may sound nice to ask senior leadership for feedback, but they rarely have the type of visibility of the work of individuals to get a sufficiently educated opinion.

It's wise to agree in advance with your team members which people they will ask for a feedback. Otherwise they might ask their "friendly" colleagues to provide feedback, and avoid people who could provide harsh feedback, or they might pick a mix of people who don't create a solid 360-degree view. If your organization doesn't have a system that allows your team members to ask people for written feedback, as a manager you'll need to speak to people personally. That can be time-consuming, but it's time well spent. People generally appreciate it if you check in with them to hear whether they are happy with the "service levels" your team member provides, and they are typically open to providing constructive feedback that helps your team member to grow. You'll build a much richer view of the "what" and the "how" of the work of your team members. I think it's good practice to be transparent with your team members that you are having these conversations with and who you are speaking to. It's also valuable to share feedback you've heard, even before a formal performance-evaluation cycle starts. You as a manager should be the last person to write feedback, because you need to incorporate the perspectives of all people consulted in your feedback. You do this in your manager assessment.

Assessments

The ultimate output of a performance-evaluation cycle is normally an assessment from the manager. But before that assessment can be written, several inputs need to happen first. The 360-degree feedback mentioned in the previous section is one of the sources of input. Most organizations also ask individual team members to submit information about projects they worked upon and achievements they believe they had. They are then asked to reflect on their achievements and the feedback they have received.

When you make written self-assessments a part of your process, it is wise to provide people with a maximum word count. Otherwise some people would start writing books. It's also valuable to give people a fixed format. For example you could say people can submit up to five accomplishments. I typically ask people to describe projects in the following structure:

- *Objective*: what is the objective you worked on?
- *Actions*: what are the actions you took?
- *Result*: how did those actions help achieve the objective?

If you have a solid system for OKR-writing, it should be relatively easy for people to write about their achievements in this format. If they end up writing something that doesn't look like it's aligned with their OKRs, that's a signal that something might be wrong. They may have gone off track.

People can also reflect on the set of "how attributes" that are applicable to their role and level or grade. They can mention one thing they believe they do well, and one thing they want to improve. Whatever structure you provide, make sure you limit the word count for each section. It increases the fairness of the process, because all team members then work within the same boundaries. It also encourages people to invest in the quality of notes over the quantity.

You don't need a formal system to handle self-assessments the way described here. You can easily run a process like this by providing people with a text document that is a template for their self-assessments, and you can write manager assessments for them in a similar template.

Your manager assessment should include your interpretation of the impact people had through delivery upon the "what", and your assessment of their performance on "how attributes." In both areas you can use information from feedback given by peers and stakeholders, and from the self-assessments that your team members wrote. You can also include information about feedback you already gave to people earlier, and observations about how they acted (or didn't act) upon that feedback. Try to use specific examples as often as you can. When your organization requires you to assign a rating, your assessment should clearly summarize how your observations resulted in deciding this was the right rating. Whenever you can, include actionable recommendations that can lead to increased performance over time. Finally, hold yourself to a word count the same way you would do for your team members. This forces you to focus on quality and clarity.

Whether your organization has a formal system to capture feedback and assessments or not, either way it's useful to have something in writing: from team members about themselves and from you about them. It helps you and your team members to reflect before and after performance-evaluation conversations, and it's a useful archive to build over time, for instance to avoid recency bias when deciding about people's promotions. Such an archive is also critical when you might leave and a new manager comes in, or when people move to different teams within the organization.

Rating scale

Most large organizations have some kind of scale they use to assign performance ratings to people. Some organizations do this yearly, some twice a year and some quarterly. I prefer a yearly model, because the other ones create too much admin that distracts from core work. Too frequent performance evaluations can also create situations where the performance-evaluation system "takes over" the organization and its culture. People start doing things because they worry about their performance ratings, instead of doing the right things to drive their projects with impact. The downside of an annual model is the risk that managers delay giving feedback until the performance evaluation comes. If your organization works based on an annual model, you must give extra attention to making sure that people get feedback the whole year round. The Brilliant Basics of meaningful meetings and tracking of progress on OKRs and milestones will help you with that.

A rating scale that is too granular creates an illusion of precision that leads to a lower quality of performance-evaluation conversations

Some organizations have a rating scale with four types of ratings, some with five, some might assign a number between one and ten, and there are probably many systems I am not aware of. Whatever the scale, in my personal experience it's important that a scale isn't too granular. A rating scale that is too granular creates an illusion of precision that leads to a lower quality of performance-evaluation conversations. The big question when assigning ratings is always: how do you define who is most impactful? That question rarely has a precise answer, but the answer also doesn't *need* to be precise. The difference between the amount of work and quality of work between your highest and your lowest performer is typically large. It is those big differences that you want to reward. A rating scale doesn't have to be precise to do so. A rating scale with five ratings is already hard to apply consistently, and probably the maximum level of granularity you should go for. The minimum amount of buckets in your rating scale is three. A scale with three buckets allows you to separate three types of people in your team:

- *The highest performers*: people who clearly demonstrated outsized impact;
- *The ones doing a solid job*: this is generally the majority of your team;
- *The lowest performers*: people whose work is clearly below standards.

If you work in an organization that doesn't have any performance-evaluation system and no rating-scale, I'd recommend categorizing your team in these three buckets based on the consistent criteria invented by yourself. Once you've done that, you can think about how you want to create extra reward for your highest performers, and how you want to deal with your lowest performers. A process like that already does most of the job that you want a performance-evaluation system to do. The lighter you make it, the less admin it triggers and the less it distracts you and your people from focusing on the work that delivers the most impact.

Tuning the "aggressiveness" of your rating scale

The title of this section is deliberately somewhat provocative. Of course, a performance system or rating scale is never really aggressive, and it doesn't have that purpose. But choices made about the application of the rating scale do define the amount of pressure you create in your organization. Similar to the idea of stretch OKRs, a certain amount of pressure can be a good thing, but you create damage when you overdo it.

There are several decisions about the application of a rating scale that affect the amount of pressure you create in an organization. First is the recommended distribution of ratings. Let's assume as an example that your organization has a rating scale that consists of five ratings. That could look something like the example in the table in figure 20.

Figure 20 *Examples of ratings distributions.*

	Lowest performance	Below average performance	Solid performance	Above average performance	Highest performance
Light pressure	3%	7%	80%	7%	3%
High pressure	10%	20%	40%	20%	10%

In the light pressure example, I've assumed eighty percent of the people in the organization will get a rating that is in the middle of the scale. That means the assumption is that most people do a solid job. There's only a small number of people who stand out positively or negatively. That means two things: first the amount of people whom you can reward for outstanding performance is relatively low, and second the amount of people who will be "punished" for low performance is also low. A system like this is relatively predictable for people, because they'll know they'll be in the middle most of the time. Predictability is a good thing, but it could also mean that your ability to reward high performance is so low that talented people start leaving your team.

In the high-pressure example, a total of sixty percent of all people are expected to be above or below the average. So more people can be rewarded for high performance, but also more people will be "punished" for low performance. This model is less predictable. There's more reward, but it's also likely to trigger more tension in your organization. There are also options to make the distribution asymmetric. For example you could dial down the proportion of people in the low-performer buckets, and put those in the middle bucket. That would allow you to reward many people for high performance, without necessarily "punishing" an equal amount of people for low performance.

There is no right or wrong, but you have to be conscious about the consequences of the choices you make. There are several choices you can make when thinking about a distribution of ratings:

- *Do you provide guidance on distribution at all?* You could leave it up to the discretion of the manager to decide what rating distribution makes most sense within their team. After all, they are the closest to the work of their people. The downside of this line of thinking is that different managers apply different standards across the organization. And if performance ratings are directly linked to financial reward, typically there isn't an infinite amount of money that can be spent, so you can't allow managers to score their teams as high as they want. I have a possible solution for that problem that I will share later.

- *When you provide guidance: is it a hard rule, or is it a soft recommendation?* If you make distribution a hard rule that every team must live by, you create a situation where colleagues within teams end up competing with each other. If all team members perform better, the ratings' distribution still stays the same, unless people can get promoted. A promotion brings people back to a lower score, because you are then evaluated based on higher standards at the next level. At small team sizes, adhering to a hard rule can be tricky because small sample sizes come with large fluctuations. One person too many in a particular rating bucket could shift the balance of ratings by twenty-percent points if you have a team of five people only. That brings us to the next consideration.

- *At what team size do you make the desired distribution a hard rule?* It's tempting to say, let's leave it flexible for smaller teams and only apply hard guidance once you get to a team size of about 50 or 100 people. At these team sizes, the sample becomes large enough to produce stable numbers. The problem with that, is that such a rule creates competition between teams. Managers of teams, on average, have a tendency to overestimate the performance of their teams, while underestimating performance of other teams. And most managers don't enjoy giving low performance ratings to their team members. They have personal loyalties to their people, and less so to the people in neighboring teams. Theoretically the leader of all teams could be the referee who makes sure all teams get evaluated by the same rules. However at a size of about 50 to 100 people, the leader of the team no longer has visibility upon the work of all people, so can't play an objective role. If you don't ask small teams to adhere to a fixed distribution, but you *do* apply it *across all of them collectively*, it's therefore inevitable that each team leader tries to push for one or two extra high ratings, and one or two extra promotions. If one person does that, it's not a big problem. But if one person gets away with it once, more managers will be doing it soon. From there onwards, you enter a gliding scale where the performance-evaluation process becomes a tactical game or negotiation between managers. Some managers enjoy that process, some don't. It doesn't matter: the essence is that a performance-evaluation system that is based on tactics and negotiation can never be fair and predictable. So it inevitably harms the effectiveness and culture of your team. The solution I will propose later on in this chapter solves this problem. Let's first look at some more decisions about ratings distribution that need to be made.

- *To what extent do you force people in the lower rating scores?* Some organizations enforce that a certain minimum percentage of all people *must* get a low rating. The underlying premise here is that in any sample, there will always be some low performers. If senior leaders don't see people getting low ratings, the assumption is that managers don't apply high enough standards. This could be true. Some managers dislike giving low ratings so much that they prefer to keep working with a person that is actually dragging the team down, or is just not contributing a lot of value. If you tolerate that, the performance and culture of the organization suffer. It also isn't fair to peers of those people who *are* making an effort, and *are* performing. But if you solve that problem by making it mandatory to assign low ratings, you create several problems. First, if a manager is disciplined in managing out low performers, while investing heavily in people who *can* perform, you end up punishing that team. Even though there are no low performers left, certain people will still get low ratings. When you can get a bad rating despite doing good work, that creates frustrations and psychological unsafety. Most teams I worked in therefore didn't enforce the lowest rating buckets, and I think they made the right call. It's a thin line to walk, and I cannot tell you how much pressure on this is healthy in your organization. I certainly recommend staying away from a mandatory percentage of low scores. But I also recommend not to shy away from low scores if people aren't performing. I think it's best to trust managers to make the right decision and to train them on the importance of managing out consistent low performers. When you allow for that flexibility, some managers will shy away from assigning low ratings for the wrong reasons. But the damage that does is lower than the damage of enforcing mandatory low scores in your organization.

My ideal organization

So, there are quite some choices around ratings-distribution that affect the amount of pressure you create in your organization, and whether that's good or harmful pressure. A hard rule for ratings distribution is certainly not a good idea for small teams, but when applied to large teams it nevertheless creates competition between teams. Forcing people in low rating buckets does more damage than good. Yet at the same time there isn't an unlimited amount of budget to reward people, and you want to have consistent standards across the organization, so you can't let managers do whatever they want.

Here's my ideal solution that solves most of these issues: this is what I would do if I had my own large company, and could design a performance and reward system from scratch. The first principle I would want to live by is that the manager should be trusted to make the right decisions. That's the person who's closest to the people and their work, and knows best what's right. This works up to a team size of about thirty people or so. In larger team sizes the leader of the team is mostly no longer close enough to the work of all people. A team of about thirty people will mostly have a few managers. The team leader is likely to be a manager of managers. The group of all managers at that team size, is still small enough to care about all people across the team, and they are still likely to understand as to all team members what they are doing. A small group of managers in a unit of this size, should be allowed to decide what ratings distribution is most suitable for their team, so I wouldn't provide any guidance or rule about that distribution, and I also wouldn't force them to assign low ratings. What I would do though, is give them a fixed reward budget to work with (adjusted to the size and average levels or grades in the team). That way they still operate within the same boundaries that all other teams in the organization work within.

The combination of a fixed budget, and a fully flexible ratings distribution allows a small group of managers to make the decisions that have the most positive impact as to the performance and culture of the team. For example, if there are no clear positive or negative outliers in the team, they could choose to distribute the budget evenly across team members by giving all people a similar rating. Interestingly, even if they would give all people the highest possible rating, the budget's distribution would still be equal. So there's no benefit in cheating the system. Another reason to go for a somewhat equal distribution could be that there's high interdependence in the team: in some teams, levels of interdependence are so high that it's hard to point to any individual contributor that made the greatest difference. In such a scenario, the thing you want to reward is how people pulled together in order to deliver impact as a team. Again, a fixed budget without rules for ratings distribution allows a small group of managers to make these decisions. If one person clearly stands out positively or negatively, that one person can be given a higher or lower reward, and the rest gets distributed evenly. The amount of extra reward you get cannot be linked to a particular score in a fixed way in this system. If you'd create a fixed reward multiplier connected to each score, the managers would no longer be able to be fully flexible with their ratings-distribution. For example, if five people are clearly outperforming the rest, assigning all of them a high rating would deplete the budget quickly. If managers can decide themselves what the multiplier would be, they could assign the highest rating to five people without depleting the budget. The total reward per person for high achievement becomes lower, but at least you can still reward all high achievers equally. So the managers should be able to decide themselves how ratings translate to rewards, as long as they stick to the team budget.

Now there is still a scenario in which an entire team does not perform well, or performs very well. If all teams of equal size and seniority were always given the same budget, there would be no way to adjust pay according to the performance of the team as a whole. So the person leading a group of these "autonomous decision units" should be able to change the amount of budget each unit receives. If all teams write and score OKRs well, leadership can properly see which teams are contributing the most impact and adjust rewards accordingly. In my ideal organization, I would also ensure that all managers receive feedback from their teams every six months. That would reveal the extent to which team performance (or non-performance) is related to the quality of the manager(s).

In summary, these would be the rules in my ideal organization:
- Fixed budget at a team size that is small enough for the leader and all managers to have visibility upon the work of all people, and to care about all people equally. This budget is adjusted to the average size and seniority of the team.
- This budget can be increased or reduced if the team as a whole performs well or doesn't.
- No rules for ratings distribution.
- No forced low ratings.
- No fixed relation between rating and reward.

This level of autonomy gives a group of managers the trust and tools to use the performance and reward system in the way that is best for the team.

> *Performance evaluation is not about being perfect, it's about being thoughtful*

It's unlikely that you will have every single ingredient of this ideal scenario. I certainly never had it in my jobs. But the exercise of walking through these scenarios makes you conscious about all the consequences of decisions as to the performance system. Some of these decisions aren't yours to make, but for many you can define how you apply them or even how you design them. A performance-evaluation system should never be over-engineered. If you want to create a system that is as fair as possible, the first thing to understand is that it can never be perfect. When you understand the inevitable imperfections of these systems, you can mitigate the damage they do, and maximize the value. When you *ignore* the inevitable imperfections of a system, it's a certainty that the rules of the system create situations of unfairness. Performance evaluation is not about being perfect, it's about being thoughtful. If you can say within each job level, which of your people perform at low, medium and high levels, you've done a perfect job that allows you to differentiate reward and opportunity based on performance.

Agreements and guidance to run fair and unbiased performance evaluations

The biggest problem that undermines the integrity of a performance-evaluation system is bias. Bias comes in many forms. It could be that certain styles of working or certain types of people are overvalued, while others are undervalued. It could be that the system unconsciously rewards the loudest people, rewards straight white men more, or the ones that senior leadership has most visibility on. In an international organization, there might be a bias that causes preferred treatment for people in headquarter offices, versus people working in smaller offices. Reducing bias and unfairness is best done through best practice- sharing between managers, training, data checks and some supervision of senior leadership and HR.

Let's start with training: when companies think about training for managers to make the performance-evaluation system more fair and effective, they often think too narrowly. Managers might for instance be asked to do unbiasing training, or follow a training about giving high-quality feedback. But most unbiasing of performance evaluations happens before the performance-evaluation cycle starts. OKR-writing is for instance the moment when people are set up for success by assigning the right stretch-opportunities that help them to grow, and to build on their strengths. If a manager assigns the highest-profile projects to the people whom they trust, because these people happen to spend most time with the manager, that's a bias in the performance system. On top of that, you only know which projects and OKRs are good stretch goals for each person when you have regular and genuine conversations about career and personal growth with people. Unbiased access to the manager and equal airtime in meetings, can only be created through a thoughtful cadence of meetings, with thoughtful meeting norms. The way a manager uses one-on-one meetings and builds trust-relations defines whether people have equal access to high-quality feedback all the year round. One of the reasons why women and minoritized groups get less opportunities, is because some managers shy away from giving them an honest feedback, often out of fear of saying something wrong. These are all things that happen outside of performance evaluations, but they strongly define whether there's equal opportunity and reward or not. So when you want managers to contribute to fair application of the performance system, you need to train them as to all Brilliant Basics, not just on performance management. Unbiasing training is also important, yet people forget the principles over time, and therefore often still don't act on it in the moments that matter. So it's a good practice to remind managers of most common biases, and how to counter them, every time a performance-evaluation cycle opens. In appendix 3 you can find a practical unbiasing checklist from Google's re:work-website that can be used as a reminder to unbias performance evaluations. I'll cover the topic of unbiasing deeper in part II of the book.

> *Most unbiasing of performance evaluations happens before the performance-evaluation cycle starts*

It's also valuable if the senior leader of the organization joins sessions where managers discuss best ways to apply the performance-evaluation system. The senior leader can share observations from previous performance cycles, things that went well, but also things that went less well. A leader can for instance show data about potential biases in the system. In my organization I always compared ratings distributions by gender in order to check for bias. I also checked if people who worked in large markets, near leadership, were getting higher scores than people working in smaller countries. I'd check whether people on senior job levels or grades were getting higher ratings. The higher the grade, the closer the proximity to leadership. Most of these data checks are checks you can do by hand, in an excel-sheet or even on a piece of paper. In part II I go deeper into data checks that help tracking progression on initiatives pushing for more diversity and inclusion in the organization.

I am not in favor of senior leadership interfering with decisions about ratings or promotions for individual people who are several layers lower than those in the organization. If a leader runs a large organization, they can't be close enough to the work of all people. So when they become involved in those decisions, they inevitably introduce proximity bias. But a senior leader can make powerful contributions by doing data checks and zooming in on edge cases, in order to see whether consistent criteria were applied. Once the checks have been done, and the right critical questions were asked, managers should be trusted to make the right decisions.

Performance-based rewards
When you have identified which people are your highest performers, it's nice if you can reward them for their impact and efforts. Laszlo Bock is the former Vice President of People Operations of Google, who wrote the book *Work Rules* where he shares his philosophy for the design of the Google organization. When he still worked at Google, he was the driving force behind the idea of Google's re:Work website, where Google "open sourced" a lot of their organizational and cultural ways of working. An interesting and provocative quote from his book is "pay unfairly (it's more fair!)." With that quote, he makes a similar point that I made earlier in the book. The difference in impact between your highest and lowest performers is typically very high. In his philosophy you should match that with differentiation in reward. I agree almost entirely with that statement. I believe that effort and impact should be rewarded, and lack thereof should be dealt with.

I've however also seen that for many people high pay leads to adjusted expectations for reward. People typically don't look at their salary as an absolute number. They look at it relative to what they think their peers earn. If you work in an organization where everyone gets paid very well, people can still be unhappy with their salaries. The perception that others might get more reward out of the performance and reward system than you do, can even undermine the work pleasure for people who would have been perfectly happy if the performance and reward system hadn't existed. Every time a big email goes out celebrating all the people who got promoted, ninety percent of the organization is watching it realizing that they did not get promoted. If people trust that your performance evaluations and promotion decisions are fair, they won't be bothered to see colleagues around them being promoted. They might even be happy for these colleagues. But if there's any doubt about the fairness of people's ratings and promotion decisions, every celebration of a colleague's promotion is a slap in the face.

> *Every time a big email goes out celebrating all the people who got promoted, ninety percent of the organization is watching it realizing that they did not get promoted*

So yes, I do believe high performance should translate into higher reward and I believe low performance should have consequences, but I am conscious that financial reward is only a small part of the puzzle and too much emphasis on it can have adverse effects. It's the sum of all Brilliant Basics that counts. As a manager, if you make an effort to understand your employees by having genuine conversations about career and personal growth, and you give them projects that match their intrinsic motivations, you treat them with respect, create trusting relationships, give feedback and opportunities to grow, create a team culture where people can feel a sense of belonging, and performance reviews are fair and predictable. Then you will have already delivered about ninety percent of what it takes for people to feel valued and motivated. Getting financial reward based on great performance can then be the "icing on the cake" that keeps people happy. But without all the steps before it, it's hard for people to feel valued, no matter how high their financial reward.

There are many non-monetary forms of reward. Many of those are more powerful than money. In my experience, anything that empowers people and helps them grow is a valuable source of non-monetary reward. Examples are access to coaching, mentorship, rotations, education and talent programs. The ability to run side projects, to work on bigger projects, to train peers, to coach or manage junior team members, or to see your ideas get funded are also powerful ways to reward people for high performance, in a way that salary and high bonuses cannot buy you. I also use flexibility and autonomy as reward mechanisms. If people prove they are intrinsically motivated and can make the right decisions that create a positive impact, I give them more flexibility and autonomy. The more you do that, the better talented and motivated people perform, and the longer they stay with you. This includes the flexibility for people to choose when, how much or where they work. If you have the opportunity to reward high performance with financial reward, you should definitely do so. But don't forget the Brilliant Basics, and make sure you think hard about all the non-monetary ways you can create value for people to reward their performance.

Running fair and predictable performance conversations

A performance-evaluation cycle typically ends with one-on-one conversations between managers and their direct reports. I have recommended earlier in this book to keep performance conversations and career conversations separate, so I'm assuming in this chapter that the performance conversation is a separate conversation.

The performance conversation typically covers at least the following topics:
- A summary of the "what": the impact the team member had by delivering on OKRs.
- A summary of the "how": an evaluation of skills, behaviors and attitudes the team member applied while delivering on the OKRs. Ideally this analysis of the "how" is based on "how statements" that have been formulated by job grade or level.
- An explanation of how the "what" and the "how" together have resulted in the rating you have given to your team member. If your organization doesn't have formal ratings, as a manager you'll still provide some kind of value judgment that indicates to your team members whether you consider them to perform at the high end of the spectrum or the low end of the spectrum.
- All of the above should be explained by referencing specific examples of things you've observed or learned through feedback from others. And it should come with actionable feedback: what are examples of things your team member can do to keep growing and performing better over time?
- Finally, there should be an explanation about how the performance evaluation affects reward and opportunities. This last part is in many organizations a conversation at a later moment. This could be an explanation about the way the evaluation translates into financial reward, it could be a promotion, and it could be that you have various growth opportunities you offer as reward

for great performance. On the negative end of the performance spectrum it could be that you need to give people a warning, or put them on some kind of improvement plan.

These topics are not a one-way street. In fact, I often start my performance-evaluation conversations by asking people what their own reflections are, and what their expectation is in terms of rating. If I did a good job throughout the year, people will mention most of the things I am about to say and they arrive at the right rating. To avoid surprises, I often ask myself the following question during the year: "If I had to rate my team member today, and had to communicate that rating, what would the rating be and how would I explain it?" In fact, I even rate all of my team members every few months or so, simply as a self-reflection. If you think about people individually, you might believe they deserve a certain score. If you think about all cases collectively, you might discover that your total set of ratings is too far removed from the rating guidance of your organization. It makes you aware of the trade-offs you need to make, and you still have the time to make them in the fairest possible way. Sometimes I discover there's information that is lacking. There's still enough time at this point to gather the information by asking for it, or to observe it directly.

Doing this exercise regularly forces you to think about what feedback is important for your team members. Imagining giving people a rating, while knowing you haven't landed all important feedback, gives you an uncomfortable feeling. If you feel this, that's a sign there is feedback you should deliver right now. You could even say literally: "If I had to rate you right now, this is the rating I would give and here is why." People will appreciate the honesty, if this is a conversation you have with them well ahead of the performance evaluation.

I've seen many managers having this "managing-expectations conversation" only one, two or three months before the performance evaluation. This is often when they realize a rating is going to be a negative surprise to people, so they still hope to fix this. If you do it that late, it will feel like a tick-the-box action to people. They might even feel deceived, because at that moment they can't change the situation anymore. If you do this, it has to be done at least four or five months before the performance evaluation happens, and there needs to be a real opportunity to still act upon the feedback and influence the rating. If you ask yourself regularly how you would rate people right now, and act on it, you will not have to deliver any surprising feedback or ratings during performance evaluations.

When you give people your assessment and feedback about their performance on the "what" and the "how", that is also a two-way street. You can share your observations and reflections and then ask them whether this matches theirs: Do you recognize this? Do you agree with my interpretation? If not, what is your interpretation of the situation? If you can run the entire conversation in a dialogue that way, a performance-evaluation conversation can actually be a pleasant experience for people. If you successfully made the conversation fair and predictable, and you made it to a proper dialogue, people will be likely to react with positive surprise. Performance-evaluation conversations aren't often pleasant for people.

The reward conversation at Google was always easy, because reward was mostly automated once ratings were established. When your organization isn't very structured as it comes to rewards, you may end up in negotiation conversations. People may ask for more salary, bonuses etcetera. To me this is one of those areas where you need to do the job *before* you enter the conversation. Establish clear criteria for yourself as to who gets a raise, how much and based on what criteria. Manage people's expectations throughout the year based on those criteria. Then apply them consistently in performance evaluations. If people try to use the performance-evaluation conversation as a negotiation moment, you can use that as an opportunity to reiterate the principles by which you decide upon reward, how that is based on the performance evaluation, and why you believe the performance evaluation was fair. If you allow yourself to enter negotiation any other way, your reward system becomes biased towards the loudest people, whereas it should be rewarding people who get the highest *impact*.

What if a team member doesn't agree with your evaluation?

Every now and then, there are outliers where expectations are far out of tune. If you execute well on Brilliant Basics, you will have few of those. But if you're not getting to a point where you and your team member agree upon the outcome of the performance evaluation, don't dwell on it for too long. Summarize the conversation, and the reasoning that made you decide this was the right rating. Don't promise anything that you can't deliver on. That will make the situation even worse. If you have been thorough in your assessment, there shouldn't be any situations where the rating you assigned is fundamentally wrong. You can suggest sleeping a night over it, and plan an extra hour to talk things through later on. That helps your team member to recover from the shock, and allows you to reflect whether you really believe your decision was fair. If not, you can think about ways that you can rectify this. If you do believe your decision was fair, you can think about what's the best way to still land it. The message might be a lot easier to land after your team member recovered from the initial negative surprise. If the person still fundamentally disagrees at the next conversation, you can refer your team member to the official channels where a complaint can be filed. Most large organizations have processes for this. I personally never had to use them. If you are thoughtful about your approach, the odds of that happening are small. And even if it does happen, it's mostly a moment where you can agree to disagree. Your decision still stands. It's up to your team member then to reflect on whether they can live with that or not. If you worry about your team member leaving, because of a rating you gave, to me that is a signal that there might be something wrong with that rating. If you are however convinced the rating you gave is fair, and you know you delivered well on all Brilliant Basics, it's easier to accept that a team member might leave. It might be the best decision for them and for the team.

Actionable feedback & coaching

When is the right moment for giving feedback? Many managers, including myself, sometimes delay giving feedback to people because it doesn't feel like the right moment. But the risk is that no moment ever feels right to land feedback, especially when you know it's difficult feedback. I hope by now it's clear that you should definitely not wait giving feedback until the official performance evaluation. In fact, the performance evaluation conversation is the worst moment to give feedback: the fact that it is a formal evaluation moment makes it a somewhat unsafe moment, which triggers a mindset where receiving and digesting difficult feedback is harder for people. When you work in an organization with a highly formalized performance-evaluation process, you can even feel that when the performance cycle is nearing. If you give people difficult feedback in the last few months before a performance-evaluation cycle starts, they worry more about how it might backfire in their performance rating, than thinking about how to change their attitude and behavior. You have much more opportunity of landing difficult feedback in a way that changes people's behavior positively, when you do it well ahead of the performance-evaluation cycle.

> *The performance evaluation conversation is the worst moment to give feedback: the fact that it is a formal evaluation moment makes it a somewhat unsafe moment*

So earlier is better, but how do you find the right moment? Have you ever had this happen to you: someone comes to you while you are in the midst of something and says "Do you have some time? Is this a good moment to give you some feedback?" Can you remember such a moment? What was the first reaction you felt? Chances are that somewhere inside you felt a somewhat defensive reaction. You probably started to wonder what you might have done wrong. It depends on the tone of the person saying it, and on the level of trust in your relationship. Imagine this happening while there's a difference in seniority between the two people. If this is a team member saying this to a manager, it's likely to be less threatening. But if it's a manager saying this to a team member that is one or two levels down in the organization, chances are that this remark triggers at least a wee bit of worry in people.

When you do trainings to learn about giving feedback, they often teach you to check in with people: "Is this a good moment to give you some feedback?" But the word *feedback* triggers negative emotions with people, and it therefore reduces your opportunity to land difficult feedback with them. And you don't even *need* the word *feedback* to check in with people and to give them feedback. In fact, I have almost never used the word *feedback* in my relationships with team members, yet I still scored a 100 percent in my manager feedback- survey on the statement "My manager gives me actionable feedback on a regular basis." I did so by asking people about their reflections of a certain moment or action, by sharing my thoughts with them, honestly and in a direct manner, positive and negative, and always with personal care. I rarely called it feedback though. People experienced value out of the questions I asked, and the thoughts I shared with them. They knew I was making an effort to help them to grow, so it felt like valuable feedback.

The word *coaching* has similar challenges as *feedback*. Has someone ever said to you "let me give you some coaching"? How does that feel? Again, it depends a bit on the relationship with that person, but in most situations this will feel at least somewhat patronizing. It diminishes a person's sense of self, and makes them less open to coaching. When used wrongly, the word *coaching* implicitly says "you need some coaching, because there's something wrong with you and I am the one that knows what's right." Similar to giving feedback, coaching a person is easier when you don't call it *coaching*. This is particularly true when you are a manager. It's different if a person has actively asked you to be their coach. But as a manager, people may or may not want you to be their coach. They may or may not trust you, or find you sufficiently credible. So it's better to avoid the word, and instead just focus on asking the right thoughtful questions in order to help people reflect on their projects, situations and themselves. These are actually coaching questions, but you don't have to explicitly say that.

In many organizations and for many managers, giving more feedback and coaching people seem to have become goals in themselves. This is because feedback and coaching are critical contributors to high performance, so many organizations send all of their managers to trainings, and encourage them to give more feedback and coach more. These managers then often overdo it, at the wrong moments, with the wrong intention behind it, and it makes things worse rather than better. Feedback is not about "giving feedback" and coaching is not about "being a coach." In both cases it is about asking people the right questions at the right moment, that help people reflect on situations, problems, opportunities and behavior (or absence of behavior). And it's about sharing valuable thoughts with them, so they can find a better way forward for themselves.
Feedback typically is not about the person. If you make it about the person, that's often what makes people defensive. So focusing on people's behavior is always better. But most of the time, conversations about people's projects and OKRs are the opportunities for landing feedback and coaching people. You start talking about strategies, choices to be made, people to approach, creative ideas, possible solutions, etcetera. By going through topics like these, inevitably you also touch upon the behavior of your team member. Sometimes even without you or them noticing it. When you provide valuable feedback on a broad set of topics, these topics become your "entry doors" that create opportunities to give feedback on people's behaviors, and you'll be able to do it without having to say "let me give you some feedback."

Feedback can be positive as well as negative. I've often heard leaders say "giving positive feedback is easy, giving negative feedback is hard." That's not true: both are equally hard. Sure, it's easy to say "well done, thank you!" but that is not positive feedback. It doesn't specify what it was exactly that made what a person did well, and how they can use that knowledge to do even more things well or even better. Feedback is only relevant if it is specific, personal and actionable. You have to deliver it in a way that resonates with the receiver, so the person is encouraged to reflect, and so it affects attitudes and behaviors. That's equally hard, whether it's positive or negative feedback.

> *You have to deliver it in a way that resonates with the receiver, so the person is encouraged to reflect, and so it affects attitudes and behaviors. That's equally hard, whether it's positive or negative feedback*

A book about feedback that I found valuable as a manager is the book *Radical Candor* by Kim Scott. The essence of the model is described in figure 21. Feedback needs to be direct and clear, but it also needs to be delivered with personal care. When you combine these dimensions, people change and grow. If one of the two is missing, you end up in the quadrants of obnoxious aggression, which leads to defensiveness or ruinous empathy, which then leads to ignorance. Both aren't useful and are often even damaging to the effectiveness of the team, and in some cases to the relationship with team members. If both are missing you are in the quadrant of manipulative insincerity, which leads to mistrust.

Figure 21 *The Radical Candor feedback framework by Kim Scott.*

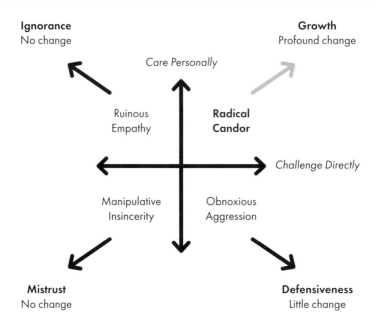

When you search for "Radical Candor" and "Kim Scott" on YouTube, you'll find some nice speeches by her that are worth watching. And the book is certainly worth a read as well.

Summing things up: consider erasing the words *feedback* and *coaching* from your dictionary. Instead, just spend time with people to understand who they are, what they do, how and why they do it. Have ongoing dialogues with them about their work, their ideas, their strategies, their actions, their fears, their working-relationships and more. Listen well and share honest thoughts and reflections with people. Ask how they look at those thoughts and reflections. Ask questions that help them to reflect and find ways forward for themselves. When you do it like this, feedback and coaching are closely related to each other. You might start coaching to solve a problem, yet at the same time you're likely to also give people feedback about their role in relation to that problem. You might start coaching a person to help find a strategy for maximizing impact of a project, and implicitly give feedback about behaviors or attitudes that could make or break the success of the project. Allow feedback and coaching to work implicitly, and you'll be more effective. Always do it with genuine intent: intent to understand the person and help them find a better way forward.

> *Managing low performers starts with giving them a genuine opportunity and support to become solid or high performers*

Managing low performers
Everything I have written until now has been focused on helping people be the best they can be for themselves, the team and the organization. But the Brilliant Basics also help you to manage low performers, because managing low performers starts with giving them a genuine opportunity and support to become solid or high performers.

Below are three principles that help you manage low performers in a respectful manner:
- 100-percent commitment to consistent performance standards
- 100-percent commitment to human respect
- invest first, judge later

Most of the time, when people don't perform well in a job, they can be turned around with the right levels of personal care, direction and support. It could be that they're just on the wrong project, or didn't get the right guidance, or there's something wrong in their support environment. They might have lost faith in themselves, or lost faith in the team or in leadership. Maybe they struggle with prioritization, or with strategic decisions. Maybe they moved from manager to manager, and clarity or motivation got lost on the way. It could also be that events in people's private lives affect their performance. When someone doesn't deliver what you expected, the first step is always to zoom in and understand. In organizations that look upon themselves as a high-performing organization, people can sometimes conclude too fast "this is a low performer." If managers arrive at such a conclusion without understanding and investing first, people who could have performed fine, spiral down fast.

The deep career conversations that are the first Brilliant Basic, are a powerful tool to figure out what could be wrong. The fact that you take several hours of personal time out of your schedule signals positive intent, and creates a circle of safety. The conversation framework helps you find out what drives a person, what gives them energy and what drains it, what they think they're good at and what not. This conversation will give you ideas for projects you can give this person, in order to test what they can do and what they enjoy. If you can come out of a conversation with some agreed actions or projects, and positive hope from you and your team member, you have started a potential journey of recovery.

From here it can go two ways: first, you see it starts to work, and you keep tweaking projects and guidance until you see your team member build up confidence. When that happens you can gradually fade out the extra guidance you are giving this person. Second, the person doesn't perform as well as you hoped. This means you have to keep giving this person extra attention, first to figure out if different input and guidance can make things better. If this doesn't work, agreements about deliverables need to be underlined more thoroughly. This means you're making it explicit and clear that the team member isn't delivering on expectations. That clarity opens the door to having honest conversations: Why is it not working? Why is the support not helping? Why are agreed deliverables not being delivered? What gets in the way? When you gradually narrow the space for people to get away with not delivering what was agreed, it will become clearer whether there is a lack of will or a skills-gap that is just too hard to overcome.

If a person has a will to perform, yet a skills gap that is too hard to overcome, I do not look at that person as a low performer. It's just a person who is in the wrong job. It's still better if this person finds a different job then, and you can even help with that. But there's no need to make things nasty. Besides the fact that there is no need to treat the person badly, it also isn't good for the team. When you treat a person that has positive will, as a low performer because they lack a skill, and then you manage them out in a way that is painful for them, the other members will see that too. Some of them might be friends of this person. They might see that the person isn't performing, but they also know this person is trying hard and doing their best. Seeing such a person being treated badly by the leader is demoralizing. This harms team norms for respectful interaction with each other, and can lead to a turnover amongst your higher performers.

> *If a person has a will to perform, yet a skills gap that is too hard to overcome, I do not look at that person as a low performer. It's just a person who is in the wrong job*

A problem with *will* is harder. If you as a manager have invested lots of personal time and care in a person, yet that person still refuses to play ball, I do consider such a person a low performer. Your real low performers are the people who cannot be managed without power, that only do what you ask from them when they know you are watching. Similar to the previous scenario, I think such a person needs to find a different job. The main difference is that I would not be willing to *help* them find it, and I wouldn't write a positive recommendation. I wouldn't feel good luring a peer manager in another organization into hiring a person that I know has a lack of will to do great work. This person might even be damaging to colleagues, due to political behavior. You don't want to be the one who handed that problem to another manager and team. The problem with a lack of will, is that people go to great lengths to hide it. When not managed tightly they can successfully get away with such behavior for quite some time, sometimes for years, which encourages them to keep a poker face. They will pretend to listen to feedback, and do the minimum to make you feel they acted upon it. But they will not fundamentally change their ways of working. The only way to get them out is to make it sufficiently painful for them so they consider leaving, or to gather a large amount of documentation that proves their low performance so clearly that they can be forced to leave.

The formal way to do this is called a *PIP* in many organizations (Personal Improvement Plan). Your organization might have a different name for it, and there might be various flavors with different levels of severity. The PIP that I know is one where "improvement plan" actually isn't the right name. If you have been thorough in your investments in a person, by the time that person needs to be put on a PIP, they will have ignored all your guidance and feedback for several quarters in a row. You already know that they are not going to turn around. So the PIP is mostly a way to formally document your expectations of a person in a language they can't wiggle themselves out of. It also states clearly what the consequences are if they don't deliver on the expectations. And then you go through several months of micromanaging this person, essentially to prove they aren't delivering on the PIP. That's a painful experience, both for the team member and for the manager. It's also time-consuming and costly to the organization, because it easily takes four to six months to get to the point where you can end someone's contract. And even then, they might still have a right to get some kind of financial compensation, and lawyers might need to be involved.

There's a phrase in my native language, Dutch, that says "gentle healers make stinking wounds". It applies very much to this problem. As a manager, you should try to avoid getting to the stage of a PIP. A PIP is a stinking wound. That doesn't mean you should allow low performers to get away with not delivering. You should still achieve a situation where they leave the team, but ideally you do it in a way that is faster and less painful.

> *Your real low performers are the people who cannot be managed without power, that only do what you ask from them when they know you are watching*

Below are ten "layers of defense" that prevent you from ending up in at PIP-stage with your team members:

1 Hire the right people.
2 Give people time and support to *ramp up* effectively in their job.
3 Find people's intrinsic motivation through meaningful career conversations, care, and giving them projects that stimulate their strengths and passions.
4 Create a productive supportive environment for people.
5 Create clarity of direction and expectations through vision, plan and OKRs.

6. Ongoing tracking of progress and honest actionable feedback the whole year round.
7. Fair and predictable performance evaluations—and don't shy away from low ratings if people really have not delivered.
8. Support people with too large skill gaps by finding another job where they can shine.
9. Have tough and honest conversations with people who lack will, and try to agree upon an exit with them.
10. PIP.

> *You can avoid being a "gentle healer" leaving a "stinking wound"—but it's even better to avoid needing a doctor at all*

Hiring is a topic I will cover in part II of this book about high-performing teams. Defense layers two till seven are all Brilliant Basics I discussed previously. When you execute well on the first seven layers of defense, you rarely end up in a situation where an exit is the only option. In layers eight and nine, you need to get to a situation where the team member realizes that the current situation in your team isn't going to work for them, and chooses to leave voluntarily. The problem is that some people only arrive at that conclusion when their current situation is sufficiently painful for them. A settlement can help to reduce some of the pain of leaving, yet when people don't experience their current situation as a problem, they're less likely to accept a settlement. If you as a manager refuse to tighten the screws on people, because you find it hard to be tough on people, no settlement will ever feel attractive enough to leave voluntarily. PIP then becomes the only way out. Or not doing a PIP, but that will mean that you and your team get stuck with a person who drags the team down, and this might even cause damage to people.

Layers eight and nine are where you can avoid being a "gentle healer" leaving a "stinking wound"—but it's even better to avoid needing a doctor at all. Layers one to seven prevent the need for a doctor. When you've arrived at the stages eight and nine and realize that a PIP will do even more damage, it's easier to accept that you've got to do what you've got to do as a manager: you need to make the current situation sufficiently uncomfortable. I've gone through this process only a handful of times. It felt painful, because it goes against my nature and some of my values, but I knew this was the least painful route for all involved, so I could do it with a good conscience. For a person with a fundamental skill problem it means making them painfully aware that they're not up to the job, while at the same time showing them a way forward, where they could perform much better and be happier. For people with a will problem this means narrowing all their options to wriggle themselves out of accountability: this requires you to set extremely clear expectations, verbally communicated and repeated in writing. You need to give them tough feedback and warnings, verbally communicated and repeated in writing. Meanwhile you need to keep your HR-business partner informed, and take their advice. When you reach the stage where you think you've tried everything, and the situation has become sufficiently painful for your team member, you can try to open the conversation about an exit settlement. When your team member realizes the alternative is a PIP, which is going to be an even worse and longer version of what they already went through, they might accept a settlement. Typically this releases people from duty instantly, which is a relief for all involved. Depending on the settlement and the country they are in, they will still get paid for a few months, which gives them time to find something new for themselves.

> *The one thing that is always in your power, is to be thoughtful about how a person's exit affects your team members*

In all exit scenarios, you must stay respectful to the person. It's the right thing to do and it sets norms for your team. When you can, give people a worthy exit. It doesn't mean you have to pretend they did a great job. In fact it's better if you don't pretend. Your team members will know what you're saying isn't true, so it harms your credibility. It also doesn't mean everyone that leaves needs to get a big expensive dinner. Some genuine words typically do the job, and maybe some nice cards written by team members to say goodbye. In your speech, you can focus on what's good about a person, maybe acknowledge it wasn't an easy journey, and then part with respect. Closures like this make it easier for everyone to move on with positive energy.

The only exception here is when the person you managed to get out was a damaging person. In that scenario, don't give them a good farewell. In severe cases this can be damaging. I've heard of a scenario where a senior leader was known for sexual harassment issues. The person was fired, yet still received a company-wide email saying "Thank you for your great services!" Many people got hurt by that message. It would have been better not to write anything. In most situations when someone did something serious that crossed the code of conduct of the organization, there are limitations in what you are allowed to communicate. That's tough for a team leader who needs to communicate about such a person's exit. You can choose not to communicate about it at all. That at least avoids the situation I just described. In some cases it's valuable when you speak one-on-one with a few people you know who interacted closely with the damaging person. You can let them know you can't share details, but that people's stories have been heard, and that you hope the problem is solved now. In tricky situations, speak to your compliance team to understand what you can and cannot share. You have to assume that everything you share with one individual, will eventually make its way through-out the grapevines. So if you are genuinely not allowed to share certain information, also don't do it in confidentiality with one person or a small group of people. The one thing that is always in your power, is to be thoughtful about how a person's exit affects your team members.

Closing remarks

Fair and predictable performance evaluations conclude part I of this book about the Brilliant Basics that are the foundations for high-performing teams. Many of the topics that relate to the performance-evaluation system are often seen as the responsibility of HR. But the way people experience the performance-evaluation system is primarily through their manager. The manager applies the rules, communicates about them. and can influence them. So you have to own it. You don't need to be the expert, but you need to reflect upon it, experiment with different ways to apply rules, share experiences with peer managers, and challenge the system when needed. The same is true for all other Brilliant Basics. The quality of your execution on those Brilliant Basics shapes most of how your team members experience the organization. That's a large responsibility, but also a great opportunity.

The Brilliant Basics are an investment in high-quality input, to get the highest-quality output

I have often heard from managers that they don't have the time to do all the things I advocate. For instance, many told me they couldn't afford to spend several hours or even a day on a career conversation. I acknowledge that the job of a manager is fragmented and full of conflicting demands, so you're always time-poor. But managing is an investment game. Output is a consequence of input. When you try to get a team to perform by demanding output, yet you don't invest enough in giving them high-quality input, you'll never get there.

Problems will keep circling back, solid or high performers leave, while low performers *refuse* to leave. When you fail to invest early, things will keep popping up that demand your time at a moment that you no longer control. The amount of time you lose then will be larger than what your investments would have cost. And I haven't even mentioned loss of opportunity: a high-performing team that works based on intrinsic motivation often delivers you more than you ask for. They come up with solutions you didn't think of. And a high-performing team attracts more great people. This is also why part I of the book is much longer than all the other parts: everything you do is easier and faster once the Brilliant Basics are in place. The Brilliant Basics are an investment in high-quality input, to get the highest-quality output. Helping a team perform at the highest level is very much like nurturing a young tree.

A young tree doesn't grow faster if you pull it really hard.
In fact it's more likely to die. Nurture it and it will grow into something bigger and stronger than yourself. Teams are the same: top-down pressure and lack of care suck the energy out of teams. Personal care, trust, safety, clarity, encouragement and meaning bring them to the highest level of performance.

Critical points

- The first four Brilliant Basics do most of the work to make fair and predictable performance evaluations possible.
- Having a performance system is better than not having it: it helps you reward your highest performers and deal with your lowest performers.
- A performance system can never be perfect, but something is better than nothing, as long as you don't over-engineer it.
- When you don't have clear criteria for assessing people on the "what" and the "how" and for assigning reward, you inevitably create bias in your system.
- 360-degree feedback, data checks, and oversight by leadership and HR can help prevent bias.
- Managers should never give feedback during performance evaluation conversations, that wasn't shared before at a moment when the team member could still act upon it.
- Don't force a fixed ratio of low ratings on your teams, but don't shy away from low ratings either.
- It's your job as a manager to minimize the damage of the performance system, and maximize the value.

PART II

GREAT TEAM LEADERS, HIGH-PERFORMING TEAMS

PART II

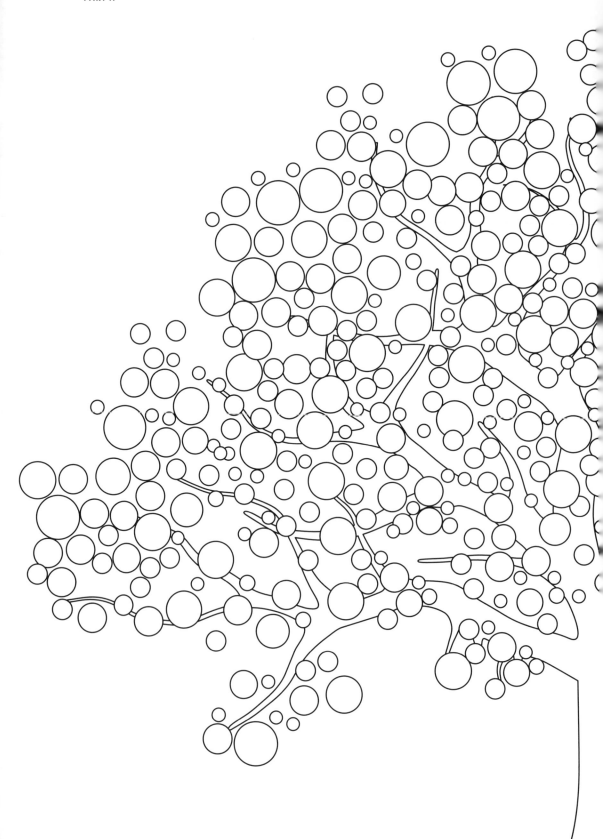

We're now getting at the part of the book about high-performing teams, but when you apply the principles of part I you've already achieved most of it. When executed with consistency, genuine intent, and personal and situational awareness, the Brilliant Basics become a flywheel for trusted relationships and intrinsic motivation. These basics cover about two-thirds of the habits that make a team effective. Without these, it's impossible to create high-performing teams. The rest can be achieved by putting *focus* on psychological safety, innovation, meaning, diversity and inclusion. The remainder of this book is about that last 33 percent, and about scaling team effectiveness in order to create an effective organization.

Google's People Analytics Team published a famous piece of research about high-performing teams under the codename *Project Aristotle*—a tribute to Aristotle's quote, "the whole is greater than the sum of its parts." The goal was to answer the question: "What makes a team effective at Google?"

The People Analytics Team evaluated more than 180 Google teams, ran over 200 interviews, and ran more than 35 statistical models in order to find a relation with various output KPIs. They found that the number one factor that drives team effectiveness is *Psychological Safety*. Safe teams beat their targets by seventeen percent on average, while unsafe teams miss their targets by nineteen percent. The analytics team found four other attributes of high-performing teams. Below is the total list:

1 *Psychological safety*: team members feel safe to take risks, and be vulnerable in front of one another.
2 *Dependability*: team members get things done on time, and meet Google's high bar for excellence.
3 *Structure and clarity*: team members have clear roles, plans and goals.
4 *Meaning*: work is personally important to team members.
5 *Impact*: team members believe their work matters and creates change.

Dependability, structure and clarity, and impact are all covered by the five Brilliant Basics in part I of the book: there's nothing extra you need to do in order to establish these last four attributes of high-performing teams.

When it comes to "meaning," it is tempting to attribute this to having a lofty mission about the value your organization brings to the world. Google actually has a fantastic mission: "To organize the world's information, and make it universally accessible and useful." I know many Google employees who derive meaning from that mission. The founders of Google wrote it down at the start-up-phase, but it's equally relevant today. However, if you look at it from the perspective of the daily work of your team members, the organization's mission is not the primary source that drives a sense of meaning.

There are many things that contribute to a positive sense of meaning for your team members. The Brilliant Basics play an important role there. Meaningful career conversations help uncover what is meaningful to each individual, and you can match the projects people work on with that. If there isn't enough connection between what people want and what the team needs, you can have honest conversations early on, so people don't end up "drowning" for too long in feelings about the lack of meaning. Meaning is also driven by the feeling of having impact, and of working effectively together within a team culture that feels good. Reversely, it's demoralizing to work in a team where you see the same mistakes repeating themselves, where the same challenges are discussed over and over again without being solved, or to see people consistently not respecting each other's boundaries. It's demoralizing if dynamics like these result in a too high workload, without a solution looking as if it's near. The Brilliant Basics prevent all of these things from happening, laying the foundation for a positive sense of meaning as to your team members. You can add to that by creating an inspiring mission or vision for your team and organization, so I will cover that in part III when we get to the topics *vision* and *leadership*.

In this part of the book I will focus on psychological safety. Psychological safety is inseparably linked to topics related to diversity, equity and inclusion, because psychological safety can't exist if it isn't there for everyone. When team members see other people in the organization get treated badly or in unfair ways, it reduces their own sense of safety as well. If it happens to someone else, it can happen to them too.

Before I go deeper into psychological safety, it's worth also covering dimensions for which Google's People analytics team found they didn't correlate significantly to team effectiveness at Google:
- Colocation of teammates (sitting together in the same office)
- Consensus-driven decision-making
- Extroversion of team members
- Individual performance of team members
- Workload-size

- Seniority
- Team size
- Tenure

This list is a good reason to reflect upon common assumptions:
- Do we really need to make coming into the office mandatory?
- Can we make decisions in smaller groups?
- Do we acknowledge the effectiveness of more introverted people well enough?
- Does our performance-evaluation system reward team performance over individual performance?
- Do I trust that people who manage their workload effectively can be equally or more impactful than people who do lots of overtime?
- Am I willing to pick a talented junior person over an experienced team member when allocating high-profile work?
- Do I really need more people to solve the workload-issues we have? Or is it a problem of prioritization and team effectiveness?
- Do I hire enough external people who can bring in fresh perspectives?

Psychological safety is inseparably linked to topics related to diversity, equity and inclusion, because psychological safety can't exist if it isn't there for everyone

Psychological safety

Now let's dig deeper into the dimension that is the strongest driver of team effectiveness at Google: psychological safety. The bit "at Google" is important here, because the same research might produce different outcomes in your organization. The research team doesn't provide a clear rationale as to why they believe psychological safety is the number-one dimension at Google, and how that would translate to other types of organizations. My theory is that it relates to the use of stretch OKRs.

I already mentioned that Google aims for stretch OKRs, because they found people deliver more impact when focusing on big bets, as opposed to deliverables that are obviously feasible. I also mentioned this inevitably leads to an unnecessary high workload and stress, when you don't make thoughtful use of priority labels. Psychological safety is the final dimension you need, in order to work effectively with stretch OKRs. Focusing on stretch OKRs and big bets means there's more ambiguity and risk, which results in lower safety. When you want people to take more risks, you need to provide them with safety. When people aren't sure whether they can achieve stretch OKRs, and they worry what might happen if they only achieve seventy percent, they won't accept stretch OKRs. Or they might accept them, but feelings of stress while executing might undermine their effectiveness, and their ability to come up with creative solutions for problems. So it's not surprising that psychological safety came up as the number one dimension for team effectiveness at Google.

> *When you want people to take more risks, you need to provide them with safety*

Now you might say that many traditional stable organizations aren't like Google, and therefore they don't need people to focus on big bets, and hence don't need stretch OKRs. I think it's worth reflecting on that in the context of all changes happening in the world. Almost every organization nowadays is under pressure to go through some kind of transition: digital transformation, the shift to sustainability, shifting cost structures, increased ethical standards and changes in legislation are just a few. The required organizational transformation typically isn't the first one, and it won't be the last. Very few organizations can still afford to "cruise along." In that context, every organization needs at least some of their people to focus on big bets that help anticipate required change, so org-transformation can happen early and fast enough. I will explain in more detail in part III why every organizational transformation inevitably triggers more work and more risk for employees. For now, I think it's enough to conclude that psychological safety is likely to be the number one driver of team effectiveness for all organizations that are going through some kind of change. This is what links the three parts of the book:

- Brilliant Basics do two-thirds of the work to establish the five dimensions of high-performing teams: they are the foundation.
- Psychological safety, diversity, equity and belonging are the remaining drivers for team effectiveness.
- High-performing teams, and managers that can create and nurture those teams, are key drivers of organizational change, because they are able to take risks and deliver on big bets.

This relation is summarized in figure 22.

> *Psychological safety is likely to be the number one driver of team effectiveness for all organizations that are going through some kind of change*

Psychological safety does many good things for your team:
- People are more comfortable delivering stretch goals and taking risks.
- They can carry a higher workload, without feeling overwhelmed.
- Less fear means people have clearer minds for creative thinking and problem- solving.
- People are more likely to raise problems or challenges early.
- They share more information with each other.
- People are more likely to ask for help and get help.
- They resolve problems together, rather than pointing the finger at one another.
- People can challenge each other and come up with difficult feedback, without undermining relationships.
- Your team members are not afraid to challenge you more, so that you make better decisions and grow as a person and professional.
- The team is more inclusive to all types of people.

Figure 22 The Brilliant Basics are the foundations for establishing the five attributes of high-performing teams.

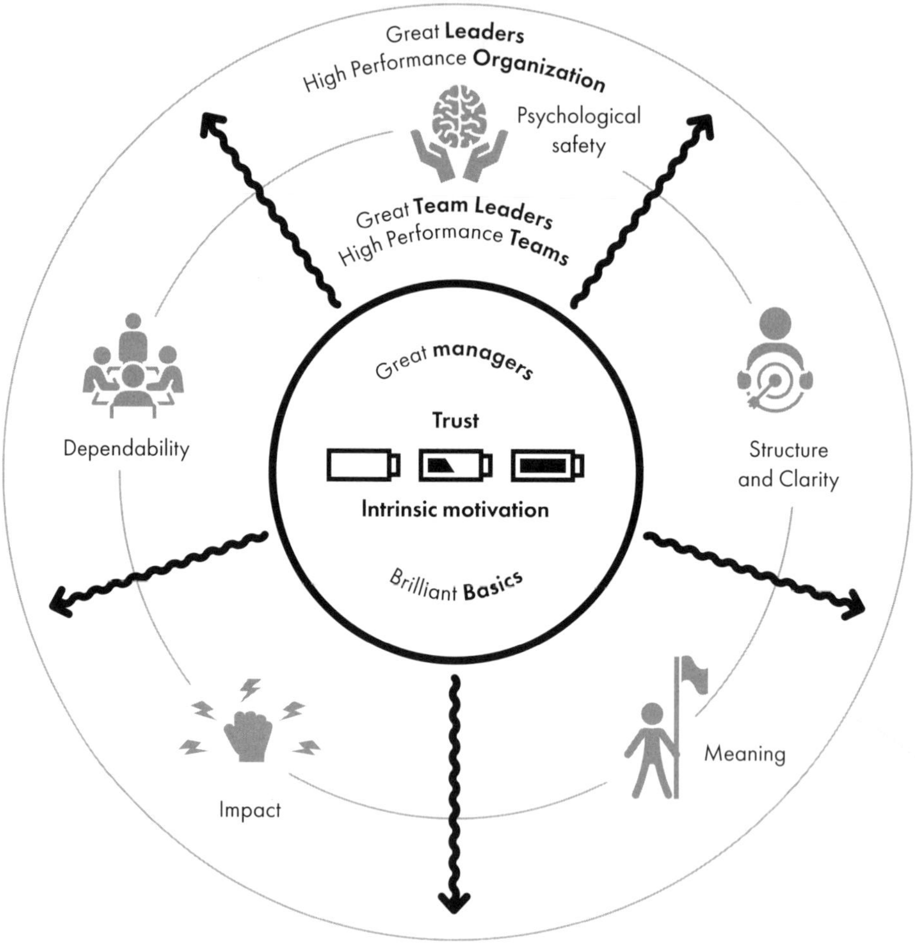

So psychological safety is critical for achieving the highest levels of team performance. That sounds nice, but it's easier said than done. In the next sections I will therefore cover how you can make psychological safety a reality.

Combining psychological safety with high performance standards

Stretch goals and big bets inevitably come with ambiguity and mistakes. How do you hold people accountable for achieving stretch goals, and how do you deal with mistakes without undermining psychological safety? How do you deal with situations of conflict between team members without undermining safety? How do you remove low performers from the team, without their peers fearing they might be next? How do you create safety for all types of people with completely different backgrounds, personalities, work preferences and communication styles?

Let's start with dealing with mistakes. It starts with investing early: the earlier you invest in building trusted relationships with your team members, the better. Ideally you already have some funds in your "trust account" by the time the first difficult situation emerges. Using deep career conversations to get to know your people at the early stages of your relationship with them, helps you to create a first "safety buffer". You will have a better understanding of your team members, which helps interpreting the situations and assessing what input works most effectively for each team member. But it also helps them to know *you* better, which means they're more likely to understand where you are coming from, when you have to land difficult feedback with them.

Next, it's important to use the word *blame* as little as possible. Whenever something goes wrong, what matters is what the best way forward is, and how to learn from what happened. Not whose fault it was. There is a nuance to this, because some mistakes do need to have consequences in the performance evaluation of a person. For example, not delivering on a P0 OKR, without any escalation or communication is something that can have consequences for performance evaluations. And if you wait with feedback about this until the performance evaluation, it's going to be a surprise at that moment. So you have to act upon it somehow. *How* you act on it makes a big difference to the psychological safety of the team.

When you first learn about something big that went wrong, you may well feel frustrating thoughts. "How is this possible? I clearly communicated the importance of this OKR! Why did you not communicate about this before?" When you allow those thoughts to become words in the heat of the moment, it's likely you will express them in a way that does damage. You'll pick the wrong words, you'll have a tone that indicates frustration, and it will all happen when a team member is most likely already banging their head against the wall due to their own frustration. So, the feelings of guilt and worry appear at that moment. It's even worse when this happens in front of other team members. So it's important to learn to "bite off your tongue" at such a moment. Your first reaction should be something like: "OK, tell me more about what went wrong. What are all the consequences? What have you done already to mitigate the damage? What more do you believe should happen? Do you need support with that?" For that moment, it's enough to leave it at that.

It could be that you end up discovering in such a conversation that your communication about priorities wasn't as clear as you thought it was, or maybe the team member tried to escalate to you earlier but you didn't listen. When you manage to create a safe environment, your team member is more likely to fully disclose all relevant information about what caused the problem. This will help you find more effective solutions together. And lowered stress helps your team member concentrate with a clear head on solving the situation. As a result the problem will be solved better and faster. The final benefit is that both you and your team member will have cooled down by the time you have a more thorough debriefing-conversation that includes potential negative feedback for your team member.

> *When you avoid unloading frustration in the heat of the moment and support solving the problem, your team member is more likely to be open to your feedback*

Once the problem is solved, with the full overview of all information and with a cool head you can still deliver negative feedback when that is needed. If you had a role to play in information falling between the cracks, you can apologize for that, but you can also let your team member know how you would have expected them to deal with this situation. When you avoid unloading frustration in the heat of the moment and support solving the problem, your team member is more likely to be open to your feedback. Sometimes a situation like this can even increase trust between you and team members, because you've worked through a difficult situation together in a respectful and effective way.

Do this consistently and your team will develop respect for you. They will learn to hold themselves and others to high performance standards while remaining respectful. When things go wrong between people, you won't see them escalate. Instead you'll see them work to resolve the situation together effectively and respectfully, and they will give one another feedback. Less problems will land on your desk as a result. Whenever you see team members working through a mistake or problem together in a respectful manner, don't forget to compliment them for demonstrating great team dynamics.

Dealing with conflicts

Let's have a look at another type of situation that can undermine psychological safety. Imagine three of your team members having a conflict. One or more of them escalates the issue to you during your one-on-one meetings. What do you do? My first line of defense is always to keep them responsible for solving the problem amongst themselves. I might ask "Have you delivered this feedback to this person directly already?" If not, I will ask to do so first. When they already delivered the feedback, I would be curious what the response was, and what other things the person has already tried to resolve the situation.

Now imagine this: Despite nudging all three individuals to give one another honest feedback and to resolve things amongst one another, the problem keeps circling back to you. On top of that, the problem undermines effective project collaboration, and the conflict is starting to affect team culture. If you would follow my recommendation from the previous section, to focus as little as possible upon who the guilty person is, you'd hold all three people equally accountable. That might result in each of them getting a lower rating in their performance evaluation. Now imagine that one of those three is a highly manipulative person, who has been sabotaging collaboration to a point that it became impossible for the other two team members to resolve the situation. If you would hold all three people equally responsible for the problem, you may have punished willing team members for a problem created by the manipulative person. Even worse: it would send a signal that people can get away with bad behavior, and that you as a leader don't have people's backs when someone deliberately makes their work hard. Your entire team will be affected, because people are likely to talk about such situations together, and because the manipulative person will most probably keep doing whatever that person did.

There are situations where you just cannot afford to stay impartial: you have to cast judgment and "pick sides." In situations like these you have no other choice than to zoom in and spend as much time as needed to uncover what is going on. And you have to consider that at least one of the people involved isn't telling you the full truth about the situation, so you need to dig hard. When people are skilled at manipulation, it can be very hard to discover who did what. But I do find that people like that, often leave a trail of damage that extends beyond that one situation which reaches your desk. Other team members or stakeholders will have experienced challenges with this person too. The main problem is that people may not dare to tell you. This is particularly true if the damaging person is more senior than the people who were affected. The more psychological safety you establish in your team, the faster you will figure out what's going on. With high psychological safety, people from various sides will proactively come to you if a person is a problem. Often they won't know about each other's stories, because a manipulative person typically makes sure that every "victim" thinks they are the only one. You will be able to stitch up the stories though, and form an image of what really happened.

So when you spend enough time and establish enough psychological safety, you're likely to untangle all bits of conflicting information, and so you get to understand who was the problem. If it was primarily one person, you will know who to hold accountable. You need to discuss this directly with that person. In severe cases you may need to involve HR. It would also be good to have a conversation with the other team members, to reassure them that you understand what caused the problem and are acting upon it. You may not be able to share all details about the situation, but the assurance that you dug deep enough to understand their challenge, will be highly valuable to them. And it will re-establish safety.

When you dig deep and discover it is genuinely a problem in which all three people were equally responsible, it would be good to let each person know what your assessment is, how you arrived at that assessment, and what the consequences will be. Do this as soon as possible after you have formed your opinion.

Moments of truth for psychological safety
People making mistakes and situations of conflict are examples of "moments of truth" for psychological safety: your actions in those moments define whether people experience psychological safety, or not. When your actions in those moments send the wrong signals, there are few words left that can repair that damage: you can't create psychological safety by just saying it exists.

Another example of moments of truth are exits: every time a team member leaves, you have an opportunity to reinforce psychological safety. It doesn't matter whether people leave of their own choice, due to a reorg, or whether they for instance needed to leave your team due to low performance. You can always spend some aware time allowing people to leave with respect and with some kind words. I mentioned earlier that it's probably not a good idea to give a damaging person a send-off like that. Instead of giving these people an exit ritual, you can spend time giving your team a context about why the person is leaving, without sharing confidential information. When you don't communicate anything, people will start guessing. They might even think they are next. Exit-rituals are a good way to ensure safety around exits. In my team we always send around a slide-deck where people can write a goodbye card for the person that is leaving. We give it to the person on the last day, so they can read people's messages. The slides people create are often full of pictures and memories. Habits like these create moments of closure. These moments communicate over and over again that every person matters, even if they are leaving.

People making mistakes and situations of conflict are examples of "moments of truth" for psychological safety: your actions in those moments define whether people experience psychological safety, or not

Reorgs are also critical moments of truth. Both before and after the reorg, it's almost certain that people will experience psychological unsafety. In the period before it's the anticipation of the unknown that is most difficult for people. In the period after, jobs may be lost and people may have moved managers or projects. Some people might be lucky: they may have kept their jobs, or maybe their job even became bigger. Yet they still will have seen other people lose their jobs. I've come out of several reorgs with a bigger team and a bigger job, yet I still needed to recover from the fact that the colleagues around me lost their jobs. The context and support you provide before and after a reorg, defines how fast a team can move on, and be safe and effective again. It can easily take six months or so, for a team to be fully up- and running-again.

"Moments of truth" can also be triggered by big societal events. For example, the moments when *MeToo* and *Black Lives Matter* came up, were moments when my team felt a need to share experiences in a safe space. I organized virtual gatherings at these moments, where people could exchange thoughts if they wanted to, and where I shared my personal thoughts too.

Spotting moments of truth is a matter of situational awareness. The more you are in tune with your team, the more likely you will be to spot moments of truth, that are an opportunity to demonstrate through behavior that psychological safety exists in the team. When you miss out on these moments, at best it's a missed opportunity, at worst it damages safety. And that damage is hard to undo. Psychological safety also helps making it easier for you as a manager to spot moments that matter—because your team members will start helping you. Whenever there's something on people's minds, people will come to you, and make you aware that it might be a good idea for you to add value or to mitigate damage.

Psychological safety is often in the details. Small behaviors, even facial expressions while you say something, can make a world of difference whether a situation feels safe to people or not. Small acts of kindness, like a hand-written Christmas card or a chat message to say thank you, can have profound impact when applied consistently. And sometimes, the moments when you *don't act* or *don't* say something are the moments of truth: for example if you don't intervene when team members treat each other disrespectfully, or if team members leave and you forget to spend time and attention on it. Google published a valuable checklist for psychological safety, which I included in appendix 4 of this book. It might help you to spot tangible things you can do to create and nurture psychological safety.

> **Critical points**
> - Psychological safety is the number one trait of high-performing teams at Google.
> - Safe teams beat their targets by seventeen percent on average, while unsafe teams miss targets by nineteen percent.
> - Whether or not people experience Psychological Safety is defined by your actions in moments of truth. Examples are moments of mistakes or conflict.

DEI: Diversity, Equity, Inclusion

When I first started educating myself on the topic of diversity, equity and inclusion, I struggled with the terminologies people use. I had a hunch what people meant by diversity and inclusion. But equity was a concept that needed more explanation for me, to understand the full breadth of the concept. Equity, in the context of professional organizations, is about fair treatment, equal access to opportunities, progression and reward. And someone's identity cannot predict the end result.

'Belonging' is another term that has an important place in this list. People often speak about an "inclusive culture": cultures can be less inclusive or more inclusive. I look at Belonging as the highest level of Inclusiveness you can achieve.

The analogy below has brought further to life for me what different terms mean:
- *Diversity* is about all differences and variations within a group, or: "being invited to the party."
- *Inclusion* is about valuing the perspectives and contributions of all people, incorporating the needs and viewpoints of the full diversity of the organization, or: "being asked to dance."
- *Belonging* is about feeling *seen* for your unique contributions, *connected* to your co-workers, *supported* in your daily work and career development, and *proud* of your organization's values, or: "dancing like nobody's watching."

The dance-analogy helps you to understand how teams and organizations can "feel for" different kinds of people.

When I became a manager for the first time, one question I asked myself is: "Should I have a strategy for diversity and inclusion?" At the time I only had six people in my team. This led to follow up questions: Should I do something special for the two women in the team? Or for the only black person? But shouldn't I then also do something special for the only Finnish person in my team? Somehow it felt against my principles to do this. The size of my team was small enough for me to be in direct contact with all the individuals of my team. And who says these two women have certain challenges, for the only reason that they're women. Who says the men in my team *don't* have challenges that are common among women?

Creating a diverse and inclusive team is about knowing how to manage individuals, as unbiased as you can

I decided to *not* have a strategy for diversity and inclusion. Instead I focused on my full day career conversations, making large investments in getting to know my team members. I knew I would have an opportunity, to see whether or not the way I ran my team was inclusive. Besides the manager feedback-survey, Google also has an annual employee satisfaction-survey called *Googlegeist*. That survey contains lots of questions about diversity and inclusion within the team. I decided I'd focus my efforts on knowing the individuals first, and to use Googlegeist to evaluate whether more was needed. About nine months later, the Googlegeist results came out: I had the highest scores on almost all statements that related to diversity and inclusion. I concluded: creating a diverse and inclusive team is about knowing how to manage individuals, as unbiased as you can.

Being raised by lesbians

The way I was raised heavily influences my views of diversity, equity and inclusion. My parents divorced when I was five years old. My mother discovered she was bi-sexual. About a year later she met the girlfriend she lived with for the rest of her life. So, I was raised by two women from the age of six. My older sister and I referred to my mother's girlfriend as our "spare mother." But she's very much like a real mother. Nowadays she's the grandmother of my children. People often asked me whether it was strange to be raised by two women. At that young age though, the situation you live in is "normal" for you, so it never felt strange. As I grew up I never really noticed how being raised by two women had shaped my views about the world, people and myself.

I remember people often asked me: "Which of the two is the man in the relationship?" I'd always answer them with my reflections, and never thought much about that question. It's only about seven years ago, when I was nearing forty years of age, and started leading initiatives on diversity and inclusion, that I realized how offensive this question really is. And a stupid question too: there is no man in the relationship. People use labels of all kinds to organize the world so it makes sense to them. Gender labels are part of that. We cling to these labels so much that we even apply them in situations where they don't make sense. And we do it all the time: it's completely normal in most working environments to say that a woman is demonstrating "male leadership behaviors" when she's tough and dominant, and to say a man is demonstrating "female leadership behaviors" when he's empathic and caring. When you think of it, it's actually pretty offensive: it implies it's not manly to be empathic and caring, and that it's not female to be strong and dominant.

Our biases are hidden in the language we use, even in the context of advocating for equality. For instance, when we encourage women to use their "female qualities" to be better leaders, we reinforce the biases that also lead to women being judged for being "too manly." Our organizations would be more inclusive, if we could eliminate all biased language. One simple question helps with that: Would I have used the same language if I were speaking to ...? ...if I were speaking to a man? ...if I were speaking to a white person? ...if I were speaking to a straight person? ...etcetera. If the answer is "no," the language is likely to be biased.

I realized through these reflections how profoundly my view upon people and the way we apply labels to describe them is influenced by being raised by two women. When I think of groups of people, for example men and women, the mental framework in figure 23 comes to mind for me.

Figure 23 *Bell curves comparing two samples of people.*

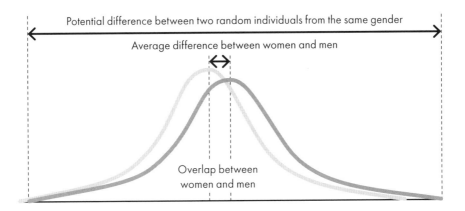

These are two bell curves. One represents a sample of women, the other of men. This could for instance be a comparison about particular cognitive abilities. Many statistical phenomena can be described through a bell curve. The "belly" of the curve is the average within a sample. The further you go away from that average, the less likely that this data point is to occur. When there's more variety in a sample, the bell curve becomes flatter and wider. Researchers have a tendency to focus on averages within a sample, yet it's often the variation where the real insight is.

When you apply that thinking to the comparison between men and women, these two bells could represent the data points about their ability to listen, to negotiate, to lead, to solve problems or any other skill. The average difference between men and women is quantified by the distance between the two vertical dotted lines in the middle. The difference is likely to be small in most cases. You can perform effectively in many different ways in most jobs. The more ways there are to be effective, the less likely it is that women and men on average would perform at different levels. And even *if* there is a difference, it could go in both directions.

> *The more ways there are to be effective, the less likely it is that women and men on average would perform at different levels*

The difference between women and men will certainly be much smaller than the amount of variation of data points that exists *within the female sample* and *within the male sample*. The maximum of that difference is depicted by the two vertical dotted lines on the outer edges of the figure. The difference between *two random men within the male sample* is likely to be larger than the *average difference between* women and men. Similarly, the difference between *two random women within the female sample* is likely to be larger than the *average difference* between women and men. The area where the bell curves overlap is where men and women are similar. That's the largest area. And I haven't even gone into the question whether gender is binary at all, so this is a simplified version of reality. When you plot it out in a graph, this insight is a no-brainer. But in everyday life, we talk about differences between men and women as if they are the most normal thing in the world, and we often make them bigger than they really are, and ignore the variations between individuals far too easily. In doing so, we perpetuate unconscious biases.

You can apply this reasoning to the comparison of any type of group. Black people versus white people. Germans versus Americans. Introverts versus extraverts. When you compare the groups as to traits or skills that are needed to be effective at a certain job, the difference between *two random individuals from the same group* is likely to be larger than the *average difference between the different groups*. The only exception to that rule is when the skill you measure on is highly correlated to how you classified the groups. When you compare Germans and Americans on their ability to deliver a workshop in the German language, I'm pretty sure you'll find a large difference in skill.

> *When you make assumptions about an individual based on the group that person is part of, and based on what you think you know about that group (for example about the personal traits or skills of that group), you are more likely to be wrong than right*

So when you make assumptions about an individual based on the group that person is part of, and based on what you think you know about that group (for example about the personal traits or skills of that group), you are more likely to be wrong than right. If you base your decisions upon such assumptions, these decisions are also more likely to be wrong than right.

When you interact with individuals, whether it's in job interviews, performance evaluations, salary negotiations or any other kind of meeting, you need to work hard to unbias yourself so you see the full person, and not what you think you know about that person based on the group you think they are part of.

Micro- and macro-actions

So what about diversity and inclusion initiatives that focus specifically on women or minoritized groups. Those are examples where you do "label" people based on the groups they belong to. Is that still OK then? Can't you just solve these problems by unbiasing yourself, and focusing on the individuals? This is where the difference between "micro-actions" and "macro-actions" comes in. I define micro-actions as moments of action when you can look a person in the eye: essentially any type of meeting where you are in direct contact with a person. I could manage diversity and inclusion in my team by focusing on deeply knowing the individuals, because my team was small enough to do so. If my team would have been twice the size or larger, that wouldn't have been enough:

I would have had to add a set of macro-actions. Macro-actions are the moments when you set a strategy or make decisions about a group without having the option to directly engage with all individuals in that group.

It's easiest to explain the difference through the example of a hiring process. Imagine you're trying to unbias the hiring process of your organization to push for a better female representation at all levels. This requires conscious steps at various stages of the hiring process.

- *Macro-actions* happen, for instance when you set a target to have a fifty-fifty gender balance in your pool of candidates before you enter the interview stage. This shouldn't be controversial, because you're not giving any kind of preferential treatment. You're just creating equal access to the opportunity.
- *Micro-actions* happen at the interview stage, because this is where you can look people in the eye. By doing your due diligence at the macro-stage you've created a situation of equal access to the opportunity. From there onwards, the only thing you need to do is to focus on hiring the best candidate. If you would do anything else, you'd be giving preferential treatment because of having the goal of hiring more women. That leads to sentiment that the only reason a person was hired is because there was some kind of a target for gender balance. There shouldn't be a need for preferential treatment at this stage, because there isn't any reason to believe women would qualify less for the job. The only thing that is required from interviewers during the interview stage, is to be as unbiased as they can be. Educating yourself about unconscious bias, and taking actions to mitigate against biases, are what I consider micro-actions.

> *Macro-level is where you can set targets for representation and other diversity and inclusion related to KPIs. Micro-level is where you should ignore any targets or KPIs that exist*

When you work like this, it shouldn't matter whether the best candidate at the end of the interview stage is a woman or a man, or what skin color the person has. When you consistently generate diversity in your pool of candidates at the macro stages of the process, and you consistently unbias the micro-stage of the process, over time you should be hiring with similar representation as the population available for any given role. When you track the data over time, and you see hiring is still skewed towards certain audiences, you can be certain there's still a bias in the system somewhere.

Macro-level is where you can set targets for representation and other diversity and inclusion related to KPIs. Micro-level is where you should ignore any targets or KPIs that exist. Instead you should focus on removing unconscious bias first, and then on hiring, rewarding or promoting whoever is the best candidate. When you handle macro- and micro-level this way—with focus, structure and discipline—you can progress any topic in relation to diversity and inclusion without giving anyone preferential treatment.

Don't try to boil the ocean

When organizations put effort upon representation in hiring, often they focus upon gender and ethnicity and sometimes on sexual orientation. I still remember my first internal reaction when I learned about these initiatives: Why are we focusing on gender and ethnicity? Why not on all dimensions of diversity? Why not on introverts versus extroverts? It seemed against my principles to focus on only two dimensions of diversity. But then I started leading a variety of projects in this area, and I realized how hard it was to make progress when you look at a larger scale. And not everything is allowed. For instance, in Europe you wouldn't be allowed to build a pipeline for the interview-stage based on ethnicity. It's also not allowed to build a pipeline based on sexual orientation: you'd have to ask people to state in their resumé what their sexual orientation is. That would be outrageous. And it really isn't about any of these dimensions. It is genuinely about diversity of thought and backgrounds in all thinkable ways. But you have to start somewhere. If you try to change the hiring-practices in a large organization by focusing on all dimensions of diversity at the same time, you'd most likely be less impactful, and it would be hard to track progress. Aiming for gender balance gives you focus, and makes progress more likely and measurable.

I discovered two other things:
1 The fact that you narrow your focus to a relatively small amount of dimensions of diversity, doesn't mean you aren't delivering impact on the other dimensions. When you succeed in making your organization more accessible and inclusive for a few types of underprivileged groups, you end up making your organization more inclusive in general. For instance, many of the practices that help you take gender bias or ethnicity bias out of processes, also reduce other biases in the process.

2   The fact that you focus your macro-efforts on a relatively small amount of dimensions of diversity doesn't stop you from focusing your micro-efforts on *all* dimensions of diversity. Micro- and macro-decisions and activities happen in parallel, and they support one another.

Don't put too much on your plate. Pick a feasible set of priorities, execute them with discipline, track progress with data and hold people accountable

So don't be afraid to focus when you work to improve diversity and inclusion upon a large scale in your organization. Don't put too much on your plate. Pick a feasible set of priorities, execute them with discipline, track progress with data and hold people accountable. Meanwhile keep unbiasing yourself in all your micro-interactions with people.

Making diversity and inclusion actionable
When people talk about diversity and inclusion, the topic often sounds big, idealistic and unachievable. But when you break it down to actionable dimensions, the amount of things an organization needs to do is actually manageable. There are various ways you can categorize it. Below is how I prefer to structure what organizations need to do:
- unbiasing hiring
- unbiasing performance evaluations, reward and progression
- creating a culture of belonging

Let's zoom in on each of those.

Unbiasing hiring
Hiring is probably the topic where it's easiest to make fast progress, when it comes to pushing for a more diverse representation. You can solve unbiasing of hiring in a few quarters when you really want to. And measuring progress is straightforward. I know there are certain job profiles for which making progress is harder: for example, there are many tech-related jobs where the supply of qualified people isn't diverse in all dimensions. However, the fact that making progress is hard for certain types of jobs should never be an excuse to park the

topic in general. It makes it even *more* important to solve the problem fast for all the other jobs. You do this by taking focused actions in each step of the hiring process. The typical steps most organizations have are:
1   writing and posting job descriptions
2   sourcing (finding qualified candidates)
3   evaluating candidate pipeline
4   interviewing & deciding
5   offer stage

Macro-actions for unbiasing hiring
Your organization might use slightly different categorizations or names for these recruitment stages, but it's likely they align roughly. The first three steps in the list of hiring stages require a strategy for macro-actions. At this stage you're not assessing every individual person in a great deal of detail. You're mostly scanning and funneling to end up with a small pool of qualified candidates, that can be included at the interview stage where they will be evaluated more thoroughly. As mentioned, you could set a target to end up with a fifty-fifty gender-balance, and a diversity of backgrounds in the pool of candidates that goes to the interview stage.

> *The fact that making progress is hard for certain types of jobs should never be an excuse to park the topic in general*

This starts with writing the job description in an unbiased way. There's lots of research that proves the way you write job-descriptions affects the diversity of the group applying to them. An obvious example: when you specify in your job-descriptions that only people who went to certain specific universities qualify, and those are universities that only privileged people can afford, you're likely to get a non-diverse sample of applications for your role. There's also proof that too long lists of qualifications make women less likely to apply, compared to men. Women are more likely to doubt whether they qualify, when you overdo it with your list of qualifications. Other examples that lead to bias in applications are the use of biased language or too much jargon. When you search on the internet, you will find lots of articles with great recommendations about unbiasing job descriptions.

Next is sourcing: what sources of candidates will you explore to find qualified candidates? In most large organizations, this is something a staffing professional does for you. But you can make sourcing from diverse talent pools easier for them. First, don't limit them too much. When you want only candidates from specific competing companies, you're likely to tap into a pool of people that isn't diverse if those companies have limited diversity in their organizations. Second, you can give them sufficient time. When you force a staffing team to come up with a pipeline for the interview stage in one week, they're unlikely to come up with a pipeline that has sufficient qualified people as well as sufficient diversity of backgrounds. Finally, many organizations have referral-arrangements to encourage existing employees to bring in people from their personal network. Referral mechanisms also have a risk of bias. If the current representation in your organization is poor, a referral system is likely to retain status quo, because you're hiring people similar to what you already have.

> *If the current representation in your organization is poor, a referral system is likely to retain status quo, because you're hiring people similar to what you already have*

When you evaluate the pipeline of candidates that comes through, keep an eye on gender balance, and whether you believe there's in general sufficient variation in backgrounds in the pool of qualified candidates. When this is not the case yet, give your staffing partner more time to keep sourcing, and consider whether you've been too restrictive with your criteria.

When you take all steps above, a staffing member should be able to find you a pool of high-potential candidates that has a fifty-fifty gender-balance, and that is diverse in several other dimensions as well. The amount of extra time to get to a diverse pool of candidates is lower for most roles than managers often think. When I was leading efforts to improve hiring practices, we were able to completely solve issues with gender representation in hiring with only an about seven days longer time to hire. It was just a matter of putting focus on it in a structured way.

Micro-actions for unbiasing hiring

Once you enter the interview stage, you are in the realm of micro-decisions. From this phase onwards, you should completely ignore the fact that you have an objective of creating gender balance in your team or organization (or other KPIs you have goals on). The focus should now be on unbiasing the interview process, and on finding the best candidate for the job.

Unbiasing starts with a diverse interview panel: preferably you ask one or two colleagues to interview the same candidates. Those should be colleagues that look at people differently than you do yourself. All interviewers, including you yourself, should have gone through an unbiasing training. If your organization doesn't offer this, it's easy to find a good training for free online. LinkedIn Learning has good courses for this. It's a good habit to remind yourself of most common biases, and ways to mitigate against them before starting an interview process. Appendix 5 provides an overview of the ten most common biases that affect hiring. It was created by Equalture, a company that supports organizations with unbiased hiring. When you search on the internet for their article "10 Unconscious hiring biases & how to avoid them" you can read how you can counter these biases.

Next, you need to use what is called "structured interviewing practices." Some hiring managers run job interviews by asking people about things in their resume. That way each conversation follows a different structure, and it's hard to form objective criteria for comparison between candidates. When I prepare for interviews I define three or four skills needed for the job. I translate these skills to questions with scenarios or challenges that people would encounter in the job. For instance, I might have one question about dealing with difficult stakeholders, one question about solving problems, and one question about dealing with ambiguity. If the role includes managing people, I will also have a question about a particular aspect of team leadership. When you have multiple interviewers, it's wise to agree who interviews on what. At Google there are fixed processes for this. One interviewer will typically focus on role-related knowledge, one on leadership, one on general cognitive-ability and another on *Googleyness*. When you're curious what Googleyness means: a lot has been written about it online. Unbiased interviewing requires a consistent set of questions that is based on consistent criteria to assess candidates, and that is applied the same way across all candidates. This gives you the most objective set of information to compare candidates.

Finally, it's decision time: use all information available to you, including the information from the other interviewers, to make a decision that is as objective as possible. Ask yourself: which candidate is most qualified for the job? When two candidates are closely matched in terms of qualifications, ask yourself one more question: which of these candidates would add the most unique value to the team, compared to the people I already have? When still in doubt there's a final question that helps: which of these candidates is likely to surprise you most? You will have found your new team member when you know the answer to these three questions.

Unbiasing performance evaluations, reward and progression

The Brilliant Basics, when executed diligently, solve for unbiased performance evaluations, reward and progression:

- Deep career conversations get managers to invest in knowing their team members, and reduce the risk that biases affect their perception of individuals.
- OKR-writing ensures people have equal access to high-profile work.
- Meaningful meetings and team norms ensure people get equal access to guidance and quality feedback, and that they have equal opportunity to be seen and heard.
- Diligent tracking of progress on OKRs and milestones, prevents situations where people go out of sync with team goals, or where quality-feedback is delayed.
- Fair and predictable performance-evaluations result in an assessment of people's impact, that is as objective as possible.
- When all these steps have been taken, the only thing left is to use the available information in order to make objective decisions about reward and progression based on the impact that people have.

Building a culture of belonging, and measuring progress

The only thing left to do, when you succeed at making hiring, performance evaluations, reward and progression unbiased, is to create a culture where all people can develop a sense of belonging.

You may notice that one element is missing in my list of focus areas for building diverse and inclusive organizations: retention isn't part of the list. This is because retention automatically gets solved when all other dimensions are solved. When you build an organization with diverse representations of people, you give them equal opportunity in performance evaluations, reward and progression, and you create a culture of belonging where you should no longer see higher churn than average amongst women and minoritized groups. Retention is still a good output-metric to check though: when you see there's more churn in certain groups of employees in your organization, you know there are still things you aren't doing right, when it comes to diversity, equity, and inclusion.

When I thought about the topic of belonging, my mind went back to a moment my mother shared with me, at the age of sixteen, how the process of discovering that she was bi-sexual had worked for her. She told me she had looked in her heart and realized: "Why limit yourself to half the world, when you can find the space in your heart to open up to the entire world?" You can apply that principle to organizations too. You will only have the opportunity to open up to all available talents if you create more space for all types of people, regardless of their gender, skin color, or sexual orientation, if it does not matter whether they are introverted or extroverted, assertive or caring, young or old, physically challenged or not, etcetera. We can only create that space when we are willing to let go of the structures of our traditional thinking.

Belonging is the ultimate end result you achieve when you get all other things right. This framing is useful when you think about measuring the progress of your efforts. Measuring progress is critical if you want to hold people accountable. Coqual is an organization focused on creation of diverse and inclusive workplaces. They collaborated with Google to measure the concept of belonging at work. I've included their measurement framework in appendix 6. These are your ultimate KPIs that help you see whether your efforts were successful or not. It's worth checking whether employee-satisfaction surveys in your organization cover similar metrics or not. If not, consider including some of these metrics in your own manager- feedback survey. When you combine this data with data about representation and reward at all levels of the organization, you have a good basis to assess how the organization is doing on diversity, equity and inclusion.

When measuring KPIs like these on an organizational level, the main problem is many of these metrics move only slowly over time. That can be used as an excuse not to make progress. So you also need short-term KPIs to track progress, and hold people accountable. In hiring you can track gender balance at the interview stage during hiring and after acceptance of the job offers. That helps you see whether managers started with a diverse pool of candidates or not, and whether there's bias in hiring decisions. It works best if you can split this data by job-level or grade. It's often at the higher seniority levels that things get skewed, resulting in non-diverse leadership teams. During performance evaluations you can check similarly whether ratings and promotions are applied without bias at all levels. When you run a large organization, you can zoom in on various managers or leaders. It's relatively easy to see who makes an effort and who doesn't. When one particular leader doesn't play along, you'll see "skewed data" in the entire organization under that leader. In some countries you might be able to split data by more diversity dimensions than just gender. That might for instance make it possible to look at differences between ethnicities. In most organizations you can clearly see in the data that various groups of people have a worse experience than other groups of people. You can only split data in more diversity-dimensions if the data set is large enough, so that it doesn't create privacy issues. On top of that, employees may need to give explicit permission to use certain data points. Also, what is allowed by law varies by country. There's an increasing number of companies that offer services to help organizations track progress on Diversity, Equity and Inclusion. When you take this topic seriously, it's worth looking into this.

When managers or leaders aren't contributing to the creation of a diverse and inclusive workforce, they should be held accountable in their performance evaluations. Only then will you make tangible progress on Diversity, Equity and Inclusion.

Triple-A: Activism, Allyship, Action

Awareness of topics related to equity and inclusion, in society and at work, often starts with activism by a relatively small group of people. Those people are often the ones that are affected by the problem. At some point, some of them are sufficiently fed up with the problem that they start speaking up. At first, they typically aren't heard. Speaking up might even backfire. There are still countries in the world, where speaking out for equality can result in being punished. At work too, you can be at risk if you speak out about inequality. There are still many organizations where being one of the first to speak out, can reduce your chances of being rewarded and progressing your career. You may even lose your job because of it.

> *How do you protest within the law when your voices aren't being heard, decade after decade, while people are still being killed?*

It can take a long time before people start hearing a minority of activists, and even longer before they start *listening*. And even then, it doesn't mean actions are taken. In the examples of slavery and racism, people have raised their voices for decades. You'd think problems at work don't take that long, yet we still haven't solved topics like racism, gender-equality and *MeToo*-issues at work, even though these have been going on for decades and people have been raising their voice about them. When George Floyd was murdered by a police officer in 2020, protests became violent. Buildings were damaged and shops were raided. People complained: "This is not protesting, this is just criminal behavior!" And of course, I understand this is not how protests should go, and that innocent entrepreneurs faced significant damage and cost. But how do you protest within the law when your voices aren't being heard, decade after decade, while people are still being killed?

This is why allyship is important. Without allies, minoritized groups can stay in this phase not being heard while still being punished—forever. At some point, more privileged people need to stand up and tell their peers to listen and to act. That too comes with a risk. I know that by experience. I've gone through two periods of about two years each, where I found myself escalating stories of people who were being damaged—to my manager, to senior leadership and to HR. In each of those cases I wasn't being heard initially, and I had to keep banging the drums for about a year before I got signals the message was starting to land. And it took about two years until I knew what the consequences would be. If the person I was escalating stories about had had strong connections with the right people, this could have cost me my opportunities for advancement. I knew that, but I decided I didn't want to work for this company if this was the outcome. So I didn't care about losing my job. I was also in the luxury position to have saved enough money, so I could do without work for several years. That's a luxury many people don't have, and it's part of my privileged position. In the end, the problems got dealt with in a way that did justice. I didn't know that during the journey though, and it took about two years in each case before action was taken, so I had gone through periods of extreme stress.

Still, I had a privileged position in this situation. Relative to the people who came to me with stories, my position was more senior. My chance of being heard was probably greater, and the risk of negative consequences was probably lower. Societies and large organizations can only fundamentally change when a critical mass of people contributes to that change. Minorities cannot solve the problems alone. If there is one minority that can have a big impact, it's the minority of senior leaders, but these are typically people from privileged backgrounds. Only when privileged people in all layers of society and organizations speak up, actions will happen. And even then, it often goes slower than you would like, but every small step is a big win as to these topics.

When the MeToo-movement came up, there was a wave of protests across Google offices to support the movement. The great thing: senior leaders actively made space for these protests. Many of them canceled meetings so people could join protests, and some even joined themselves. Many of these leaders were white straight men. I saw this as an encouraging moment. The fact that leadership creates space for activism, isn't a given in large organizations. I know there also were moments in the press where Google colleagues felt there was no space to protest, so it doesn't always go right. But this was certainly a positive example in the offices where my team members worked.

When you want to create a diverse and inclusive organization, which is a prerequisite of building a high-performing organization, you need to be a triple-A organization:

- *Activism*: You need to create a safe space for people to raise their voice and be heard.
- *Allyship*: You need to mobilize allies and hold people accountable for their contributions—this starts with senior leadership.
- *Action*: You need to have a clear strategy for making diversity, equity and inclusion actionable, and for tracking progress.

> *When you want to create a diverse and inclusive organization, which is a prerequisite of building a high-performing organization, you need to be a triple-A organization*

If one of these three is missing, it can take decades before you succeed at your efforts. Meanwhile people will keep being damaged and your organization won't be performing at the highest level, because it isn't utilizing the full pool of talent available to the organization.

You could argue I am not an expert on topics of racism, gender-equality and other minority- issues, and that is actually true. There are many people who are more expert on this topic than I am. Much better books have been written on these topics. In fact, there is some risk I wrote things that aren't entirely correct. But that risk is part of being an ally. Most allies are not experts. And you don't have to be. Just make an effort to educate yourself as well as you can, and then do what you can to make a positive difference. As a manager, you have the biggest influence of all people as to how your team members experience the organization. And if you don't step up as an ally, who will?

Critical points
- Psychological safety only exists when it exists for all types of people.
- Diversity is "being invited to the party." Inclusion is "being asked to dance." Belonging is "dancing like nobody is watching."
- Managing DEI requires a clear strategy on macro- and micro-level, and both levels should be executed in parallel.
- Targets are set and measured on macro-level, and at this level you focus on a limited amount of diversity dimensions.
- On micro-level you ignore that you have DEI targets: instead you focus on unbiasing in favor of all dimensions of diversity.

- When the principles above are applied consistently, you can solve problems in DEI without giving preferential treatment to specific groups or people.
- For an organization to become fully diverse and inclusive, you must apply a triple-A mindset: create space for Activism, mobilize Allies and hold them accountable, make DEI Actionable and track progress.

PART III

GREAT LEADERS, HIGH-PERFORMING ORGANIZA-TIONS

PART III

Almost all large organizations nowadays are going through some kind of transformation: digital transformation, cultural transformation, transformation to become more sustainable, to become more responsible as an organization, or to become more efficient and effective. An increasing number of organizations now actively strive for a balance between people, planet and profit.

Anyone who has worked in or with large organizations as a driver of organizational change, knows organizational transformation is tough work: It's hard to know where to start and where to go, It always goes slower than you want to, often to the point where you wonder whether any change is happening at all. I worked with Google's largest advertisers across Europe, the Middle East and Africa, supporting them with digital transformation and organizational transformation for ten years, and discovered many universal patterns and barriers. One of those patterns was the fact that many people who work in large organizations think their organization is the only one that has certain problems, and that they are slower than the organizations around them. This increases their frustration with challenges that are actually just common and inevitable things which any organization faces when going through a change. Almost all large organizations struggle with silos, data integration, making space for innovation, scaling innovations, general slowness and rigidity of the organization, lack of vision and direction, legacy-technology and processes, measurement of ROI (return on investment), having the wrong targets and KPIs, organizing data into actionable insights, internal politics and competition between teams, lack of people with the right expertise, cultural challenges... I could go on like this for a while. Do you recognize these challenges? I hope it's a relief to know you are not alone.

When Sundar Pichai, CEO of Alphabet, was asked in an interview about the threat of competition, he replied: "I've always believed that if you focus too much on the competition, you tend to get it wrong. Large companies in particular fail because they stumble internally." This analogy explains well why it can feel so frustrating to push your organization through change: you stumble over the internal organization, over and over again.

Interestingly, leaders always say it is hard to bring along employees, and employees always tell me their leadership isn't sufficiently supportive at great changes. I've learned by experience that the most effective and fastest way to change a large organization is through middle-management. This is the layer that can make the vision of leadership actionable, that can make sure people get the right direction and support, and that the right culture is established. When you apply all the principles of the parts I and II of this book, you've become the most powerful driver of change that any large organization can have, particularly when you pull together with the managers around you.

> *When you apply all the principles of the parts I and II of this book, you've become the most powerful driver of change that any large organization can have, particularly when you pull together with the managers around you*

People know what needs to be done… and still they don't do it

Another insight I built up by working with many organizations on transformation challenges, is that most people know what needs to be done, what changes need to happen in the organization. That isn't true for everyone: some just follow the boss without thinking critically themselves, they might do whatever the organization always did, or they might focus on their own job and not on the bigger picture. But most people I meet are not like that: they do care about the bigger picture, they do see the things the organization systematically does wrong, and the things the organization is not doing, but should do. Many of them even made efforts to push the organization to change, but even the best of them need to acknowledge they have to pick their battles. Some people may give up trying to change the organization, even when they know what needs to be changed. When people know what needs to be done, yet bump into boundaries over and over again, people lose a sense of meaning in their jobs. There are two underlying causes for the barriers that many people in large organizations encounter, which I have observed in almost all the organizations I have worked with:

1. Universal limitations of data.
2. People tend to do what makes their bosses happy, and that's not always a good thing.

In the next sections I will cover what those universal limitations of data are, and how that can create situations where it's not the best idea to do what makes your bosses happy. I will also discuss what leadership can do to prevent such a situation.

Universal limitations of data: a game of prison break

I spent a large part of my career working in the industry of research, data and insights. Data also plays an important role in digital transformation. I've heard many leaders wish for a "magical red button" that aggregates all their data, analyzes it and predicts based on ROI (return on investment)—calculations what the best decisions for their organization are. I've also seen many suppliers of research, data, technology and consulting, promise that red button:

- "Our ROI-model takes all data sources into account, and predicts exactly what marketing mix is best for you."
- "Our technology platform integrates all types of data you can think of, and produces dashboards a toddler can read, so all decisions are based on ROI."
- "Our Artificial Intelligence-solution predicts the outcome of decisions by looking at all types of data you have, and learning from it, so your people don't have to do that work."

These products, tech-platforms and services are often of high complexity. It can be extremely hard to get your suppliers to explain to you what the limitations of the system or service are—or even to acknowledge that there are limitations in the first place. The result after implementation is typically not as rosy as the picture that was painted. That's partly because implementation is often more complex than it first seems. But it's also because there are three universal limitations of data that no system that relies on data ever can get round:

1. *Short-term impact is easier to measure than long-term impact.* This dilemma often emerges in marketing organizations as a tension between performance marketing, which is typically focused on short-term ROI, and brand-building which focuses on the longer term. Performance marketeers always complain that the ROI of brand-building-efforts is too hard to prove, but anyone who works in a marketing organization long enough knows it's hard to be sustainably successful when you don't have a strong brand.
   This limitation of data also makes it harder for organizations to invest in long-term bets like sustainability, transformation or innovation. These topics often require investment now, while pay-off is uncertain and takes a long time. When organizations optimize all their decisions based on data, their teams tend to prioritize short-term tactical actions over investments in the

long-term journey, even when their leaders encourage them to invest in the future by painting beautiful future scenarios.

2 *Measuring within a channel is easier than measuring across channels.* Marketing ROI is easiest to prove when a consumer clicks on online-advertising, and then buys a product online and on the same device. As soon as the user buys on another device, measurement gets less accurate. You can solve for some of that when users are signed in on multiple devices, but it gets even less accurate when the purchase happens in a brick-and-mortar store. Again, you can make corrections in your data to solve it, but the calculations inevitably become less accurate. Wrong decisions get taken when you ignore the fact that these inaccuracies exist. This problem is also behind the issue of silos that many organizations face. It's easy to optimize the efficiency of conversations from a medical specialist in a hospital. When you isolate your view on one type of specialist-area, you might think the hospital is becoming more efficient. Yet when you talk to patients you might hear they end up getting sent from specialist to specialist, causing bad patient experiences. When you scrutinize the data about all types of specialists, you will see that systematically forwarding patients to one another also creates a higher collective workload. Building a model to optimize efficiency of conversations across all types of specialists is hard. The same problems occur when consumers are sent from one team to another, when trying to solve a problem with your organization. Each team optimizes for their own KPI, and individually it looks like they are efficient. Yet the damage to the customer relation, and the waste of effort across teams are harder to measure.

3 *Data cannot accurately predict impact as to things you've never tried.* Data tends to be based on things you have already done. Predictions about the future are extrapolated from what you already know. Even predictive data models are based on data from the past. Too much focus on data can therefore paralyze fundamental innovation within your organization. You will get stuck in incrementally improving methods that have been tried and tested in the past, and hence will gain a few percent each year, but are unlikely to make any *radical* improvements. If you want to build an organization that is "future-ready", you must be open to experimentation, even if the data cannot prove that the experiment will work. If the data could predict with certainty whether an experiment will work or not, it wouldn't be experimentation.

The three universal limitations of data make their way into our technology platforms and dashboards that organizational leaders use to make decisions, and into the processes by which we optimize the output of teams. This leads to suboptimal behavior of teams, including siloed behavior. When a leader tells

me with pride "we make all decisions based on data," I know employees in that organization probably struggle with:
- breaking through silos
- investing in long-term bets
- pushing fundamentally new innovations

The only way to make effective data-based decisions is to start with understanding the boundaries within which the data can provide accurate answers. The tighter we optimize behavior of teams without acknowledging limitations to our data, the less teams will prioritize behaviors that help our organizations to be future-ready.

> *The tighter we optimize behavior of teams without acknowledging limitations to our data, the less teams will prioritize behaviors that help our organizations to be future-ready*

The result of this problem is that many leaders, without intending it, ask one thing from their teams yet incentivize something else:
- They might incentivize sales-teams to be customer-centric, while rewarding them to sell specific products because that makes it easier to measure sales success. This often results in sales teams pushing products, instead of listening to client-needs.
- They might encourage teams to break through silos, and collaborate more across teams, yet at the same time put pressure on those teams by optimizing their activities with KPIs that reward siloed behavior. When people have a lack of time and need to choose whether to invest in cross-team collaboration or achieving their KPIs, they often pick the latter.
- They might encourage their teams to serve consumers holistically at all stages of the consumer journey, while online- and offline-sales are handled and optimized by different teams with different KPIs. These teams often end up competing with each other, even though they serve the same consumers whose journeys seamlessly mix online and offline channels.
- They might ask for more innovation, while also demanding that you prove the ROI will be good, before you get permission to invest in new innovations. ROI-predictions for things an organization has never done are rarely accurate, so people in large organizations often end up innovating "below the radar" without permission, or they drop the idea altogether.

Leaders who want to create agile organizations that can change as fast as their environment need to lead, based on:
- data
- mind
- heart

Data needs to be used within the boundaries of its accuracy. The *mind* stands for strategy: in the areas where data is less accurate, you need to create logical strategic frameworks that set direction, and that quantify achievement of milestones. These strategic frameworks should be supported by "proxy KPIs." Proxy KPIs are estimators of ROI, that solve the lack of accurate data. For example, it is difficult to measure the ROI of customer satisfaction directly. Therefore, many companies have established KPIs for customer satisfaction, such as five-star-ratings and Net Promoter Scores (NPS). They measure these KPIs and make business-decisions based on them, but without directly measuring their financial impact. People often find it hard to accept proxies as hard KPIs, because they fear the inaccuracies. But making decisions based on fake precision of data is much worse than making decisions based on thoughtful proxy KPIs. Finally, the *heart* stands for the moments when you have to do something because the creative idea is beautiful, or when it's the right thing to do. Sometimes you just need to extend trust to people, when they come to you with ideas. If you do that at the right moments, people typically surprise you. They often overdeliver in a way you would never have seen if you had tried to optimize their work based on data.

> *People often find it hard to accept proxies as hard KPIs, because they fear the inaccuracies. But making decisions based on fake precision of data is much worse than making decisions based on thoughtful proxy KPIs*

Organizational transformation: breaking out of the prison

Pushing for organizational change requires people in your organization to take on more work and more risk. New ways of working rarely work well with existing processes and structures in an organization, so people end up shopping around for support and permissions, and they end up knocking on people's doors in order to unblock the barriers. And it's always uncertain what the reward for all that extra work is: you don't know in advance whether new ideas will work, and due to the universal limitations of data they rarely fit within the existing frameworks for measuring success and assigning reward.

The limitations of structures, processes, legacy technology, and KPIs make our organizations into prisons for those trying to forward change. Driving change in large organizations is like trying to escape from prison. You need to break through walls, find loopholes, and secret supporters. You hope that your manager and leaders help you with that, but some leaders are more like prison guards. Good managers and leaders are in a continuous connection with people in all layers and parts of the organization, and they are conscious of the barriers that structures, processes, systems and KPIs create. Bad managers and leaders are primarily driven by the dashboards and KPIs available to them, which means they are trapped within the same prison, and can't create an environment from which they may safely break out of.

The least you can do as a manager and leader is to scrap as many barriers for change as you can. That makes it safer and easier for people to push change. But simply "making it safer" is a really low bar to set. It means that people will not be punished for doing the extra work to further the organization. In many organizations this is the maximum you can expect when driving change. For intrinsically motivated people that's often enough encouragement to keep on going, because it provides a sense of meaning to help making your organization future-ready. That's more rewarding for those people than grinding and optimizing existing processes that you know are outdated. But it would be nicer and more fair, and better for the organization, when driving change comes with an extra reward.

This is where the principles of *Managing Without Power* are critical. When you apply these in the context of transformation, you create the levels of safety for people to take more risks, focus on longer-term bets, and come up with more innovative ideas. You set direction and measure progress, so you know which people contributed to the most difficult change projects, and thereby need to be rewarded. You create space for team members to cross the boundaries of teams, by agreeing joint OKRs with peer managers. When a critical mass of your managers knows how to manage without power, everything their teams do has a ripple effect, because it is based on intrinsic motivation. Even if you wanted to, you wouldn't be able to stop these people from challenging the boundaries of the organization. And that's exactly what you need to create: an organization that is able to transform over and over again.

So, when you are a leader from a large organization, and you want to reduce the risk and effort it takes for people to drive change—while increasing reward for these efforts—you need to create as many great managers as you can, who know how to apply the Managing Without Power principles. This can be be done in several ways:
- Train your managers, and give them a common language and toolkit that helps them to create a culture where change is inevitable.
- Reward and promote your best managers by measuring manager-feedback and including that feedback in the performance evaluations of managers.
- Create communities amongst your managers: encourage the best to train the rest.

Critical points
- Everything that relies on data is bound by three universal limitations of data:
  - Short-term impact is easier to measure than long-term impact.
  - Impact within a channel is easier to measure than impact across channels.
  - Data cannot accurately predict impact for things you never tried.
- Imperfections of data dashboards, of the KPI's and processes we use to optimize behavior of teams, make our organizations into prisons: it's hard to invest in long-term goals, to break through silos, and to innovate.
- Leaders can create more space for their employees by leading with data, mind and heart, and by creating a critical mass of managers who know how to manage without power. This can be achieved through training, manager-communities, and reward and promotion for the best managers.

Five enablers of organizational transformation

We've looked at what managers and leaders can do *generically* to make it easier for people to drive change in their organization. But it's worth going one level more specific. When my Google Digital Academy team built our portfolio of programs about organizational transformation for the first time, we spoke to many customers, to experts within Google and in the industry, and identified five themes of organizational transformation that are relevant in most organizations.

- Vision and leadership
- Customer centricity
- Tech, data, and automation
- Culture of innovation
- People operations

When a critical mass of managers in your organization succeeds in creating high-performing teams, they've charged the batteries of trust and intrinsic motivation within their teams, and in doing so their teams became a source of energy that can push the boundaries of the organization. As a leader you can channel that energy by setting a focused strategy for change in each of these five transformation themes. Let's dive deeper into each of them.

Vision and leadership

In my first four years with the Google Digital Academy team, I never had a vision for my team. Or better said I had a vision in my head, but it wasn't written down on paper. Nevertheless, I scored 100 percent on statements that related to having a vision and strategy. That score was almost entirely based on executing consistently on the Brilliant Basics, while being highly conscious why our team existed, and what unique role we played versus other teams at Google. There were about twenty other teams at Google that did education in one way or another. Most of them focused on education as to Google's products. We were one of the few helping customers solve digital-transformation challenges. We did so with the purpose of enabling Google's sales teams to become more consultative in how they sell, so we invested in problem-solving and action-planning workshops, where sales reps could spend quality time with customer teams. Everything I communicated to the team, annual plans I made, OKRs I set, came from that sense of purpose, and people felt there was a vision, even though there wasn't one on paper.

Figure 24 *Great managers build high-performing teams that are a source of energy in order to drive change: you can channel that energy through the five enablers of organizational transformation in the outer circle of the model.*

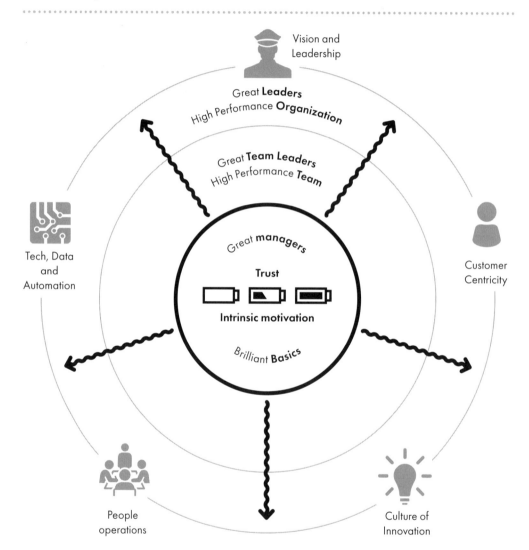

I've been in many manager-trainings about writing a vision and mission for your team. People often end up debating the difference between vision and mission. I've seen many managers and leaders struggle to get words on paper that sounded sufficiently inspiring. The definitions and wordsmithing don't matter as much as people often think. Yes, when you write a vision or mission for an organization or brand, it pays off to hire a fancy agency to help you find a "light bulb-insight" and inspirational wording. But most managers and team leaders are not in a position where they get to define a vision or mission for an entire organization or brand. When it comes to teams, most team members don't necessarily want visions and missions. They want to have a sense of direction, prioritization and meaning for the group they are part of, and for their individual roles. Visions and missions can play a role establishing those things, but often they're just words on a slide. A vision or mission only has meaning to people when it helps them understand why the team exists, why their role exists, and how it defines where we go, what we do and what we don't do.

> *When it comes to teams, most team members don't necessarily want visions and missions. They want to have a sense of direction, prioritization and meaning for the group they are part of, and for their individual roles*

I find Simon Sinek's golden circle a powerful instrument to summarize all of these things for a team. It works at all team sizes. It was originally designed to help brands define their value-proposition by starting with the "why." Sinek argues that companies often talk too much about *what* they do and *how* they do it—and they lose the customer's attention as a result. Precisely by starting with *why* you do something, you bring people into your story, and your real reason for existence. "Why" is therefore the center of the model in figure 25: your organization's purpose, cause and beliefs are the starting point of your story. In the "how" you explain which strengths, values or guiding principles differentiate you from the competition. Finally, in the "what" you explain what products or services you provide. When you're not familiar with the framework, search for "Simon Sinek golden circle" on YouTube, and you'll find many movies of him explaining it.

As a team, you may not sell services or products, but you do have a reason for existence, and you have internal or external customers for whom your team performs activities. Therefore, the model works very nicely for teams. Below is how I applied the framework to my Google Digital Academy team. I made edits to the original wording to remove things I shouldn't share.

Figure 25 *The "why, how, what" framework from Simon Sinek's book Start with Why is very suitable for writing a team vision.*

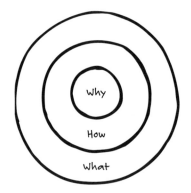

Why
Your purpose, cause or belief.

How
The strengths, values or guiding principles that differentiate you from the competition.

What
Products sold, or services offered.

Why

We believe Google has a unique opportunity to support customers with digital transformation, because Google…

- builds the technology that shapes the future
- has access to unique insights
- has unique ways to run a large organization, while retaining a remarkable startup- spirit

How

Google Digital Academy brings Google account-teams and customers together in order to offer inspiration, solve business-challenges and develop deep partnerships… creating time together that transforms.

What

We support consultative selling by creating and running scalable or semi-scalable action-planning workshops, that solve digital-transformation challenges for large customers.

The wording is not as smooth as Google's mission "To organize the world's information and make it universally accessible and useful," but it doesn't have to be. The last thing I want is managers and leaders getting stuck finding the right wording. If you haven't written a vision or mission for your team, give it a try this way: sit down for two hours or so with a clear head, and put your thoughts on paper.

Exercise: Making your vision meaningful and actionable with your team

It's nice if you can get input from your team also for your vision. I find that works best after I wrote a first draft myself. I'd typically do this on a team offsite in a session of about two hours, where we polish the "why, how, what" together, and then spend time exploring how it defines what we do and where we go. Below is how you could run a sequence of exercises about this with your own team.

Step 1: Likes and dislikes for the "why, how, what"
Print your draft "why, how, what"-statement on a large piece of paper, and hang it on a wall. Below it, hang two sheets of paper: one with the text "What I like," and the other saying "What I don't like." Or to make it more playful, you could have one with a smiling emoticon, and the other with an angry or sad emoticon, or a happy or grumpy cat. You can play around with that. Give all people post-its. Give them five minutes to read the statement, and five minutes to write down one thing they like about the statement, and one thing they don't like about it. Get people to stick their post-its under the sheets of paper. Observe when the group is ready reflecting and writing. If it's faster or a bit slower than the amount of time I mentioned here, that's fine—but don't drag it too long. Now have a look at the post-its, read them out to the group, and ask people for clarification where needed. This is an opportunity to have a discussion about various parts of the statement. Don't try to rewrite the statement on the spot with the group. You only have to make sure all voices are heard. Then you take the action-item to capture everything that was written and discussed, and use that to rewrite the statement and share it for a final check with the team after the offsite. The end result won't be "perfect," but it will be good enough to create direction and meaning. The discussions you had are equally important to what you end up writing on the paper. This exercise should take you about thirty to forty minutes.

Step 2: Defining where you play or don't play
A vision is only meaningful if it helps the team understand what we do and what we don't do as a team. This exercise is an easy way to clarify this to your team, while allowing them to reflect on what it means for their personal roles. In your preparation for this exercise, print three sheets of paper saying the following things:
- Where we play
- Gray zone
- Where we don't play

The areas where your team plays have activities that are clearly core-work for your team, and typically things other teams should *not* be doing. Areas where your team does not play have activities that you believe other teams should be doing, or that aren't important enough for the organization to focus on. Very often a team gets loads of requests from internal and external stakeholders about activities they shouldn't engage in. Agreeing where you don't play helps team members say no at the right moments. There's always a gray zone, activities where you might make an exception when it helps opening a door or building a relationship, or it might be that it's not a priority now, but is likely to become a priority in the near future. For activities in the gray zone it's good to discuss under what circumstances you say "yes" and when you say "no."

Next, you need to create a few more sheets of paper: each of them should contain a domain of work that members in your team focus on. When you are a manager of managers, these domains could be the ones each team under you works on. For instance, in my Google Digital Academy team, one part of the team focused on Executive Workshops, one part on marketing workshops, and one part on the processes and ecosystem required to scale our workshops. You could also pick domains based on the strategic pillars in your annual plan, or the objectives you use in OKR-writing. Whatever structure you choose, people should already be familiar with it. On the offsite, use the sheets of paper to create a grid like the one in figure 26 on a large window or wall.

Ask people to have the "why, how, what"-statement in mind, and reflect upon things they do in their roles, and the requests they get. Explain the meaning of "where we play", "where we don't play," and the gray zone with some examples. Write the examples on post-its while you explain them and stick them where they belong. Give your team members ten minutes to write post-its for their own roles, and stick them in the right place in the grid. Finally, ask one representative for each of the domains to talk the group through the activities on the post-its. This allows that person to express an opinion: Why should the team play there or not? Or why is something a gray zone? This exercise doesn't just help people to understand when to say yes and when to say no. It also makes them aware of the boundaries of other people in the team: when should they respect someone else's "no"? So, it's a great exercise to make direction, prioritization and team norms actionable. This exercise should take you about thirty to forty minutes. Don't allow it to drag on much longer. You're not trying to set perfect prioritization. You're just training people to apply the principles. You can make priorities more distinctive in the OKR-writing later.

Figure 26 *Exercise to determine where you team can play, and where it can not.*

Step 3: Defining where you go
The last step is about looking ahead. Assuming you run an offsite about every six months or so, it's sufficient if you look ahead at the next six months. In your preparation, create a similar grid like the one in step 2. On the vertical axis you use the same activity-sites as the previous exercise. For the horizontal axis you now print six sheets of paper with the next six months of the year on them. Make a grid like the one in figure 27.

Ask people to take the "why, how, what"-statement in mind, and the agreements you made about where the team plays or not. Ask them to think ahead about the deliverables they want to achieve in the months ahead. Give them time to write deliverables on post-its, and stick them on the right part of the grid. When you see all people are done, ask each team member to walk the rest of the team through their highlights in five minutes. Whether you can afford to cover each individual in this exercise depends on the amount of people in the group. Even when you can afford the time, it's not wise to cover more than six

Figure 27 *Exercise to look ahead with your team for the next six months.*

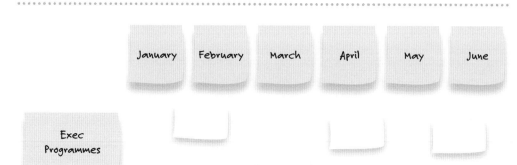

to eight individuals. Otherwise this step starts dragging for too long, lowering energy-levels that you need in order to run a good offsite. If the group is larger than six to eight people, you have two options. One is to run this exercise in subgroups, for instance: one group per knowledge domain. People will then be solely presenting within their subgroups. The other is to ask one representative for each knowledge domain in order to talk the group through the highlights. The benefit of the first option is that sub-groups can cover the road ahead in more detail. The benefit of the second option is that the entire team becomes aware of each other's priorities for the coming months. You can assess what's most valuable for your team.

There is also a nice version of this exercise that looks *back* in time: the wall of celebrations. It's worth considering as an opening exercise on the offsite. The only thing you need to do is create a grid like the one in this exercise with the six months prior to the offsite. Instead of knowledge domains on the vertical axis, you might have one sheet saying "work" and the other "personal". People can then write post-its to celebrate achievements or things that happened at work and in their life. It's a nice way to get to know one another, and to boost energy at the start of an offsite.

The simple set of exercises above ensures that a team vision is more than a few words on a slide. It helps you define the vision with input from your team. It makes actionable on a team level and individual level how the vision defines what people do or don't do, and where they are going. It helps people understand each other's work and boundaries, and empowers them to make decisions. That's all you need. You don't need to be an experienced facilitator to run these exercises effectively. You can repeat parts of these exercises over time, perhaps with small variations, in order to keep the team on track. It's important that you reinforce the vision and the things discussed when you write OKRs. And every moment when the team is under pressure to prioritize there is an opportunity to refer to the mission and things discussed, in order to emphasize how these define the prioritization-decision at that moment.

> **Critical points**
> - Teams want to have a sense of direction, prioritization, and meaning. A vision or mission can help, but most of it is achieved through the Brilliant Basics.
> - A vision or mission is only relevant if people see how it defines where the team plays and doesn't play, how prioritization decisions are made, and how their role is affected. Without those things, visions and missions are just words on a slide.
> - Simon Sinek's Golden Circle is an intuitive tool that helps drafting a team vision without overdesigning it.
> - You can use offsites to align the vision with team members, and to agree how it defines what topics and activities people should and should not focus on.

Customer centricity

I rarely meet leaders or professionals who don't want their organization to be customer- centric. Still, few large organizations are genuinely customer-centric, so customer centricity is a topic of attention in many organizations. I know that not all teams interact with customers directly, but even when you are a team that is 100 percent internal, you still have internal customers. Customer centricity is often seen as a cultural problem, yet it's more often a problem of structures, processes and incentives.

There could also be a cultural problem, however you can't solve that without first solving all problems in structure, processes and incentives. And when you solve the other problems first, things that seemed to be cultural problems are

likely to be resolved too. The key-problems below are examples of common issues with structures, processes and incentives that make customer centricity hard to achieve in large organizations:
1   The fact that an organization is large, makes it inevitable that you split tasks between teams.
2   In large organizations, leadership is no longer close enough to the work of all people, so output of teams is optimized based on KPIs. These KPIs are inevitably imperfect due to the universal limitations of data.
3   Reward-systems encourage people to deliver as to their KPIs, yet typically fail to acknowledge the imperfections of the KPI-system.
4   Optimization-efforts reduce the stretch that teams have to invest extra in customer- centric behaviors that aren't covered by the KPIs they are evaluated on. People give up "doing the right thing."

> *Customer centricity is often seen as a cultural problem, yet it's more often a problem of structures, processes and incentives*

The result of the above challenges is that people demonstrate siloed behaviors, or other behavior that isn't customer-centric, often even against their own wishes of being more customer-centric.

Now let's look at things managers and leaders can do to take away friction on the points mentioned. The first problem is unavoidable. You can't solve customer centricity in a large organization by putting all people in one big customer-centric team. The lack of structure would result in even less customer-centric behavior.

The remaining three challenges can be counter-balanced though:
- Joint-technology platforms between teams can make it easier to integrate data and to steer on KPIs that are less siloed. When data about the customer gets integrated, you get a single *view* on the customer. When that data then gets used to steer the work from teams, you create a single *voice* towards the customer.
- Leadership can create KPIs that quantify customer satisfaction, and make reward of teams at least partly dependent on the success on these KPIs. Many organizations measure customer satisfaction at least to some extent.

But in most organizations I know, customer satisfaction is not taken into account when evaluating performance and reward for employees. And even when it is taken into account, it's often treated as a secondary input. There's no point encouraging people to be more customer- centric when there is no incentive to do so, and while organizational structures make it hard to do so.

- Managers across teams can agree to joint OKRs and projects that reduce the presence of silos: when senior leaders sponsor these projects, they become career opportunities for the people contributing to them.
- Managers and leaders can prioritize more rigorously using OKRs and priority-labels, so that people aren't loaded with work to the point that they can't afford to invest in "doing the right thing." They could aim to always leave twenty-percent "customer centricity time" for people to invest in behaviors that aren't incentivized by their KPI-structure, but that are helpful to customers.

When structural barriers to customer centricity are removed and customer-centric behaviors are rewarded more, the only thing left is for leaders to consistently role-model customer-centric behavior themselves. Ideally, leaders in all layers of the organization make time at least every six months to speak directly with customers, whether internal or not.

> **Critical points**
> - Customer centricity is often treated like a cultural problem, but it is more often a problem of structures, processes and incentives.
> - Optimization on inevitably flawed KPI's leads to situations where people demonstrate siloed behaviors, or other behavior that isn't customer-centric, against their own wishes.
> - Joint technology-platforms, customer-centric KPIs, joint-OKRs between teams, and twenty-percent "customer centricity time" can make it easier for employees to be customer-centric.

Tech, data, and automation

Almost every form of organizational transformation requires some kind of change as to the use of technology, data and automation. These three also depend on one another. Technology is often needed to integrate data, and to disclose it to organizations. Automation is often informed by data. When data isn't integrated, automation results in a faulty output. When technology-platforms aren't integrated, automation can merely be applied to narrow tasks that only benefit small parts of the organization.

There is one big problem: the people having the most profound knowledge of the latest developments in tech, data and automation are often the younger people in the organization. Those people are still at an early point in their career, and are therefore in relatively junior positions in the organizations. They are often the ones making choices about the use of technology in an organization, yet they primarily do so looking through the lens of the work in their own teams. Different teams then pick different technology-platforms, data can't be integrated, and automation doesn't work at the benefit of the organization as a whole.

> *Tech geeks often have a 'language problem': they speak figuratively in a binary code of zeros and ones*

Thus you need to find a way to elevate tech-decisions to higher levels of seniority in the organization, so that choices can be made from a holistic strategic view-point. But this also means that you need to create stronger connections between senior decision-makers and junior tech-geeks, so that their knowledge is taken into account. That brings me to the second challenge. Tech geeks often have a 'language problem': they speak figuratively in a binary code of zeros and ones. Even with the best of efforts, it can be very hard to understand what people are explaining when they are experts in a complex domain. As a leader you often find yourself bombarded with acronyms and abbreviations, while the only thing you want to know is: "How does this affect the decision I need to make?"

A digital maturity framework is an example of a solution to such a problem. An example of such a framework is the Digital Maturity Benchmark, which the Google Digital Academy team launched together with Google's marketing team and the Boston Consulting Group. This example is meant to be used by marketing organizations. The framework defines for six dimensions at what level of digital maturity an organization is. There are four levels of maturity that you can see above the columns in figure 28. If you work in marketing, you'll recognize the terminology used in the first column. *Audience* refers to the use of signals to target people as to advertising (or to applying other types of personalization). Mature organizations have integrated their data so that they get a holistic view of their customer. *Assets* refers to the communication-vehicles:

Figure 28 *Digital maturity framework by Google and Boston Consulting Group.*

	Nascent	Emerging	Connected	Multi-moment
Audience	Limited use of first party data, single broad targeting, upper or lower funnel	Use of first party data, segments defined based on personas, mid-funnel targeting expanding to other end of the funnel	Use of first and third party data, segments based on business, lower, mid and upper funnel targeting	Complete view of customer, segments based on Lifetime Value, full funnel targeting
Assets	Basic use of features on search, limited creatives, no focus on mobile	Multiple creatives optimized with automation, improvements on basic mobile-web performance	Extensions used, video ad sequencing, dynamic creatives in remarketing, optimized mobile web performance	Customized messages, audience-based strategy for creatives, optimal and always improving mobile web experience
Access	Most of us spend on one single inventory/channel, buying through direct reservation, limited quality settings	Several channels, use of generic keywords, part of video/display bought programmatically	Leveraging most channels and formats, automating generic search with DSA, leveraging DSP and ad server pre-bid quality controls	All digital media is programmatic, comprehensive and unified audience strategy, sophisticated and systematic usage of brand controls solutions
Attribution	Intra-channel measurement, no online-offline tracking, limited test & learn	Occasional brand lift surveys, track micro-conversions, some use of A/B testing	Systematic check of viewability/audibility on video, non-last click attribution integrated with bidding, deduplicated cross-channel measurement	Complete online/offline measurement, use of data-driven cross-channel attribution, always on use of A/B, incrementality on key campaigns
Automation	Manual bidding, no use of feeds	Automated bidding rules, simple and low-quality feed	Full-auto smart bidding on all channels on search and display, media buying and bidding depending on operational feeds	Full-auto smart bidding on all channels to omnichannel lifetime value, dynamic buying and bidding depending on feeds and margins
Organization	Client teams working in silos	Key functions working together, though IT remains separate, Defined test & learn process	Regular cross-functional teaming, including IT, Multiple, sequential test and learn pilots	Agile teaming and experimentation part of business as usual

video-ads, banners, search-ads, or for instance a website. Digitally mature organizations use signals to personalize messages in an automated way. *Access* refers to how media-space is purchased. The online-media space is highly fragmented, so purchasing systems need to defragment the buying process. *Attribution* refers to the way you assess the impact of ads. Mature organizations have ways of assessing impact that go across online- and offline-channels. *Automation* is about removing manual steps from the processes of targeting ads, buying ad-space, customizing messages, etcetera. *Organization* refers to the ability to break through silos, and work in more agile ways. When you don't work in marketing, the information in the individual cells may not mean a lot to you. And that's OK. I mainly mean to illustrate by a specific example what a maturity framework may look like.

This maturity-framework is supported by a public and free survey that enables organizations to assess the digital marketing maturity of their own organization. You can find this survey at digitalmaturitybenchmark.withgoogle.com. The survey gets regular updates as technology advances. Each cell in figure 28 comes with a set of detailed actions to get to the next level of maturity as to that dimension. When you take the survey, you get the set of recommended actions that bring you to the next level. This particular survey is only suitable for marketing organizations. Depending on the nature of your organization, you might need a different flavor of a maturity framework. Almost all consulting companies have a variety of maturity frameworks for different purposes, and some organizations create their own.

There's lots of value you get from having a good maturity framework, particularly when it allows you to assess your own organization by means of a survey:
- It translates "tech language" into a strategic roadmap for the organization.
- It avoids fragmentation of technology platforms by elevating tech-decisions to a leadership level.
- It helps leadership to set an aligned cross-functional ambition.
- It helps identifying the steps to achieve that ambition.
- It gives teams a common language to contribute to the ambition.
- It helps to quantify the results of your investments to make the organization ready for the future.
- It helps to track progress, so that you can reward people for contributing to that progress.

If you're not yet working with an organizational maturity framework, it's worth considering this when you find yourself struggling with one or more of the issues mentioned.

> **Critical points**
> - Technology choices should be elevated to higher levels in the organization, which means that leaders should link up more with junior specialists in their organization.
> - A maturity framework can bridge the gap between a specialist language, and a strategic point of view, and can help set the direction and track the progress of transformation.

Culture of innovation

The innovation challenge has similarities to the challenge of customer centricity. Almost all leaders I meet want their people to be more innovative, but almost all professionals say it's too hard to innovate in their organizations, and that leaders don't support innovation enough. It's one of those areas where wishes and reality don't often align. Another similarity with customer centricity is that innovation is frequently seen as a cultural issue, even though other barriers in the organization are a bigger problem that should be tackled first. So, I'd like to start with those barriers.

It starts with the people you hire. I mentioned earlier that Google doesn't hire people for a specific job, instead they hire them for a journey with Google. That makes what you're looking for in the hiring-process fundamentally different. When you hire for a specific job, you will look for people with the exact experience and knowledge to effectively execute that job. When hiring for a journey you look for people who can learn new things, deal with ambiguity, create new stuff, and reinvent themselves when necessary. Next time you write a job-description, consider removing some of the ingredients that demand highly specific knowledge and skills, and replace them by ingredients that are signals that someone can grow along with the organization over time.

Next are the organization's structure and the workplace. This workplace includes the physical and the virtual space people work in. Innovation often comes from connections between people and related worlds. It often requires cross-functional teams to come up with great ideas. How easy is it in your offices for people to bump into each other over lunch, coffee or tea? How easy is it for any random person in your organization to reach out to another colleague, regardless of what team and office they are in? Do you have forums set up where managers get together to exchange ideas about priorities and opportunities? Do teams have joint OKRs or projects that are sponsored by senior leaders, and that are considered a career opportunity? How easy is it for people to find information from all parts of the organization, and to collaborate on documents together?

And finally there's reward. Or even the opposite of reward: risk of punishment. Is it attractive for people to invest in big bets? Or is it safer for them to focus on the OKRs they are confident they can achieve? Are people encouraged to spend time on P2 OKRs? Or are P2 OKRs symbolic additions to the list that keep being deprioritized quarter after quarter? Is learning from failure rewarded? Or is failure more likely to be ignored or punished? Do you use "how-statements" in performance evaluations, that help reward people for working through ambiguity, for proactively identifying opportunities and for solving problems with a high complexity? Do the KPIs you use to measure team effectiveness and efficiency allow space to invest in long-term bets?

> *When you ask for innovation without making it easy and attractive to innovate, you deflate and frustrate people*

There's no point in thinking about the culture of innovation without solving the above topics first. When you ask for innovation without making it easy and attractive to innovate, you deflate and frustrate people. Deflation and frustration are the worst mindsets for people when it comes to innovation, because they are reductive mindsets. A culture of innovation requires playfulness, safety, openness, time, and a willingness to grow and collaborate: the same things you establish when you work on the Brilliant Basics and the enablers for the high-performing teams that were described in part I and part II of this book. The best way to establish a culture of innovation is therefore to create a critical mass of managers who know how to manage without power. Once you have that, you no longer need to ask for innovation, because intrinsically motivated teams push the boundaries of the organization—whether you want it or not. The only thing left for leadership is to channel the energy of those teams, by removing blockers on the five enablers of the transformation described in part III, and to reward employees and managers who drive change and innovation.

The culture of innovation is not something you actively create, though you can easily break it. Culture of innovation is something that emerges and grows under the right conditions

From here on, it's mostly a matter of creating space for ideas to emerge, and to be invested in. It's a matter of going out of the way. The culture of innovation is not something you actively *create*, though you can easily *break* it. Culture of innovation is something that *emerges and grows* under the right conditions. It does so when:

- You hire people who can grow along with a changing organization.
- You remove barriers to the physical and virtual connection and collaboration between people.
- You allow information and ideas to be easily shareable and findable.
- You approach prioritization of people's tasks in a way that leaves time for them to invest in big bets early on.
- You reduce risk, and increase reward for working at complex or ambiguous opportunities and ideas.
- Managers know how to manage without power.
- Leaders know how to lead with data, mind and heart.

Critical points
- Similar to customer centricity, innovation is often seen as a cultural problem, even though it's more often a problem of organizational barriers.
- Innovative organizations don't hire people for a single role. They hire for a journey into the organization.
- They make it easy for people to connect with one another face-to-face and virtually, to exchange information and to collaborate.
- Reward systems should be designed, so that they make it safe and rewarding to invest in stretch objectives and long-term bets, to work through ambiguity and to learn from failure.
- Culture of innovation cannot be created, but you can easily break it. And you need to create the right conditions for it to emerge.

People operations

The people analytics team that published the studies about great managers and effective teams, plays an important role in Google's strategy for people operations. The reason: things that work in one organization might not work in another. The advice I wrote in previous sections and chapters may or may not work in your organization or team, because your situation might be different. So, it's wise to experiment with different approaches to learn from them. Data can help assess whether something is working. The manager feedback-survey is a good example of measuring whether the changes you make in the way you manage and organize your team are having the desired impact. A digital or organizational-maturity survey can help to assess progress on a transformation roadmap. Data-drivenexperiments are another way of using data to learn what works for you.

Google runs data-driven people-experiments all the time. These experiments are sometimes big, and sometimes small. Solutions are sometimes complex, and sometimes surprisingly simple. Laszlo Bock wrote about this approach extensively in his book *Work Rules!*. I'd like to illustrate the approach with some examples. Let's start with one that seemed complex, but that had a surprisingly simple solution.

In Google's engineering organization, employees can nominate themselves for promotion. Google discovered at one point that women nominate themselves less for promotions than men do, yet when they did nominate themselves they were actually more qualified for promotion. Apparently women were unjustifiably more hesitant to nominate themselves. This resulted in an unfair difference in promo-ratios between men and women. It seemed a complicated puzzle to figure out why this problem existed. A Google leader decided to share the data openly in an email, with some background about why women seem to be more reluctant to put themselves forward. It solved the problem instantly. Women then nominated themselves at equal rates to men. Yet over time that equality faded again. They discovered that this email needed to be sent with a certain frequency, in order to keep the ratios of self-nomination equal over time. It's a great example of running data-driven experiments. First, Google used data to analyze the situation. They noticed in the data that something was wrong. They tested a solution and measured whether it made a difference. They iterated it until they saw in the data that they consistently got it right.

Now, let's look at a more complicated example. In the early days, Google was notorious for their extreme hiring-process: people had loads of interviews, with lots of weird brain-teaser- questions. How many ping-pong balls fit in an airplane? How would you estimate how much paint there is on all Dutch highways combined? That last one is actually a question someone asked me at my interview process. Media even wrote articles about how to beat Google's interview-process, and how to answer these brain-teaser questions. The amount of hours that employees were putting into the hiring process were a huge investment. Yet there was no certainty that these practices led to a better prediction as to whether or not candidates were qualified for the role. The people analytics team decided to dig into this problem.

Luckily, Google is very structured as to how they record interviews, and how people's performance ratings are stored. That meant there were two great data sets available:
- One with information about the number of interviews and questions asked;
- One with performance ratings in the period after hiring.

By correlating the number of interviews and the questions asked with performance ratings after hiring, the team could see how many interviews and what type of questions would lead to the best prediction of performance ratings after hiring. The prediction did not get better when there were more than four interviews, and the brainteaser-questions also didn't improve the prediction. Since then, Google has adjusted their hiring process. People have less interviews, and job-interviewers get guidance about what questions are most effective. So, no more ping-pong balls or highway paint.

When you understand the principles of data-driven experiments, it's a powerful way to find your own unique effective manner of running your organization. It helps you to test which bits of advice work for you, and which don't. Often you will find that advice can work only when you make some tweaks to make it to your own. So, next time you need to make a people's decision for your organization, ask yourself the following questions:
- What's the exact question I am trying to answer?
- What metrics would help me see whether I found the right answer or not?
- What hypotheses do we have about this question?
- What existing data sets do we have that might shed light on these hypotheses?
- What experiment can we run to create additional data in order to test the hypotheses?
- How can we iterate upon the experiment until we get it right?

> **Critical points**
> - Data-driven experiments are a powerful way to learn what people-strategies work best for your team or organization.
> - Sometimes you can use existing data sources to find an answer. Occasionally you need to generate data through a process of testing and learning.

Epilogue

Now it's up to you...

Why so many people complain about their managers

People often complain about their managers, yet I don't believe this is because managers don't try, or don't have good intentions. Sure, some bosses are not nice people, but most managers and leaders I meet genuinely want to do right by their people. It's just a tough job, for many reasons. First, your job is highly fragmented. You're expected to set a strategy, but are often also involved in projects, and are buried in the administration that comes with being a manager. Meanwhile your people come to you with ideas, problems, conflicts and desires—and you want to be accessible to them. Secondly, you're torn between conflicting demands. You need to serve your team, but also to satisfy senior leadership and stakeholders. You need to aim for long-term bets, but are also expected to put out short-term fires. Team members on average will always have slightly too optimistic expectations when it comes to career and reward, so you can never satisfy all people. You'll even need to every now and then enforce decisions you don't agree with. And finally, there's rarely good and practical guidance and training to help you figure out overal what approach to management works best for you, while facing these conflicting demands.

This book is my attempt to provide managers with a holistic toolkit and practical guidance upon how to bring most value to their teams and organizations. I run courses and trainings where I bring managers and leaders together in order to explore how to apply the principles of *Managing Without Power* so that peer managers can exchange ideas, and learn from one another. I find it particularly rewarding to work with large groups of managers that are active in the same organization. It allows you to create a community that can positively change the culture and effectiveness of an organization within a relatively short time.

Yet even with the best of guidance, it's impossible to get it right all the time. Even with my track-record of high manager scores, I can easily think of a few people who probably don't look at me as one of their great managers. There are too many conflicting demands, too many questions you can't know the answer to, too many decisions that can't be entirely right, and there are always limitations when it comes to time and resources. I've advocated for acts of kindness towards your team members in this book, but kindness is equally important for yourself.

Managers and leaders are often ambitious people. Otherwise they wouldn't have earned the positions they hold. That ambition often comes with an attitude of toughness towards oneself. Yet the skill to survive in jobs that comes with a continuous pressure of risk, complexity and a high workload very much depends on your ability to recharge at the right moments. Only a relaxed brain, supported by a healthy body, consistently comes up with creative ideas and sharp strategic thinking. It's the same in sports. When people see champions compete at the highest level, they mainly think about how hard these people train. But the ability to compete at the highest levels in sports is the sum of your ability to train hard and smart, eat and drink healthily, and to take rest in order to allow your body to recover. In team sports, the team dynamics is also a critical contributor, and even individual athletes cannot be champions without a great support-system around them. So take care of yourself, recharge regularly, and build your own support-system, for instance by regularly connecting with the peer managers you trust.

It's time for a new narrative
There's something fundamentally wrong about the way we think about performing at the highest level in our professional lives. There's a set of limiting beliefs that blocks us from seeing how humaneness and performing at the highest level can go together, and are even inseparable. There's a story we get told over and over again in our lives, that somehow resonates deeply within us, but that is damaging when you put it at the heart of your belief- system: that story is called the Heroes Quest.

The Heroes Quest-story's framework can be found in the majority of movies, TV-shows and books. Once you see the framework explained, you instantly recognize all the examples where you've encountered it. The story often comes in four stages, although there are variations on it:
- The calling
- The commitment
- The quest
- The homecoming

The story obviously starts with a hero. Only at that moment, we don't always know yet that this is a hero. It might even be an anti-hero. Somewhere at the opening of the story there will be *the calling*: a push or a pull. Some kind of pain pushes the hero's out of their existing life, or this happens at some kind of opportunity. Whatever the push or pull is, it may not instantly lead to action. It tends to take a few nudges to get over the barrier in order to leave the current life. Then there's this one moment when the penny drops: something happens that triggers *the commitment* to leave the current situation and move into the unknown. Now it's time for *the quest*: a journey of adventures and challenges, where friends are met and enemies faced, with wins and losses on all sides. The quest ends with a *homecoming*: this could literally be a journey home after a battle, but it could also be a moment of emotional acceptance, or a death that puts an end to a journey of suffering. Whatever it is, it is a form of closure. Stories that don't provide a sense of closure, can often leave you frustrated at the end.

Pick a random movie you recently saw, and you'll almost certainly recognize *the Heroes Quest*-framework in it. James Bond leads a hidden life on a remote island, having retired from his work as 007 after the woman he loved got murdered by his enemies. Suddenly someone from the secret-service approaches him at his hidden address, for a job that only 007 can do (the calling). Of course he refuses. There's too much pain. He will never go back to that life. Then he meets a girl, they connect deeply, but she sees the pain Bond carries with him, and convinces him to let go of it. He visits the grave of his ex-girlfriend one more time. A bomb explodes while he stands by her grave. He realizes the new girlfriend must have betrayed him, and that this must have something to do with the job the secret service wanted him to do. This is the final trigger to step back into the job as 007 (the commitment). Next is the quest with lots of action, tracing the enemy, set-backs, explosions, injuries, and confrontations with the pain of the past. In that journey he discovers the new girlfriend hadn't betrayed him. It was a setup. They find their love for each other again (the homecoming). In this case there's a surprising twist at the end: Bond gets infected with a special DNA-based poison. If he ever touches his girlfriend or her daughter, which turned out to be *his* daughter, they will die. He knows he can never be with them, yet he can't live without them. He explodes together with the base where the enemy was mass-producing the DNA-based poison. That was the last movie of Daniel Craig as James Bond: *No Time To Die*.

The Heroes Quest-story romanticizes pain and suffering. It says you come out stronger when you plough through it. In movies, most injuries completely heal again. James Bond gets shot, tortured and beaten countless times—through-out all the movies in the series. He falls off buildings and cliffs. At the end of each movie, he's typically significantly wounded. The next movie mostly depicts him recovering from physical and mental wounds, but he always heals (except however in this last movie with Daniel Craig). Even when people have lasting injuries in movies, they become part of the person's character in a way that is romanticized.

The same is true when we cover sports on TV. We see all the people who became champions, but we don't see the ones that dropped out because of serious injuries, and that could never practice their sports again. Every now and then, one of the champions gets seriously injured. It's only when they recover that we consistently keep seeing them in the media, reinforcing the idea that you can achieve anything if you work hard enough. It reinforces the idea that you can compete at the highest levels, as long as you are willing to suffer and work through pain. Yet for every champion we see on TV there are at least 99 that dropped out because of permanent injury. These are not people who were less talented, or that worked less hard for it. They were just unfortunate. And they don't fit our *Heroes Quest-story*, so we ignore them.

This belief that competing at the highest levels can only be achieved through pain, and that those who can't stand the pain didn't try hard enough, or weren't talented enough, also defines how many large organizations are run. It's swimming or drowning. If you don't swim, you're probably a low performer and need to be managed out. Burnout probably means you weren't up to the job. People often fear speaking about the pressure they feel, because it might be perceived as weakness. As a result, many people think they are the only ones that feel this pressure. Every now and then, cases make the news of famous bosses, trainers or celebrities that bullied and abused people. These are cases that are excessive enough to be newsworthy. We are then disgusted, and go back to normal. But in that "normal," we damage many more people in many more small ways. That "normal" is also the fertile ground allowing the extreme cases we see on the news to emerge over and over again. I covered examples of micro-pressures earlier in the book, or small acts of political behavior. It's behaviors like these that can cause a death by a thousand cuts, and a culture where excessively damaging situations arise from time to time. Even if this doesn't happen, I still find it strange that it is considered normal by many people, that you need to "put on your thick skin" in the morning before you go to work.

This approach might work in organizations where a relatively small group of talented and thick-skinned people can lead the organization to success, and when enough people want to work for this organization so that there's always a stream of new talent when people drop out. But in most large organizations you can't succeed with only a handful of people, and most organizations don't have an abundant stream of new talent available to replace people who were collateral damage. You need 95 percent of your people to be the best they can be for any large organization to be sustainably successful. And the five percent of low performers that can't be turned around, needs to be managed out in a way that doesn't undermine the psychological safety of the other 95 percent.

We can only build inclusive, safe and thereby high-performing organizations, when we get rid of the current version of *the Heroes Quest*-story. The way the current version is used in our organizations can be summarized as: "When you work hard and endure pain, you can play at the highest level." Besides the fact that it isn't a very healthy story, it also doesn't acknowledge the element of luck and privilege that some people have, and some don't. I was born in a country where great education was available to me. I was born without any disabilities. There were no wars during my lifetime, and there was always enough food and great healthcare. Due to the economic welfare in our country, there were also enough jobs available to build experience and grow. I've probably enjoyed loads of privileges in that journey without ever noticing it, just because of being a white straight male. I could say the success of my career is all because I worked so hard. I did work very hard, but take any of these privileges out of the equation, and I might not have achieved what I achieved.

It would be nice when a new version of this Heroes Quest is one that acknowledges not all people start with equal opportunity, one that brings all types of people along on the journey, so they can collectively bring our organizations to the highest and most beautiful standards of achievement. It should be a version that acknowledges high performance is a sum of hard work, healthy habits, time to recover, and creating a strong team culture. Here's what I think the Hero's Quest-story can be:
- *The Calling*: appreciate the talents and privileges given to you.
- *The Commitment*: work hard, learn and grow, and take care of yourself and those less-privileged than you.
- *The Quest*: do impactful and valuable work together, and support one another in overcoming obstacles and losses.
- *The Homecoming*: leaving the team, the organization and world in a better shape than you found it, and bringing beautiful memories with you.

Imagine how different our working-environment would be, and how much more effective if all organizations would be run, based upon the beliefs of this *Heroes Quest-story*. This story-arch would fuel a belief-system that enables us to create genuinely high-performing organizations, because we genuinely harness the potential of all available talent, and do impactful work in a way that is sustainable.

> **Critical points**
> - The Heroes Quest story-framework resonates deeply within humans, but the version most people know romanticizes pain, and gets us to believe organizations can only perform at the highest level, when we accept it's a game of the survival of the fittest.
> - It's time to start believing in a more inclusive and sustainable version of this story-arch, and thereby become truly high-performing organizations.

Staying true to your values

When you are successful at building a team in line with the principles of this book, it's likely that you become a "safe haven" for the people working under you. It's not easy for any professional to find a team or organization where you can do great work, with great people, in a great team culture, and under a great manager. Great people are therefore likely to stick with you, and they will tell their peers to join your team when an opportunity arises. The big question is then: "Are you as lucky as your team members are? Is *your* leadership creating the same great working-environment for you?" If "yes," you're in a great place. It probably means you are working in an organization, with enough critical mass of great managers and leaders, to have a great working-environment in many pockets of the organization. It could also be that you are lucky to work under a particular great manager or leader, who shields you from pressures in the organization. In that case, if that person leaves, the situation can change fast. Either way, you're still within the most favorable scenario.

The more likely scenario is one where you are the person shielding your team from pressures in the organization, and you are the one supporting people to break through the barriers with a view to the organizational change described in previous sections. You're likely to be in a position where you are trying to change things about the organization in order to create a better environment around your team, to make the organization more effective and inclusive. Those changes rarely go as fast as you want. Where do you find the energy to be the driving force for positive change in both the organization and for your team, when no one is creating it for you?

To me, the answer to that question is in the meaning of work. What makes work meaningful is different for each person, so the answer to that question is by definition personal. I experience meaning if:
- I see the potential to create something beautiful and impactful: this could be the output we produce as a team, for example a portfolio of high-quality workshops, but it also includes the potential to build an effective team and organization with a great culture.
- I believe the organization has enough good people to make it worthwhile contributing to improvement of the organization's culture and effectiveness.
- I learn and grow.
- I like most people I work with.
- I feel valued by my manager and leadership.

It's worth listing for yourself what your main drivers of meaning are in your work—if you haven't done so yet. Reality is that most of the time, most of these drivers won't be exactly what you want them to be. Yet when you are experienced enough, you know that no organization is ever perfect. If you run away from something because it isn't perfect, you're likely to find something else that also isn't perfect. This still doesn't mean though, that you should accept all things you don't like about your job. When you're faced with things that make you less happy, you always have three options:
1 *Change it*. This can mean convincing others to see or do things differently. Or to finding a way to work around the problem, so that it is no longer there.
2 *Accept it*. Accept that the problem cannot be solved, and try not to be bothered by it.
3 *Leave*. Walk away from the situation, which could mean looking for another job inside or outside the organization.

Failure to choose from these three, inevitably leads to unhappiness. As a manager and leader, you will be regarded as someone who lacks purpose and vision. This makes you less strong as a team leader. So, when I'm faced with something I don't like, the first questions I ask myself are: Can I change this? And if yes, is it a battle worth fighting? Sometimes I know I could change something if I tried hard enough, but I also know how much effort it would take. That effort will go at the cost of something else, for instance at the cost of investing in building a beautiful output with my team, or at the cost of spending time with my family. Even if you *can* change something, it doesn't always mean you *should*.

When the benefit of driving change outweighs the cost, then keep driving change. It will create a better environment for you and your team, and if you ever leave the organization, you will leave it in a better shape than you found it. If you can't change the problem, or the costs are too high, consider whether it's feasible to accept the situation as it is. When you find yourself thinking about the problem over and over again, during working hours or outside, that's a sign you probably shouldn't accept. The difficult part of the question is always *how long* you should allow yourself to walk around worrying about things at work. I've worked through many difficult periods where I thought it was time to leave; and then with the right amount of effort and patience a door opened in the end. It's because of that experience that I built strategies to retain energy, while investing in future scenarios that could solve the problem in my work situation.

The first step is to always go back to your personal anchors.

The anchors are things that give you meaning in work and life, and are your personal values. I opened this book describing a period where I felt I was no longer working for Google. I created a set of sneakers in Google colors in the adidas sneaker configurator. Wearing these sneakers was a way for me to remind myself what I believed Google could be, and what my personal values were. This allowed me to keep focusing on doing things I felt were most meaningful for Google, and for Google's clients. Because this meant I had to ignore some of the guidance from my leadership, I knew I was taking a risk.

The second step is therefore to reconcile yourself with the worst-case scenario and prepare for it.

The worst-case scenario is typically the one where you leave the team or the organization. I prepared for that step by starting to apply for jobs externally, but I also did so by saving enough money, so I could be without work for at least a year. You may wonder whether it's still possible to be committed to an organization when you stand with one foot outside of it. I believe you are much more effective challenging an organization when you know you can afford to leave. The hardest changes in an organization come with the highest resistance and risk. When you can afford to leave, you can face that pressure, and challenge the organization sharper, while keeping stress levels low for yourself. This makes you more convincing, and your energy lasts longer, so you can push with more patience.

The third step is to invest in actions that increase the likelihood that one or more desired future scenarios emerge.

A desired future scenario could be that you can stay in your current job longer because you still enjoy it, but it could also be that a new opportunity inside or outside the organization emerges. When I discovered after my first three years at Google that I no longer wanted to be a researcher, I invested in creating my own digital-transformation workshops and running these with big clients. This led to first getting a newly designed role as Head of Digital Transformation, and later to the opportunity to join and lead Google Digital Academy. It took a bit more than a year for that first role to emerge, and another two years for the second one. If those opportunities had not emerged fast enough, I probably would have found an external role, because I was also investing in that scenario.

The fourth and final step is to jump at the opportunity when it arises.
Even when you push for certain scenarios to happen, it's unlikely that the scenario emerges exactly the way you imagined it. So when an opportunity emerges, you'll need to assess how much of the boxes it ticks of your desired scenarios. You'll need to make a risk assessment each time an opportunity emerges, and then a leap of faith at the right moment.

> *I look at the relationship with team members as a moment in time where two journeys run parallel temporarily, until each continues their own journey again, like two travelers enjoying time together before moving on*

When you work in line with the principles mentioned, always choosing between change, accept or leave, always preparing for desirable future scenarios, and always willing to accept the consequences of less favorable scenarios, you'll develop into a leader with purpose and vision. I was constantly transparent to my team about the scenarios I considered inside and outside of the team and organization; the same way I encouraged *them* to explore *their* scenarios in career conversations. Managers don't often share it with their teams when they consider leaving, but it changes the relationship when you do. I look at the relationship with team members as a moment in time where two journeys run parallel temporarily, until each continues their own journey again, like two travelers enjoying time together before moving on.

As a manager and leader, when you make consistent and genuine choices based on your deepest beliefs, and open yourself up to deep trusting relationships with all types of people on your team, people will start to follow you for who you are and what you stand for. This helps you build organizations with a beautiful and effective culture. This is because, even people several layers away from you, will follow you *and* because your personal example will help you to create a community of brilliant managers. Once you've reached this level of connection with your team members, you don't easily lose it. It will last well beyond the time these people work in your team. Team members will take "bits of you" into their future jobs, will apply principles they saw you apply, and create great working- environments the way they've seen you do it. At this level, you create a ripple-effect that doesn't just leave your organization in a better place than you found it. It also leaves the world as a better place than you found it. The principles of Managing Without Power create managers and leaders that can build organizations that create value for people, planet and profit. Inclusivity is always the "default setting," because you can't perform at the highest level if you don't know how to mobilize all talent available to you.

> *The principles of Managing Without Power create managers and leaders that can build organizations that create value for people, planet and profit*

Thank you for the time invested in reading my book. I hope you find the principles as meaningful and effective as I do. I hope they will help you build effective and human teams and organizations, and I hope they will enable a rewarding journey for yourself too. If you'd like to ask a question, share a thought, or feel I could add value to your organization, you can always connect with me through LinkedIn.

I want to leave you with a mantra I wrote for myself that helps me to stick to my values, and to do the right things when plowing through difficult periods at work:

- Pick a battle worth fighting.
- Pick a challenge worth solving.
- Pick a skill worth learning.
- Pick people worth going on a journey with.
- Treat all with respect…
  … including the ones you don't like or don't understand
  … and including yourself.
- Set boundaries when needed.
- Accept losses and learn from them.
- Celebrate success with gratitude.
- And start all over again.

Appendix

1 Google's Manager Feedback Survey

Section 1 Please respond to the following questions. Feel free to skip any questions you are not comfortable answering, or that are not applicable to you.

1 I would recommend my manager to others.

Strongly disagree	1	2	3	4	5	Strongly agree
	○	○	○	○	○	

2 My manager assigns stretch opportunities to help me develop in my career.

Strongly disagree	1	2	3	4	5	Strongly agree
	○	○	○	○	○	

3 My manager communicates clear goals for our team.

Strongly disagree	1	2	3	4	5	Strongly agree
	○	○	○	○	○	

4 My manager gives me actionable feedback on a regular basis.

Strongly disagree	1	2	3	4	5	Strongly agree
	○	○	○	○	○	

5 My manager provides the autonomy I need to do my job (i.e., does not "micromanage" by getting involved in details that should be handled at other levels).

Strongly disagree	1	2	3	4	5	Strongly agree
	○	○	○	○	○	

6 My manager consistently shows consideration for me as a person.

Strongly disagree	1	2	3	4	5	Strongly agree
	○	○	○	○	○	

7 My manager keeps the team focused on priorities, even when it's difficult (e.g. declining or deprioritizing other projects).

Strongly disagree	1	2	3	4	5	Strongly agree
	○	○	○	○	○	

8 My manager regularly shares relevant information from their manager and senior leadership.

Strongly disagree	1	2	3	4	5	Strongly agree
	○	○	○	○	○	

9 My manager has had a meaningful discussion with me about my career development in the past six months.

Strongly disagree	1	2	3	4	5	Strongly agree
	○	○	○	○	○	

10 My manager has the technical expertise (e.g. technical judgment in Tech, selling in Sales, accounting in Finance) required to effectively manage me.

Strongly disagree	1	2	3	4	5	Strongly agree
	○	○	○	○	○	

11 The actions of my manager show they value the perspective I bring to the team, even if it is different from their own.

Strongly disagree	1	2	3	4	5	Strongly agree
	○	○	○	○	○	

12 My manager makes tough decisions effectively (e.g. decisions involving multiple teams, competing priorities).

Strongly disagree	1	2	3	4	5	Strongly agree
	○	○	○	○	○	

13 My manager effectively collaborates across boundaries (e.g. team, organizational).

Strongly disagree	1	2	3	4	5	Strongly agree
	○	○	○	○	○	

Section 2 (Optional). While this is a confidential survey, keep in mind your comments are shared verbatim with your manager.

1 What would you recommend your manager keep doing?
2 What would you have your manager change?

Source: rework.withgoogle.com

2 Checklist for setting direction and expectations

A good system to set direction and expectations should…

- ☐ Have **three to five objectives that last six to twelve months**, aligned to the annual plan, and that set a somewhat ambitious direction for the year ahead.
- ☐ Have about **three key results** for each objective that are **measurable quarterly milestones**, that set an ambitious pace to achieve the objective.
- ☐ Be "**vertically aligned**," so individuals can derive their individual priorities from team and company priorities, and know what they should spend their time on.
- ☐ Be "**horizontally aligned**," so individuals know which stakeholders have dependencies on their deliverables.
- ☐ Be "**output-based**," and quantify how success is defined, so people can be held accountable.
- ☐ Include **mechanisms to make deliverables that are hard to quantify more measurable** (e.g. defined project stages for a creative development process).
- ☐ Have clear **priority labels**, so people can manage workload, know when to escalate, and know when to say no.
- ☐ Enable **healthy distribution of workload, equal access** to high-profile work, and **opportunities for personal growth** (aligned to career plans).
- ☐ Set **clear expectations** that create transparency in order to make performance evaluations and **decisions about reward and progression that is fair and predictable**.
- ☐ Help people see a direct **link between their individual work and the vision** of the team and organization.

3 Unbiasing performance-reviews checklist

When making important decisions about employees, like when to promote someone, it's critical to recognize and address how potential biases can influence the decision-making process.

Unbiasing Checklist for Promotion Decisions

Promotion Nominations	Biases Targeted
Define what success looks like at a particular level, and don't allow extraneous data points (e.g. time in role) to affect the decision.	Stereotype-based Biases
Consider the whole bench of talent, and narrow it down from there.	Availability Bias
Consider concrete, behavioral examples throughout the current level or role to narrow the pool.	Recency, Horns & Halos, Availability Bias
Before Promotion Decision Discussions	**Biases Targeted**
Write down your own evaluation of employees before promotion committee.	Anchoring Bias
Restate success-criteria (e.g. what's expected of a person for that particular role and level).	Stereotype-based Biases
During Promotion Decision Discussions	**Biases Targeted**
Consider concrete, behavioral examples for current-level or role.	Recency, Horns & Halos, Availability Bias
Consider situational factors (in the workplace) that affected performance (e.g. lacked resources).	Fundamental Attribution Error
Consider if a promotion-decision would change if your employee was in different social group.	Stereotype-based Biases
Play devil's advocate when there are no significantly different perspectives raised.	Anchoring Bias, Agreement Bias
Listen to the devil's advocate for employees you are involved in.	Leniency Error, Self-serving Bias, Similar-to-me Bias
Consider the benefits of complementary and supplementary skill sets (i.e., the benefits of being different).	Self-serving Bias

Source: rework.withgoogle.com

Unbiasing Checklists for Performance-Review Conversations

Action	Biases Targeted
Communicate the performance expectations for your employee in that role and level.	Stereotype-based Biases
Make sure cited feedback and examples come from the entire assessment period.	Recency Bias
Discuss important work that may not have been visible.	Availability Bias
Differentiate between situational factors (in the workplace) and personal factors that affected performance.	Fundamental Attribution Error
Use multiple concrete, behavioral examples from reviewers to support *both* strengths *and* development areas.	Leniency Error, Self-serving Bias, Similar-to-me Bias, Horns & Halos
Imagine your direct report in a different social group and ask yourself whether your feedback would be the same.	Stereotype-based Biases

Source: rework.withgoogle.com

4 Psychological safety checklist

How to foster Psychological Safety on your teams

Demonstrate engagement

- Be present and focus on the conversation (e.g. close your laptop during meetings).
- Ask questions with the intention of learning from your teammates.
- Offer input, be interactive, and show you're listening.
- Respond verbally to show engagement ("That makes sense. Tell us more.")
- Be aware of your body language; make sure to lean towards or face the person speaking.
- Make eye-contact to show connection and active listening.

Show understanding

- Recap what's been said to confirm mutual understanding/alignment (e.g. "What I heard you say is..."); then acknowledge areas of agreement, disagreement, and be open to questions within the group.
- Validate comments verbally ("I understand." "I see what you're saying.").
- Avoid placing blame ("Why did you do this?") and focus on solutions ("How can we work towards making sure this goes more smoothly next time?", "What can we do together to make a game-plan for next time?")
- Think about your facial expressions – are they unintentionally negative (a scowl or grimace)?
- Nod your head to demonstrate understanding during conversations/meetings.

Be inclusive in interpersonal settings

- Share information about your personal work-style and preferences, encourage teammates to do the same.
- Be available and approachable to teammates (e.g. make time for ad hoc one-on-one conversations, feedback-sessions, career coaching).
- Clearly communicate the purpose of ad hoc-meetings scheduled outside normal one-on-one team meetings.
- Express gratitude for contributions from the team.
- Step in if team members talk negatively about another team member.
- Have open body posture (e.g. face all team members, don't turn your back on part of the group).
- Build rapport (e.g. talk with your teammates about their lives outside of work).

Be inclusive in decision-making

- Solicit input, opinions, and feedback from your teammates.
- Don't interrupt or allow interruptions (e.g. step in when someone is interrupted, and ensure his/her idea is heard).
- Explain the reasoning behind your decisions (live or via email, walk team through how you arrived at a decision).
- Acknowledge input from others (e.g. highlight when team members were contributors to a success or decision).

Show confidence and conviction without appearing inflexible

- Manage team discussions (e.g. don't allow side-conversations at team meetings, make sure conflict isn't personal).
- Use a voice that is clear and audible in a team setting.
- Support and represent the team (e.g. share team's work with senior leadership, give credit to teammates).
- Invite the team to challenge your perspective and push back.
- Model vulnerability; share your personal perspective on work and failures with your teammates.
- Encourage teammates to take risks, and demonstrate risk-taking in your own work.

Sources

- A.C. Edmondson and Z. Lei (2014) Psychological Safety: The History, Renaissance, and Future of an Interpersonal Construct. Annual Review Organizational Psychology and Organizational Behavior, 1(1): 23–43.
- A. Edmondson (1999) Psychological Safety and Learning Behavior in Work Teams. Administrative Science Quarterly, 44(2) :350–383.
- C.K. Goman (2011) The Silent Language of Leaders: How Body Language Can Help—or Hurt—How You Lead. Hoboken, NJ: Jossey-Bass Publishing.

Source: rework.withgoogle.com

5 Ten common biases that affect hiring

10 Unconscious Hiring Biases

1 Affinity/similarity bias
When we favor a candidate because we share a characteristic with them.

2 In-Group bias
The tendency that people have to favor their own group above that of others.

3 Halo effect
Your first impression of a person's qualities is based on other unrelated factor.

4 Horns effect
When after knowing or perceiving one bad thing about a person, this person seems less positive overall.

5 Confirmation bias
When we form this initial judgement of a candidate and then we focus on information that will support that.

6 Social bias
Besides stereotyping based on age or gender, also race, cultural background, sexuality and religion also often form the basis for discrimination on the labor market.

7 Illusory correlation bias
When we perceive a relationship where no such relationship actually exists.

8 Anchoring bias
When we fixate on one piece of information. As a result, giving it more weight than it de serves.

9 Attribution bias
When we evaluate or try to find reasons for others' behaviours.

10 Beauty bias
A type of bias that encourages you to prefer a candidate that is, based on norms created by society, considered attractive.

Bron: www.equalture.com

6 Measuring belonging

To score a ten on our ten-point belonging scale, you strongly agree with each component of these four elements. In other words, in your day-to-day work, you feel fully seen, connected, supported, and proud.

Seen
- My organization values my unique attributes (e.g. culture, heritage, skills, perspective).
- My organization adequately rewards my accomplishments.
- My manager recognizes my skills and accomplishments.
- My colleagues recognize my skills and accomplishments.
- My colleagues take my opinions seriously.
- I am treated with as much respect as other employees.

Connected
- I can be myself at my organization.
- Other employees at work seem to like me the way I am.
- My managers/supervisors seem interested in me.
- People at this organization are friendly to me.
- I feel comfortable attending social events at work.
- I have very little in common with most other employees at my organization.*

Supported
- My organization extends satisfactory help and support at times when I have any personal issues.
- My manager extends satisfactory help and support at times when I have any personal issues.
- My colleagues extend satisfactory help and support at times when I have any personal issues.
- My organization cares about me as much as it cares about other employees.
- My colleagues include me at work.
- There's at least one leader in this organization I feel comfortable talking to if I have a problem.

Pride
- I am proud to work at my organization.
- I feel like a real part of my organization.
- I am able to work in this organization without sacrificing my principles.
- My organization's values are similar to my own.
- I refer to "we/us" rather than "they/them" when I talk about my organization to others.
- I generally experience more positive emotions than negative emotions at work.

* Responses to this scale item were reverse-scored.

Source: www.coqual.org

Acknowledgements

Many thanks to Shuvo Saha, founder of the Google Digital Academy team, for giving me a chance to join the team and lead it, and for leading with heart and purpose.

Many thanks to my team members, for trusting me and always providing valuable feedback, for all the things I learned from you, and for the great time and memories.

Thank you Corrie Wieland and Henny van den Bosch, for taking such good care of a family that wasn't yours.

Literature

Blake, J. (2017). *Pivot: The only move that matters is your next one.* Portfolio/Penguin.

Bock, L. (2023). *Work rules!: Insights from inside Google that will transform how you live and lead.* Twelve.

Coqual. *Belonging Matters Everywhere: an examination of workplace cultures in the United Kingdom, Germany, and Poland.* Retrieved April 4, 2023, from coqual.org

Covey, S.M.R., & Merrill, R. R. (2018). *The speed of trust: The One thing that changes everything.* Free Press.

Covey, S.R. (1989) *The 7 Habits of Highly Effective People: Powerful Lessons in Personal Change*

Equalture. *10 Unconscious Hiring Bias & How to Avoid Them.* Retrieved April 4, 2023, from equalture.com

Gallup (2015). *State of the American manager*

Google. *A letter from Larry and Sergey.* Retrieved April 4, 2023, fromblog.google/alphabet/letter-from-larry-and-sergey

Google. *Project Oxygen, Project Aristotle, Set Goals with OKRs and Unbiasing Performance.* Retrieved April 4, 2023, from www.rework.withgoogle.com

Google. *The things we know to be true.* Retrieved April 4, 2023, from about.google/philosophy

Grove, A. S. (1983). *High Output Management*

Maister, D. H. (2001). The trusted advisor: *Integratie van online en offline marketing*

Merks-Benjaminsen, J. (2012). *Schizofrene Marketing: Integratie van online en offline marketing*

Merks-Benjaminsen, J. (2015). *Online Brand Identity: The ultimate guide to designing your (digital) branding strategy*

Randstad. *Why is there a global labor shortage.* Retrieved April 4, 2023, from randstad.com

Scott, K. (2019). *Radical candor: How to get what you want by saying what you mean.* PAN BOOKS.

Sinek, S. (2019). *Start with why: How great leaders inspire everyone to take action.* Penguin Business.

Zak, P.J. (2017) *The Neuroscience of Trust: Management behaviors that foster employee engagement. Harvard Business Review*